Errors

ERROR	CORRECTION SYMBOL		EXPLANATION
	Standard	Alternative	
	ev.		Evidence does not prove generalizations
	cause		Cause does not produce indicated effect
	def.		Definition needed; definition weak
	prop.		Propaganda used in place of proof
6. SENTENCES	*emph.*		Sentences unemphatic
	sub.		Subordination needed
	choppy		Sentences too short
	wordy		Wordiness
	var.		Sentences monotonous; variety needed
	sound		Sentences need increased euphony
	//		Parallelism needed
7. WORD CHOICE	*vocab.*		Poor word choice
	usage		Improper usage
	pr.		More precise expression needed
	viv.		More vivid, concrete expression needed
	fig.		Figure of speech inappropriate; mixed metaphors
8. ADDITIONAL			

Practical Rhetoric

Practical Rhetoric

O. B. Hardison, Jr.
THE UNIVERSITY OF NORTH CAROLINA

 NEW YORK

APPLETON-CENTURY-CROFTS
DIVISION OF MEREDITH PUBLISHING COMPANY

PRINTED IN THE UNITED STATES OF AMERICA

E 41068

To C.R.H. and S.F.H.

". . . in each
Are nameless graces which no methods teach."
—Pope

Preface: to the Teacher

The guiding principle of *Practical Rhetoric* is indicated by the first word of its title. Its purpose is to teach writing, not the history of rhetoric, the fundamentals of logic or the theory of general semantics. Its chief features are derived from this purpose, and its claim to offering something new to the teacher of composition rests primarily on the consistency with which the principles of rhetoric have been adapted to the practical business of improving student writing.

In general, the movement of the text is from fundamentals (organization, paragraphing, basic elements of style) to specialized techniques (methods of development, advanced principles of style, deductive logic, the term paper and rhetorical criticism). This sequence has been tested and found serviceable in the classroom, but it is not offered as a Procrustean formula to fit all needs and tastes. Variations are both possible and desirable. The order of the chapters can be changed to fit the requirements of the individual instructor, and there is, of course, no need to cover all of the material included.

PREFACE: TO THE TEACHER

Most composition courses include a semester or quarter of rhetoric and a semester or quarter devoted to either the term paper or an introduction to literature. *Practical Rhetoric* is intended to serve as the basic text for the first semester or quarter of this sequence. It can also be used in the second semester in conjunction with supplementary materials— "sourcebooks" and library assignments intended to teach research techniques, or readings intended to enhance appreciation of literature and teach principles of literary criticism.

Each chapter is designed to be read by the student at a single sitting. Each can also serve as the basis for a group of assignments that may proceed, during a period of three or four days, from reading and discussion of the chapter proper, through exercises, to application in original essays. To assist comprehension, important sections are numbered and titled, key definitions are printed in bold-faced type, and "terms to be learned" are listed at the end of each chapter. The definitions are simple, concise, and phrased in such a way as to emphasize their practical relevance, that is, their application to writing. Involved theoretical discussions have been avoided in the belief that they usually confuse the beginning writer instead of encouraging him. A corollary advantage of this approach is that the student can be held responsible on quizzes and examinations for key definitions, so that a check is possible on his mastery of assigned reading.

Throughout the text numerous examples are provided in the chapters and the exercises. These examples have intentionally been selected to illustrate the widest possible cross section of types and styles. Many selections are from recognized classics, but an effort has been made to avoid a heavily "literary" bias. Selections from newspapers, popular magazines, government publications, textbooks and research reports are used to emphasize the fact that rhetoric is important to *all* types of writing, from the most humble to the most sophisticated. Illustrative passages within the chapters are kept brief to avoid interrupting the sequence of ideas. Selections in the exercises are longer, and where practical they are complete units or essays. No selection, however, is so long as to be incommensurate with the type of essay the student can reasonably be expected to write. Finally, student essays are often included in the exercises along with the work of professional writers. These are offered for discussion, evaluation and, at times, revision. They can be supplemented by essays written specifically for *Practical Rhetoric* assignments. The result of this approach is, it is hoped, a text that is explicit without being dogmatic, stimulating and instructive in its variety without being diffuse.

The ideas presented in this text have germinated over many enjoyable years of teaching. I owe a considerable debt to numerous colleagues who have provided specific suggestions as well as intellectual stimulation. My greatest debt, however, is to my students. *Practical Rhetoric* is an embodiment of what I have learned from them and an attempt to make the lessons they have so patiently taught available to others.

O. B. H., Jr.

Preface: to the Student

The aim of this text and of the course using it is to teach effective writing. Only a few students plan careers in creative writing, but every student eventually finds himself deeply involved in problems of expression. Term papers, essay examinations and reports are regular parts of most of the courses you will take while in college. When you enter professional life, your need for writing skill will probably increase. Business correspondence will have to be answered, projects will have to be "written up," brochures and manuals will have to be composed and speeches delivered. Most of these jobs will have to be done on short notice, usually in the midst of other activities. If you write easily they are opportunities; if you write poorly they are at best unpleasant and at worst, episodes that can jeopardize advancement or threaten the success of an important project. For this reason your writing course is of central importance, both to your success as a student and to later success in your career.

The heart of any writing course is writing itself. Writing is an acquired skill, and we acquire a skill by doing, not by listening to lectures, although lectures make the process more efficient and far less painful

PREFACE: TO THE STUDENT

than learning by trial and error. The advantage of a formal writing course over all other methods of learning to write effectively—over individual experimentation, correspondence courses and in-service training programs —is that it combines a review of writing principles with regular writing assignments read and criticized by an experienced instructor. Your instructor functions for you in somewhat the same way that an editor functions for a professional writer. He knows the difference between good and bad writing, and he also knows your own strong and weak points. He corrects errors, he gives advice and he offers, in the form of grades, evaluations of what you submit to him. To take advantage of the opportunities of your writing course, you must be willing to work hard and accept and benefit from criticism. You must also be willing to experiment. The rewards of a course in writing, which will make your efforts worthwhile, are the sense of assurance that comes from competence and the realization that writing can be an absorbing, deeply satisfying activity.

The present text is not a grammar but a rhetoric. That is, it assumes that you know the fundamentals of correct expression—even though you may be puzzled occasionaly by fine points—and concentrates on matters relating to effectiveness. It consists essentially of definitions and illustrations of various writing principles, together with enough discussion to enable you to apply them in your own writing. Its principles are derived partly from the nature of written and spoken communication and partly from observation of how writers in the past have solved their problems. No principle is offered as a hard-and-fast rule to be applied mechanically in every situation. You should use each with tact and understand that each essay poses its own special problems. Writing principles must be adapted to each new situation, and any and all principles can be violated if there are good reasons to do so.

Traditionally, rhetoric has been divided into five "topics" and three "methods of appeal." The topics are "invention" (discovering material), organization, style, delivery and memory—that is, ways to remember a complicated argument while speaking without notes. Because most of us express ourselves in writing instead of delivering formal speeches, modern rhetoric has abandoned "memory" and transferred "delivery" to courses in public speaking. "Invention" is still a part of rhetoric, but is usually treated in connection with organization and style rather than as a separate topic.

The "methods of appeal" recognized by traditional rhetoric are the character of the writer, the character of the audience and logical proof.

xii

They are just as essential today as ever. To be effective, you should obviously present yourself in a favorable light by appearing sympathetic, informed and reliable. Second, you should relate your presentation to the interests and limitations of your audience. If you are writing for an audience of "general readers," for example, you should strive for a popular style and avoid technicalities that only experts can be expected to understand; if you are writing for specialists, on the other hand, your style can be more formal and the discussion more complex. Third, you should support your case with logical proof. The methods of proof are discussed in the present text in the chapters on argumentation.

The focus of *Practical Rhetoric* is on practice, not theory, and on types of writing that everyone is likely to use frequently. While many of its examples are selected from recognized literary classics, it also includes examples taken from "working prose"—manuals, newspaper articles, textbooks and magazines. If you are a prospective creative writer, you will find that it provides a solid foundation on which to build, but its emphasis is on exposition and argument rather than fiction and poetry.

Above all, it aims at being clear and explicit. There will be complications enough as you translate principles into finished essays. The chapters are kept to the minimum length compatible with clarity, and each can be read at a single sitting. Important points are spelled out in boldfaced type and illustrated. You can memorize them just as you memorize the bones in a frog's skeleton, the five most important dates of the French Revolution, or the atomic weights of the elements. To bridge the gap between explanation and practice, each chapter includes exercises keyed to the topics discussed. At the end of each set of exercises comes the real point of the chapter—suggestions for themes. You can use these as given; or, better still, you can use them as a point of departure for developing your own topics.

The first questions an author asks are "What should I say?" and "Where should I begin?" Chapters 1 and 2 concentrate on principles that are helpful in answering these questions. After the "What?" and the "Where?" comes the "How?" Chapters 3 and following do not exhaust the answers to questions about style and method, but they give several standard ones. Equipped with these you can begin the task of working out your own. It is a task that will continue as long as you have a term paper to write, a speech to give, a report to complete or a letter to answer.

O. B. H., Jr.

Contents

CONTENTS

2: THE PARAGRAPH

3: STYLE (I)

4: DEVELOPMENT BY DETAIL

CONTENTS

8: DEFINITION

9: STYLE (II)

10: INTRODUCTIONS AND CONCLUSIONS

11: ARGUMENTATION (II): DEDUCTION

12: STYLE (III)

13: THE RESEARCH PAPER

CONTENTS

14: RHETORIC AND CRITICISM

Practical Rhetoric

Organization

Organization is the writer's means of insuring the unity of his essay. We are all familiar with writing that wanders pointlessly from topic to topic, sometimes saying too little, sometimes too much and never seeming to get anywhere. Such writing lacks unity.

There are no ready-made ways of achieving unity. Each essay has its own special problems, and what is right for one many be wrong for another. Writing an essay is not an impersonal activity like solving a problem in mathematics by applying a standard formula. It requires skill, judgment and knowledge of both the subject and the probable audience.

The most important organizational tool is the outline, and the most important function of the outline is to make clear the unifying elements of the essay. To do this the outline must show both the **subject** of the essay and the author's **purpose** in treating the subject. It should also reflect the **adaptation** of the essay to the anticipated audience and the main steps in the presentation. In general, the simpler the outline can be while meeting these requirements, the better. An excessively detailed outline forces an inflexible pattern on the author before he has begun writing and risks burying the essential elements in a mass of trivia. In most cases an outline for a five-page essay should not be more than a page, and if it can be reduced to half a page its usefulness will probably be increased.

1.1   UNITY OF SUBJECT

Unity is the effect achieved when all parts of the essay contribute to the author's purpose and nothing has been left out that should be included. We might say that for each essay there is a point of ideal unity at which nothing can be added without dilution and nothing can be subtracted without loss.

To decide when this point has been reached (or approximated), the author must first of all have a clear understanding of **subject** and **purpose. Subject** in this connection means **the topic or subject matter** of the essay. It can be an idea, like "The Role of Fraternities on the College Campus"; a process or phenomenon, like "Mutation in the Fruit Fly" or "Love in Hemingway's Novels"; or an object or group of events, like "A Description of Monticello" or "Saturday Night in Chicago."

Obviously, an essay lacks unity if it treats more than one subject. The author who decides to write about the fruit fly has no business talking about fraternities; and an essay on fraternities should not wander off into a description of Monticello. One qualification is needed here, however. The requirement of unity of subject does not mean that all the

2

materials going into an essay must be directly related to its subject. Often the relation is indirect. For example, heavy industry, detergents and fishing seem, in the abstract, quite unrelated; but they all might legitimately be treated in an essay on water contamination. In this case the **subject** of the essay would be "water contamination," and manufacturing, detergents and fishing would be discussed later in connection with the causes and effects of contamination.

1.2 UNITY OF PURPOSE

The purpose of an essay is the most general point the essay is intended to convey. A statement of purpose has two parts: it indicates the subject of the essay, and it makes an assertion about the subject. "Higher Education" is a statement of subject, not a statement of purpose. "Higher education is expensive," "Higher education is broadening" and "Higher education involves administrative and teaching personnel, students, buildings and equipment" are all possible **statements of purpose.** Under certain conditions, to be discussed in connection with argumentation, a **statement of purpose** is labeled a **thesis.**

Unity of purpose is achieved when the subject is treated in a manner consistent with the statement of purpose. To illustrate, let us consider the steps involved in writing a descriptive essay on a subject of general interest. The author first must decide what he is going to describe. Obviously he should choose a subject that he knows well. Typical subjects include "My Home Town," "The State University Campus," "A Tourist Paris" and the like. Once he has reached a decision, he has limited his **subject.** Fairly soon, however (hopefully, before he begins writing), he realizes that answering one question has led to a whole set of new ones. The very fact that he knows his subject well means that he possesses far more information than he can use.

For discussion purposes let us assume that he decides to write his essay on "An Insider's View of Washington, D.C." What features of Washington should he mention? Should he describe its business districts? Its residential areas? Its recreational facilities? Its outstanding buildings and monuments? Should he discuss its people, and if so, how? Should

3

he quote from the latest census figures, should he describe typical inhabitants or should he concentrate on famous citizens? Should he emphasize the attractive aspects of Washington's political, social and cultural life, or attempt an exposé of its inadequacies? Should the essay stress "atmosphere" in an attempt to recreate the sense of living in Georgetown, Alexandria or East Capitol Hill, or should it be "factual," with statistics on sewage disposal, government agencies, median income, crime rate and output of goods and services? Should it proceed historically, moving from "Colonial beginnings" to "the outlook for the future," or should it emphasize the present?

At this point, our writer is in a peculiar but all-too-familiar dilemma. He has a great deal to say, and at the same time he seems to have nothing to say. No detail is essential, but there is no good reason for leaving out any detail. If he begins to write without formulating a definite **purpose,** he will probably fall into one of two common writing errors. Either he will try to include everything and will ramble monotonously from topic to topic until he and the reader are exhausted. Or, if he tries to exclude, he will end by excluding everything. His essay will turn into a few pallid generalities, and he will find himself complaining that there is nothing to say.

If he recognizes the source of his problem, he will solve it by formulating a **statement of purpose.** "An Insider's View of Washington" is a satisfactory **subject** and might make a good title, but it does not show purpose. "Washington is stimulating" *does* show purpose. It is general, but at least it tells the author that he should select material suggesting "stimulation" and omit material that is "not stimulating."

1.3 ALTERNATIVES; LIMITATION; ADAPTATION

Before deciding to use "Washington is stimulating" as his statement of purpose, the writer should consider **alternatives.** If he lists three or four possibilities, he can then pick the one that best suits his needs. Among many possible statements, he might list the following:

1. "Washington is a city of politicians."
2. "Washington is essentially a middle-class town."

4

3. "Washington is a city of wide boulevards, parks and open vistas."
4. "A good way to appreciate Washington is to walk from the Lincoln Memorial, down the Mall, to the Capitol."
5. "Washington had a stormy history during the Federal period."
6. "Major L'Enfant's master plan for Washington reflects the ideals of the Napoleonic era."

These purpose statements are more limited than "Washington is stimulating," and in most cases **limitation** is desirable. Hence, in most cases they would be preferable.

Limitation is not, however, an end in itself. The most important factors determining the choice of purpose statements are the interests of the author and the nature of the audience he expects to reach. Assuming that the author knows Washington well and is sincerely interested in discussing it, he should **adapt** his treatment to the probable interests of his readers. For example, "Washington is stimulating" would probably be a satisfactory purpose statement for an essay intended for the general reader; but "Washington had a stormy history during the Federal period" would obviously be more appropriate for a paper to be read to a history club. "Major L'Enfant's master plan for Washington reflects the ideals of the Napoleonic era" would be suitable for a term paper in a college course in American culture; while "A good way to appreciate Washington is to walk from the Lincoln Memorial, down the Mall, to the Capitol" would make a useful talk before a tourist group planning to visit Washington.

1.4 INTRODUCTION AND CONCLUSION

The parts of the essay are derived from the statement of purpose. They tend to fall into three sections. The first is the **introduction**, the second, the **development** and the third, the **conclusion**. Each of these sections has its own conventions. Introductions and conclusions will be treated in detail in a later chapter (chapter 10; 10.1, 10.3). For the present, the following observations may be used as guides.

The **introduction** is a service provided by the author to the reader. It is not always necessary, but it should not be omitted without very good reason. The more emphasis the author places on informing the reader, the more desirable a formal introduction. The introduction gives information needed for easy comprehension of what follows. The most important part of the introduction is therefore a **statement of purpose.** This does not have to be phrased in exactly the same way as the statement in the author's outline, but it should convey the same idea and it should be placed in a position of emphasis.

There are three other parts that may or may not appear in any given introduction. The **statement of method** tells the reader how the author plans to treat his material. Often it consists of a brief outline giving the order in which important points will be taken up. A statement of method is particularly desirable in a long essay on a complex subject. **Background material** explains points that are necessary to an understanding of the essay as a whole. The author can discuss the significance of his subject, show its relation to the reader and define important terms. Some background material is desirable in almost any essay, but it should be used sparingly. Finally, the **approach step** is a device for securing the reader's attention. It is the least essential of the standard parts of an introduction. It is usually confined to the first two or three sentences of the essay and consists of a striking fact, anecdote or intriguing generalization that will catch the reader's interest immediately.

With the exception of the approach step, the parts of the introduction can appear in any order that seems effective to the writer. Often they are intermingled. For example, it is quite common for an introduction to begin with background material, proceed to statement of purpose, give additional background material and end with statement of method. Two rules-of-thumb should be followed in writing introductions. First, they should be proportioned to the essay as a whole. For a five-page essay, an introduction of one or two sentences is too abrupt and an introduction of more than two paragraphs is probably too long. Second, introductions should be clearly separated from the main body of the essay. In a short essay, paragraphing is sufficient. In a long one, spacing and subheadings may be used to emphasize the division.

The **conclusion** is the most abused part of the essay. It is an invitation to be long-winded and repetitious. Often the author can simply write the word *conclusion* at the end of the outline and wait until the essay is actually written before deciding how to end it. The conclusion will often write itself. For a short essay, a final sentence, or at most a final paragraph, is enough. A long essay will demand more formal treatment.

The author may wish to include a **summary** of the most important points that the essay has made. He may wish to use **restatement** to remind the reader of the original purpose of the essay. And he may want to include **author's comment** in which he discusses the significance of the points made and their implications. When a formal conclusion is necessary it should be separated from the preceding material by paragraphing, spacing or still more emphatic devices.

1.5 DEVELOPMENT: METHODS OF DEVELOPMENT vs. FORMS OF DISCOURSE

The development of an essay is a series of units illustrating or proving the purpose statement. It is often called the **body** of the essay and is the longest and most important of the three general parts.

There are several methods of development, all of them depending on or deriving from **analysis** of the purpose statement. **Analysis is** discussed below (section 1.6), and the various **methods of development** are considered individually in later chapters.

In addition to **methods of development**, rhetoric recognizes four **forms of discourse**. These are **description, narration, exposition** and **argumentation**. The forms of discourse cut across the methods of development, but should not be equated with them. "Development by detail," for example, is the natural method for a descriptive essay, but it is also used in essays of narration and exposition. Again, "argumentation" can be considered either a form of discourse or a method of development based on techniques of inductive and deductive proof.

1.6 ANALYSIS

To illustrate **analysis** let us return to the essay on Washington. Having decided on his purpose statement, the writer must next divide his material into units of practical size. He will do this by the technique of **analysis**. This technique is a natural one that we use constantly in our everyday lives. When Caesar wrote that all Gaul is divided into

7

three parts, he was using analysis. When we notice that an electric fan is divided into base assembly, motor and blade assembly and blade guard, we too are using analysis. For purposes of introductory rhetoric, **analysis is the division of a large subject into smaller, logically distinct components.** Classification is the reverse process. **It is the assigning of a detail, fact or component to a larger category or class.** The statement "Most movies are romances, westerns or mysteries" is an example of analysis, and the statement *"Gone with the Wind is a romance"* is an example of classification.

The method of analysis gives the writer several options. Let us assume that he has chosen "Washington is stimulating" as his purpose statement. Both the subject half and the assertion half of the purpose statement can be subdivided by analysis. "Washington" can be analyzed or divided into a series of representative aspects, such as physical characteristics, famous buildings, parks and monuments, typical activities of Washingtonians and special events. In a short essay, each of these aspects might be presented in one or two paragraphs consisting of illustrative details.

Analysis of the assertion half of the purpose statement seems less promising but deserves investigation before being rejected. "Stimulating" is a general term. It may include such qualities as grandeur, beauty, variety, color, excitement and intellectual appeal. Clearly, it would be possible to write a short essay about Washington emphasizing these qualities.

The possibilities of the alternative purpose statements listed in section 1.3 are still more evident. "Washington is a city of politicians" leads easily to several units consisting of character sketches and anecdotes illustrating the political nature of Washingtonians. And "A good way to appreciate Washington . . ." leads directly to a unit-by-unit description of the buildings and other interesting sights encountered in a walk from the Lincoln Memorial to the Capitol.

1.7 ARRANGEMENT

When the major units have been decided on, they must be placed in some order. **Arrangement is the ordering of the main topics of the development (or body) of the essay.** If, for example, our writer has decided to treat Washington in terms of monuments, parks, politics and special events, he next must decide which should come first, which second and which last. There are three possibilities. The first is random **listing.** The writer may put the topics on slips of paper, place them in a hat and treat them in the order in which he draws them out. This might work for a short essay. Sometimes, in fact, listing is the *only* workable order. If a more emphatic order is possible, however, it should be used. The reader likes to feel that he is making definite progress with each paragraph. In a long essay, lack of emphatic order can be frustrating, if not confusing. In such a case the essay seems to wander from nowhere to nowhere.

The second possibility is to use **inherent arrangements.** These are **arrangements inherent in the subject itself. They include arrangement by space, time and process. Spatial arrangement** would obviously be appropriate for the essay based on "A good way to appreciate Washington . . . ." Using this method the writer would describe the important sights in the order in which they would be encountered by the tourist— the Lincoln Memorial, the Washington Monument, the Museum of Natural History, the Archives Building, the National Gallery of Art, Union Square and, finally, the Capitol.

Arrangement by **time (chronological arrangement)** is familiar to everyone. It is the method one instinctively uses to relate a sequence of events. It presents the events in the original order of their occurrence. Chronological arrangement would be the natural method for the essay based on "Washington had a stormy history during the Federal period," but it is obviously not suited to "Washington is essentially a middle-class town."

Arrangement by process resembles chronological arrangement. It gives the parts of a process step-by-step. It differs from arrangement by time in that arrangement by time tends to be continuous, while in arrangement by process the parts or steps in the process are sharply distinguished and their *discontinuity* is emphasized. Arrangement by process is extremely useful. It would be the appropriate method for an essay on "The Stages of Development of the Adult Frog," a manual on "How to Operate Your New Washer" or an explanation of "A New Method for Treating Victims of Severe Burns." It does not, however, seem to fit any of the proposed purpose statements for the essay on Washington.

If the writer decides that inherent arrangements are unsatisfactory

9

for his purpose, he can turn to various **logical** (or **imposed**) **arrangements. Logical arrangements are imposed by the author and are not inherent in the material treated.** There are a great many kinds of logical arrangement, and labels for them vary. Among the common ones are **arrangement by climax, arrangement from general to specific** and **arrangement based on cause and effect.** Several of the purpose statements for the essay on Washington seem better suited to logical than inherent arrangement. A "least-to-most" system would be appropriate for the "Washington is stimulating" essay, as well as the more specific essays on "Washington is a city of politicians" and "Washington is essentially a middle-class town." Using a least-to-most method of arrangement, the "Washington is stimulating" essay might begin with "physical characteristics" (least stimulating), continue with "exciting activities" and end with a particularly colorful "special event," such as Inauguration Day (most stimulating).

1.8   OUTLINING

It is useful to incorporate the purpose statement and the major units of the development into a written outline that shows the plan of the whole essay at a glance. Most professional writers use outlines for longer essays and books. Those who do not do so have developed the ability to outline automatically, without the need for notes. The beginning writer should regularly make outlines both to improve his essays and to develop his sense of form.

A few rules are sufficient for any outline, whether for a five-page essay or a five-hundred page book:

1. Item one on the outline should be the purpose statement. This specifies the unifying elements of the essay as a whole and gives the most important part of the introduction. If the writer plans to use background material, statement of method or approach step, these elements can be indicated in positions subordinate to the purpose statement.

2. Item two and those that follow indicate the major units of the development. They should clearly reflect the unifying purpose of the essay as well as the subject matter. In a book outline, they will be purpose statements for the chapters and they will eventually have their own subdivisions. In the outline of an essay they can indicate units varying in length from a single paragraph to several pages. As long as they indicate clearly how the units will be written, they need not be expanded. If they do not, further subdivision will be helpful.
3. The outline ends with a conclusion or simply a reminder to consider a conclusion when the time comes.

The myriad other rules devised for outlines can be reduced to three general suggestions. First, be consistent. If roman numerals are used for the first major heading, they should be used for other headings of the same order of importance. Second, it is useful—though not always necessary—to use parallelism between topics of the same order of importance. The repetition of similar grammatical structures is a mechanical convenience, but it helps eliminate digressions and ambiguities. Third, a preliminary outline should be treated with courteous disrespect. It is a plan, not a straitjacket, and a good writer will modify it—sometimes even abandon it for a better one—in the course of writing.

1.9 SAMPLE OUTLINES

The following outlines all have Washington as their subject. All use logical rather than inherent arrangement and all are informal. They are "working outlines" and include notes by their author on examples to be used and questions to be answered during composition. Before they could be handed in as part of an assignment they would need to be rewritten in a more formal manner, but at the beginning of a writing job "notes and queries" are helpful. The diversity of the outlines illustrates the range of possibilities inherent even in a simple subject.

Editorial notes are in brackets. The writer's notes to himself are italicized and in parentheses.

11

Outline A   [Satisfactory but rather
obvious. About par for
a "C" essay.]

[INTRODUCTION]   I. [Statement of Purpose] Washington is stimulating.
a. [Background] Explain that I have lived in Washington for
the past five years.
b. [Method] Begin with physical features, then describe typical
activities and end with special events.

[DEVELOPMENT: II. Washington is, physically, an impressive city.
II-IV]   a. Street plan.
b. Famous buildings (*Capitol, National Gallery, Pentagon*).
c. Parks (*Rock Creek Park, Potomac Park—especially the view
from Hains Point*).
III. Washington provides opportunities for many exciting activities.
a. Professional activities (*politics, law, foreign service*).
b. Recreational and cultural activities (*Washington Zoo,
Smithsonian Institute, boating on the Potomac*).
IV. Washington has many colorful special events.
a. Cherry-blossom time.
b. Fireworks display on the Fourth of July.
c. Inauguration Day.

[CONCLUSION]   V. Conclusion. (*Use the description of Inauguration Day as my
conclusion.*)

Outline B   [Better than Outline A.
Note emphasis through-
out on atmosphere.]

[INTRODUCTION]   I. [Statement of Purpose] Washington is stimulating.
a. [Approach Step] "Most tourists who visit Washington see
only a collection of buildings and monuments. . . ."
b. [Background] "I first came to Washington in 19—. In the
two years that followed, I gradually discovered. . . ."

[DEVELOPMENT: II. To begin with, Washington is one of the most beautiful cities
II-IV]   in the world.
a. A city of trees, parks and open vistas.
b. The beauty and variety of its embassies and public buildings.
c. Residential areas (*Georgetown, Spring Valley, Chevy Chase*).

12

III. Life in Washington is fun for people of all ages.
   a. Children (*Zoo, Rock Creek Park, Glen Echo*).
   b. Adults (*concerts, art galleries, libraries, sports facilities*).
IV. The people of Washington are its most exciting feature. (*Cite examples of interesting Washingtonians I have met.*)

[CONCLUSION]
    V. Conclusion. (*Decide later.*)

(*Note: This may be too much. Try developing III first. There may be enough in it for the whole essay.*)

Outline C   [More technical than Outline B. Intended for a specialized group.]

[INTRODUCTION]
I. [Purpose Statement] There were five major steps taken to provide a capital city for the United States between 1790 and 1800.
   a. [Background] The problems and debates that led the Congress to enact the Residence Bill of July 16, 1790, establishing Washington, D.C., as the site of the capital.
   b. [Method] (*Since the method is clear from the purpose statement, no explicit statement of method is needed.*)

[DEVELOPMENT: II-VI]
II. Washington and Jefferson decide on the location of the new city.
III. The work of the Presidential Commissioners and Surveyors.
IV. Major L'Enfant and his master plan.
V. Land purchases from residents of the area.
VI. The first buildings: the President's House and the Capitol.

[CONCLUSION]
VII. The capital city in the year 1800.

Outline D   [For a report in an education class. This essay would be technical and presupposes considerable research.]

[INTRODUCTION]
I. [Statement of Purpose] Washington's public school system is a case study of the results of mismanagement, inadequate support and public indifference.

13

a. [Background] Recent events illustrating the inadequacies of Washington public schools.

b. [Statement of Method] The four basic causes of Washington's inadequate school system are inefficient administration, lack of funds, improper taxation and lack of special programs for marginal students.

[DEVELOPMENT: II-V]

II. The Washington public school system is administered by an overlapping group of committees, some of them federal and some local.

a. Role of the Congressional District Committee.

b. Role of the Congressional Appropriations Committee.

c. Role of the District Board of Commissioners.

d. Role of the Board of Education.

e. Other agencies influencing education: Board of Public Welfare, Zoning Board.

III. The Washington public school system is inadequately supported.

a. *Per capita* expenditure in the District compared to *per capita* expenditures in Philadelphia, New York and Boston.

b. School construction and maintenance.

c. Inequities among school districts.

IV. High taxation and poor schools accelerate the movement of middle and upper income families to the suburbs.

a. Cite census statistics of 1930 and 1960.

b. First result: lack of effective pressure for reform.

c. Second result: lowering of the general attainment level of the Washington school population.

V. These basic problems are compounded by inadequate programs for culturally deprived children and high school dropouts.

a. Inadequate programs for preschool children.

b. Inadequate programs for counseling and special medical and psychiatric aid.

c. Inadequate vocational training programs.

[CONCLUSION]

VI. Washington's public education needs a thorough reform. Such a reform will require a revision of the structure of school administration and of taxation policies. Three hopeful signs: the "home rule" bill; urban renewal; Job Corps and other government programs.

1.10   A NOTE ON TRANSITIONS

Although **transitions** are not normally included in the outline, they are important structural elements and help to clarify organization. **A transition is a paragraph, sentence or phrase used to clarify the movement from one unit of thought to the next.** An essay with insufficient transitional material may be well organized from a logical standpoint, but will impress the reader as being choppy and abrupt. **Transition paragraphs** are paragraphs—usually brief—facilitating movement from one major unit to the next. **Transition sentences** appear frequently at the beginning of paragraphs and are also useful *within* longer paragraphs. **Transition phrases** are used in the same way but are still more common. At all stages of composition the writer should keep in mind the need for smooth transitions between the units as defined in his outline.

1.11   STEPS IN DEVELOPING AN ESSAY BY ANALYSIS

For convenience, the process of planning an essay using development by analysis can be summarized in five steps:

1. Selection of subject
2. Formulation of purpose statement; consideration of alternatives
3. Consideration of limitation and adaptation of purpose statement
4. Analysis
5. Arrangement

TERMS TO BE LEARNED

▸ Unity
▸ Unity of subject and unity of purpose
▸ Statement of purpose
▸ Development

15

▸ Analysis
▸ Inherent arrangement (definition and three kinds)
▸ Logical arrangement (definition and three kinds)
▸ Transition

Exercises & Theme Topics

I. Select two subjects from the following list. Write three purpose statements for each one. Then, using the method of analysis, suggest appropriate subdivisions for each of the purpose statements.

safety in automobile design, the freshman curriculum, cigarette smoking, professional football, the American landscape, U.S. foreign policy, civil disobedience, regulation of student conduct, modern art, censorship and pornography, poverty, creativity

II. Select two purpose statements from your answer to exercise I. Make two different (alternative) "working outlines" for each. After each outline, state the method of arrangement you have used and comment on the kind of essay that the outline would produce. Would the essay be long or short? Good, bad or indifferent? If less than good, what can be done to improve the outline? After having completed the first part of this exercise, choose the outline that seems most promising, make revisions and write it out as a "formal outline" to be handed in with a completed essay.

III. The following essay is by a professional writer and appeared originally in *The New York Times Magazine*. It is a discussion of Washington, D.C., based on the second "alternative purpose statement" listed in section 1.3 of this chapter. Outline it and comment on the effectiveness with which the purpose statement is developed.

16

"IT'S MIDDLETOWN-ON-THE-POTOMAC"

Washington is my home town. It dies at sundown; it is too hot in the summer, too damp in the winter, too dry on Sundays and more interested in politics than it is in sex, but I like it.

It is civilized in a square, middle-class way, which is to say, urbanely dull. It is ideally suited for the middle-aged family couple, being perhaps the last great city in which middle income can afford a house, a tomato patch and a canopy of dogwoods within fifteen minutes of the office.

Its society is democratic, unstartling, cosmopolitan and notably free of the small-town chauvinism of New York or San Francisco. The Washingtonian is unruffled by New York's insistence upon being thought the most thrilling city on earth or by San Francisco's claim to be the loveliest.

Being tolerant and well-traveled, he is unlikely to point out that London, Paris, Hong Kong and Tokyo have equally valid claims, but being perfectly satisfied that his own town is a bit of a drag, he would surely never argue the case for Washington's superiority.

He may feel sorry that the New Yorker cannot afford to rear his children among Manhattan's splendors or that the San Franciscan must live out his days at the far edge of Nowhere, but it pleases him to see these unfortunate people making a virtue of necessity, for he is, above all, a man with the politician's devotion to the status quo.

He might—just *might*, mind you—prefer to live in New York if he were rich, or in London if he were more adventurous, or in Paris if he were at ease in the language., But with all problems judiciously weighed—he is a very judicious fellow—and his own middle-class limitations faced up to and conceded, Washington seems the best of all possible cities.

What we Washingtonians cannot for the life of us understand is the relentless American urge to turn the town into someplace else. The Kennedys tried to make it into a cultural capital—a sort of instant Lincoln Center-Vienna-Paris-London. President Johnson's blueprints seem to call for Augustan Rome.

Most recently, Mrs. Johnson has sponsored formation of a 20-member Committee for a More Beautiful Capital. Its specific aims, aside from the worthy goal of prettifying the place, are still vague, but it is difficult to see how the basic causes of ugliness—downtown real-estate speculation, expanding traffic flow and massive slum poverty—can be relieved by attack from the top.

17

Also on the boards are tentative plans for a monumental reconstruction of Pennsylvania Avenue and schemes for brightening the lifeless expanses of the Mall area. In addition, President Johnson has asked Congress once again to make the city self-governing so that it may become a model of urban endeavor. Congress has refused repeatedly in the past, and no one is very optimistic this time, but it illustrates the incessant pressure for redoing the place.

Scarcely a week passes without a new plan for turning Washington into a "showcase" for this or that, and there are as many schemes for converting it into a "truly great world capital" as there are sociologists, art critics, architects and city planners.

This passion for reshaping the town rests on a naive misconception. The fact which the reshapers fail to grasp is that Washington is no longer the child capital in the wilderness, waiting to be molded by loving parental hands. It is not only fully grown now, but well on into maturity, set in its ways, committed in its habits and hardened in its vices. With the inner city filled to capacity and a metropolitan population of 2,300,000, its growth is substantially complete and though the "slurbs" will doubtless continue to spread through outlying Maryland and Virginia, the city's character is well formed and no longer pliant.

This explains why the Kennedy effort to implant a taste for the arts— "the culture bit," as local cynics called it—was always doomed. You can lead a middle-aged burgher to the Mona Lisa, but you cannot make him surrender the martini hour for Couperin. Faced with the challenge to do something about culture, Washington's response has been characteristic. It will build another marble monument—the National Cultural Center—isolated from everyplace that has to do with living, and unreachable except by the most daring expressway pilots.

It is the natural middle-class response to *Kultur* which will be appropriately venerated in stone but kept at comfortable arm's length from daily life. It is this instinctive middle-class reflex which distinguishes Washington from all other American cities and accounts for the placid charm that is the special quality of life here. It is the urban triumph of the middle class, the apotheosis of Zenith. No more appropriate capital could be envisioned for the nation that made a mass blessing of capitalism, and it is time for the rest of the country to stop fretting about what the city is not and to accept it as it is.

It is first of all a city of civil servants—250,000 of them. The society-page myth has it that the tone of Washington life is set by the President and his lady. It is true only for the privileged few in the orbit of official society.

In the vast sprawl of suburbia, the tree-shaded side streets of the Northwest and the huge Negro ghettos north and east of the White House, it is the 250,000 civil servants who dominate the patterns of Washington life.

The bureaucratic passion for order, safety and a neat out-basket is the prevailing force in the Washington temperament. It fears extremes, whether of dress, drink or opinion. The security police are omnipresent, and as the 250,000 must all be certified orthodox by the U.S. Government, dullness and the stolid family virtues are at a premium.

The refusal of the big Negro population to explode in protest has troubled some leaders of the civil-rights movement. It is a symptom of how firmly the cautious civil-service mentality has taken hold, for while the Negro is relatively well off in relation to other cities, there remain cruel economic and social disparities between him and the white Washingtonians.

The schools, to cite a case, are overcrowded, out of date and perpetually starved for funds. The school population is predominantly (about 85 per cent) Negro within the city limits. Technically, the schools are integrated; in fact, after a brief period of integration in the mid-nineteen-fifties, most have been resegregated by the mass move to the suburbs by thousands of young white families.

Suburban discrimination against Negro home buyers keeps the Negro population (about 106,000 families) penned within the city limits, and the integrated school system becomes blacker every year. Negro protests against the shabbiness of the schools have been notable for their absence. It is probably no coincidence that the Washington Negro has a long history of civil-service employment or that only one other city has a higher percentage of Negro families earning middle-class income ($6,000 a year or more, by Urban League standards).

The civil-service regard for the proprieties permeates more than race relations. It has eaten into the soul of the city and left it with that well-ordered small-town atmosphere which prevents life from becoming the continual social mess that it is in places like New York.

Proper dinners end at 11 P.M. Proper people bed down by midnight. Proper drinkers have two before dining and a brandy afterward. Proper conversations deal with children, schools and government. Proper opinions range from three degrees left of center to five degrees right. The likelihood of ever meeting a living, breathing anarchist, Communist or pacifist in a proper Washington living room is virtually nil, and Socialists are acceptable only if they are foreign Cabinet ministers on tour.

Occasionally one may come upon a couple living out of wedlock, but they are invariably young and planning to move elsewhere. God only knows what goes on in the suburbs, but in town at least the percentage of men

19

capable of forgetting government long enough to make a pass at a bored wife is negligible. Two or three years ago, a prominent party divorced his wife for another woman, and the town is still talking about it.

There is no liquor sold on the Sabbath. The last restaurant shuts down at 1 A.M. and on the main thoroughfares the traffic lights are shut off or left blinking until dawn. It is all very comfortable, private, quiet, relaxed and free of ugly temptation.

At night, the Washingtonian visits old friends for a proper dinner or goes to a proper reception to discuss children, schools and government with old friends he has seen at proper receptions the night before and the night before that. If he is on the town, he may go to the National Theater to see a tryout or a road show, to the Arena to watch the only original theater company in town or to one of a dozen movie theaters where he is certain to run into old friends with whom he discussed children, schools and government at a proper reception recently.

Nighttime excursions downtown, however, are rare. The town center is a marble graveyard after dark, and in the daytime, too, for that matter, unless one enjoys watching footsore tourists struggling from monument to monument.

The rhythm of life is small-town and middle-class, which makes the town comfortable. What makes it yeasty is the cosmopolitan worldliness of its people. The man across the street has just gotten off an airplane from Karachi, and the fellow umpiring the kids' softball game has spent the day over plans for putting a man on the moon. Not long ago I dined with a Middle Eastern gentleman whose Government, after harrowing indecision, had decided to send him to Washington rather than hang him after the last political shake-up.

Another woman in the same party complained that her husband had been unbearable all week because "he's been insisting on bringing Vietnam home with him." The cab driver has just delivered three men who, he tells you hootingly, have a scheme for carrying Texas for the Republicans, and the elevator operator has always just taken the British Ambassador up or the Nigerian Ambassador down.

Besides being a town of civil servants, Washington is also a town of specialists who are constantly preoccupied with the burdens of the world. This preoccupation colors their society with a judicious, almost somber respect for the realities.

As a result, conversation is rarely dazzling. The Washingtonian has small time for the brilliant flight of fancy or the free-wheeling bull session or even the philosophical gymnastics of abstruse thought. He is a man accustomed to live within the confines of the harsh possibilities and conditioned to the realization that a mistake in judgment may be disastrous. Sagacity, and not creativity, is the city's most cherished quality.

The Washingtonian is too sophisticated to believe any more in solutions. He is bred to the idea that life offers no soluble problems, but only unpleasant alternatives, some of which are less unpleasant than others. This makes him a professional and accounts for the glazed look which quickly betrays him in, say, a typical New York conversation about world problems after someone has announced that everything would turn out happily if only people would love one another.

The Washingtonian does not scorn the psychic virtues of love, but people who believe it to be a viable foreign policy strike him as out of touch with reality and decidedly lacking in urbanity. He is willing to leave such qualities to philosophers, for they are not the business of his city. Reality compels him to understatement and caution.

Caution, moderation, understatement. These are basic qualities of Washington life. It is this prevailing distaste for extremes that has saved the inner city from esthetic ruin. Long ago, some cautious spirit decreed that private construction should not be permitted to overshadow the monumental Federal skyline. Accordingly, the office-building architects are restricted to a maximum height of 12 stories.

What they have done to the city's noblest boulevards within this limitation is bad enough, but the abominations that might have been if the sky had been the limit are all too plain. Connecticut Avenue, which had a kind of Parisian grace 10 years ago, is a case in point. It is now being completely faced with squalid glass real-estate speculations designed solely to cramp the maximum number of drones in the minimum amount of space at the greatest rental profit. It is a bleak period everywhere for architecture, but Washington has at least had the luck of the 12-story limit.

As a result, for three seasons of the year when the trees are leafy, the eyesores are partially softened and the sky remains broad and open overhead.

The trees and the sky. Something must be said about each, for they are the secret charm of Washington. They are its beauty. They fill it with color and air and drama. The city's tree and landscaping division maintains 350,000 trees on public land alone. They include the elm which canopies the broadest boulevard, the red maple, sugar maple, Norway maple, the red oak, willow oak, pin oak, the linden and the honey locust whose sweetness perfumes the spring night, the sycamore, the sweet gum, the Japanese keaki, the Chinese scholartree and the malodorous ginkgo.

21

The tourists come in early spring for the fragile and unreliable Japanese cherry blossoms, but the time to see the city at its loveliest is May when the flowering shrubs and dogwood are on the bloom in 10,000 front yards, or in autumn when the sunlight turns it gold and scarlet.

The sky gives the city a sense of openness that no other great American city has. It is a low city, rising from reconverted swampland on a series of encircling hills, and L'Enfant's broad avenues let the light in. London's sky, as V. S. Pritchett has written, "encloses the mind." Washington's sets it free and suffuses it with light.

And yet, it is an unsatisfactory town to walk in. Except in Georgetown, a few areas around Dupont Circle and on Capitol Hill, distances tend to the monumental and streets to monotony. It is not a place of sudden surprises tucked away around unexplored corners but a city of vistas to be viewed from magnificent distances—from the George Washington Memorial Parkway on the Virginia escarpment, the west front of the Capitol, or the steps of the Custis-Lee Mansion in Arlington.

As the triumphal middle-class city, it is ideally viewed from a car. It is, in fact, a city built for cars and a city with extraordinary respect for cars. Its suburbs, which, with the exception of Alexandria, Chevy Chase and Silver Spring, are highly forgettable, are basically Los Angeles East.

Magnificent expressways belt and penetrate the city to speed the white middle-class civil servants between dormitory and parking lot twice a day. New beltways and expressways are constantly springing up to menace the city homeowner and make a hash of L'Enfant's original city plan. Not surprisingly, for this is also the worst-governed city in the country, the private parking-lot operators have one of the few effective political lobbies in town. (The whiskey distributors have another.)

The government of Washington cannot be described. It must be lived with for 10 years to be believed. Again, it is the kind of government ideally fitted to the bureaucratic temperament, for basically no one is in charge and no one, therefore, can be held responsible for the mess.

The central feature of the thing is an ingenious system of committees which veto each other's recommendations. This assures that nothing will be done in a hurry and that very little will be done in a single lifetime. One of its more bizarre cogs is a complex of four Congressional committees which feud among each other about how much money can be spent for things like schools.

No one who lives in the city sits on these committees. They are usually dominated by gentlemen of the rural South or by Congressmen from the suburbs whose constituents are not very interested in the city's schools but in a terrible hurry to get a faster highway built through the city's residential district. These Congressmen have just built themselves the most expensive office building in the history of humanity, and this year for the first time the Ben W. Murch Elementary School was assigned a part-time librarian to operate the library supplied by the school parents.

This nongovernment has its virtues. A great many bad recommendations for the city die along with the good. The city drifts inexorably along its placid middle-class way, full of decay and unsolved problems but, on the whole, not so badly decayed or so problem-ridden as smartly governed cities like New York.

Everyone manages to keep his temper and go on behaving with civilized propriety. Yes, the crime is bad, but not so bad as it is painted, and, of course, there are too many people left to feel hopeless and desperate, and something should be done about them, but one must accept the realities of local politics.

On the whole, life is well-ordered and calm. The out-basket could be neater, but it is not out of control. We know how to live properly here, you see. In bed by midnight. No indiscretions. Not too much passion. The Washington Senators will finish tenth again this year, but we are above the bush-league despair of small-town chauvinists like the Mets fans.

In spring the herring will run again in the Potomac, and on the first warm day in April we will walk the C.&O. Canal towpath and listen for a whippoorwill. Or drive out to Dulles Airport and look for new expressways. In May there will be the azaleas and, between now and then, any number of very proper dinners with old friends.

In June the nights will be sweet with white locust blossoms and the sky will wash the city with soft breezes off the Carolinas. There will be visitors from out of town and we will drive them down to the Cultural Center to show how culture stands with us.

What better place could there be to live if you are neither rich, nor adventurous, nor capable in French? In the summer there will be tomatoes in the back yard. Only 15 minutes from the office.

—RUSSELL BAKER*

IV.   Essays reveal their structure in different ways. Sometimes, especially in the informal essay, the author conceals his structure by omitting or

* From "It's Middletown-on-the-Potomac," *The New York Times Magazine*, February 14, 1965, pp. 32-3, 95-6. © 1965 by The New York Times Company. Reprinted by permission.

23

disguising the introduction and deemphasizing the points of transition between one section and the next. At other times, most frequently in essays written to inform, the author emphasizes structure. All good essays, however, have a definite structure that will reveal itself on examination. Read the three essays below carefully. The first is a student essay written for an introductory writing class, the second is from a handbook of literary terms and the third is an informal essay by a professional writer. Write an outline for each, showing its structure. Be sure to include purpose statement and the major sections of the development. After each outline comment on the way that the author has adapted his structure to his purpose and probable readers, on his method of arrangement and on the way that he has used his outline in the finished essay. Has he emphasized it or concealed it? What devices has he used and why?

A.   *"ON LAUGHTER"*

Laughter is one of man's most useful expressions. It is the device or instinct by which man may show his entertainment and joy, and it is a mask behind which man may hide and protect his fear and his anguish. After his first wail of surprise, the infant learns to laugh. No, perhaps this is not learned; perhaps his laughter, the baby's chortle and giggle, is his experimentation with the realization that laughter is necessary. Laughter becomes a device for expression and concealing emotion. We laugh when we are surprised by an unexpected or absurd situation; we laugh when we are contented and happy; we laugh when we are embarrassed and self-conscious, or disappointed and sad.

Perhaps the most widely recognized and accepted category of laughter is that of the comic situation. Laughter comes from an outside force, an event which is not personal, but which initiates a personal response. We see or hear of something unexpected and unforeseen; laughter results. Slapstick comedy is a fine example of the unanticipated, comic occurrence. A man shingling his roof becomes trapped as the ladder falls away; an ancient automobile sails out over a steep cliffside, and the driver leaps out holding an umbrella and floats safely down. The audience roars and screams with amusement at the unexpected event.

We talk of the little man who can never do anything right, the clown who stumbles over his baggy trouser legs every time he takes a step, and we laugh. We hear about the boy who broke his arm, and we are sympathetic; but when we learn that the rest of his family have suffered likewise within a week or so of his accident, we laugh. These are situations which are more than unexpected; they are absurd and laughable. The absurd comedy is the unexpected event extended by repetition or degree into the unbelievable and the ridiculous. The absurd borders on, or crosses into, unreality. These situations are so near impossibility that we are shocked into scornful and amazed laughter.

A third type of comic circumstance depends on the stereotype. Many comedies are built around the character who acts quite *out* of character. It is funny to observe the staid, ascetic man behave like a love-struck Romeo over a doltish, ignorant girl. The reversal of stereotyped behavior has amused people for centuries. Chaucer's audience and present-day man have laughed alike at the antics of the clerk as he woos the Miller's wife. We would not snicker and giggle if a frail old lady fell hindside first on an icy street; but an imperious, arrogant, monocled, grey-suited businessman slips and falls undignified to the same ice, and it becomes a different matter.

There are types of laughter different from the hearty, loud guffaws brought on by the stereotype reversal, the ridiculous and unexpected situations. Laughter is not merely a result of comic perceptions; it is also self-initiated and is an expression, a release, of personal emotion.

Embarrassment is often shown by that singular laugh, easily recognizable by its high pitch and muffled tone. We use laughter as a device to escape unpleasant situations. To dispel the awkwardness and the self-consciousness we feel when embarrassed, we laugh. Perhaps our laughter lessens the severity of our insecurity when we have said or done a thing which was ill-timed and unacceptable to others. We escape and hope to be able, through our laughter, to make others release us from the embarrassing circumstance. It is usually good therapy; this laughter keeps us from over-dramatizing personal experiences. However, many people become too de-pendent on escape through laughter from embarrassing or even painful events. Laughter becomes a heavy shield to hide behind whenever they feel their emotions or ideas open to attack. We use this laugh when we are afraid, and we use it when we are embarrassed.

There is a final type of laughter; it is laughter directed at nothing and to no one else. The day is clear and sweet; you love and are loved; life is good and warm and fresh. Your soft laugh is contentment. You have scaled the treacherous cliffside; you stand at the top of a peak and view the valley below and the high mountains farther on. Your strong, deep laugh is pride.

All laughter—hearty laughter at the comic, the unexpected and ridiculous; embarrassed, self-protective giggles; cynical and sharp laughter of contempt —all these are necessary, for all laughter is a deep manifestation of emotion.

25

But the pure, strong laugh of love and pride expresses, more fully than any other type of laughter, the personal response to existence, to life; and, of all the expressions laughter may release, it is the laugh most rarely heard.

B.

"THE ROMANTIC PERIOD IN AMERICAN LITERATURE 1830-1865"

The period between the "second revolution" of the Jacksonian Era and the close of the Civil War in America saw the testing of the American nation and its development by ordeal. It was an age of great westward expansion, of the increasing gravity of the slavery question, of an intensification of the spirit of embattled sectionalism in the South, of a powerful impulse to reform in the North. Its culminating act was the trial by arms of the opposing views of the two sections in a Civil War, whose conclusion certified the fact of a united nation dedicated to the concepts of industry and capitalism and philosophically committed to the doctrine of absolute egalitarianism. In a sense it may be said that the three decades following the inauguration of Andrew Jackson as president in 1829 put to the test his views of democracy and saw emerge from the test a secure union committed to essentially Jacksonian principles.

In literature it was America's first great creative period, a full flowering of the romantic impulse on American soil. Surviving from the Federalist Age were its three major figures: Bryant, Irving, and Cooper. Emerging as new writers of strength and creative power were the novelists Hawthorne, Simms, Melville, and Mrs. Stowe; the poets Poe, Whittier, Longfellow, Lowell, and Whitman; the essayists and poets, Thoreau, Emerson, Holmes; the critics, Poe, Lowell, and Simms. The South, moving toward a concept of Southern independence, advanced three distinguished periodicals, the *Southern Review*, the *Southern Literary Messenger*, and the *Southern Quarterly Review*. In the North *Knickerbocker's Magazine* and the *Democratic Review* joined the continuing arbiter of Northern taste, the *North American Review*, and then were followed by *Harper's Magazine* (1850) and the *Atlantic Monthly* (1857). Between 1830 and 1855 the gift books and annuals proved to be remunerative markets for essays and tales.

The poetry of the period was predominantly romantic in spirit and form. Moral qualities were significantly present in the verse of Emerson, Bryant, Longfellow, Whittier, Lowell, and Thoreau. The sectional issues were debated in poetry by Whittier and Lowell speaking for abolition, and Timrod, Hayne, and Simms speaking for the South. Poe formulated his

Aristotelian theory of poetry and in some fifty lyrics practiced a symbolist verse that was to be, despite the charge of triviality by his contemporaries like Emerson, the strongest single poetic influence emerging from pre-Civil War America, particularly in its impact on European poetry. Lowell wrote satiric verse in dialect. Whitman, beginning with the 1855 edition of *Leaves of Grass* was the ultimate expression in America of a poetry organic in form and romantic in spirit, united to a concept of democracy that was pervasively egalitarian.

In the essay and on the lecture platform the New England transcendentalists—Emerson, Thoreau, Margaret Fuller, and Alcott—carried the literary expression of philosophic and religious ideas to a high level. In critical essays, Lowell wrote with distinction, Simms with skill, and Poe with genius. Until 1850 the novel continued to follow the path of Scott, with Cooper and Simms as its major producers. In the 1850's, however, emerged the powerful symbolic novels of Hawthorne and Melville, and the effective propaganda novel of Mrs. Stowe. Poe, Hawthorne, and Simms practiced the writing of short stories throughout the period, taking up where Irving had left off in the development of the form. Humorous writing by A. B. Longstreet, George W. Harris, Artemus Ward, Josh Billings, and the early Mark Twain was establishing a basis for a realistic literature in the language of the common man, but it failed in this period to receive the critical attention it was later to have.

In the drama the "star" system, the imitation of English "spectacle" drama, and romantic tragedy modeled on Shakespeare were dominant. Although N. P. Willis and R. M. Byrd were successful dramatists, only George Henry Boker, with his *Francesca da Rimini*, displayed any distinctive literary talent in the theatre. *Uncle Tom's Cabin* and *Rip Van Winkle* began stage careers that were to be phenomenally successful.

At the end of the Civil War a new nation had been born in the ordeal of war, and it was to demand and receive a new literature less idealistic and more practical, less exalted and more earthy, less consciously artistic and more direct than that produced in the age when the American dream had glowed with greatest intensity and American writers had made a great literary period by capturing on their pages the enthusiasm and the optimism of that dream.

—J. F. Thrall, A. Hibbard
and C. H. Holman*

* From *A Handbook to Literature*, rev. ed. (New York: The Odyssey Press, Inc., 1936, 1960), pp. 425-7. Reprinted by permission of The Odyssey Press, Inc.

C. *"MY WOOD"*

A few years ago I wrote a book which dealt in part with the difficulties of the English in India. Feeling that they would have had no difficulties in India themselves, the Americans read the book freely. The more they read it the better it made them feel, and a cheque to the author was the result. I bought a wood with the cheque. It is not a large wood—it contains scarcely any trees, and it is intersected, blast it, by a public footpath. Still, it is the first property that I have owned, so it is right that other people should participate in my shame, and should ask themselves, in accents that will vary in horror, this very important question: What is the effect of property upon the character? Don't let's touch economics; the effect of private ownership upon the community as a whole is another question— a more important question, perhaps, but another one. Let's keep to psychology. If you own things, what's their effect on you? What's the effect on me of my wood?

In the first place, it makes me feel heavy. Property does have this effect. Property produces men of weight, and it was a man of weight who failed to get into the Kingdom of Heaven. He was not wicked, that unfortunate millionaire in the parable, he was only stout; he stuck out in front, not to mention behind, and as he wedged himself this way and that in the crystalline entrance and bruised his well-fed flanks, he saw beneath him a comparatively slim camel passing through the eye of a needle and being woven into the robe of God. The Gospels all through couple stoutness and slowness. They point out what is perfectly obvious, yet seldom realized: that if you have a lot of things you cannot move about a lot, that furniture requires dusting, dusters require servants, servants require insurance stamps, and the whole tangle of them makes you think twice before you accept an invitation to dinner or go for a bath in the Jordan. Sometimes the Gospels proceed further and say with Tolstoy that property is sinful; they approach the difficult ground of asceticism here, where I cannot follow them. But as to the immediate effects of property on people, they just show straightforward logic. It produces men of weight. Men of weight cannot, by definition, move like the lightning from the East unto the West, and the ascent of a fourteen-stone[1] bishop into a pulpit is thus the exact antithesis of the coming of the Son of Man. My wood makes me feel heavy.

In the second place, it makes me feel it ought to be larger.

The other day I heard a twig snap in it. I was annoyed at first, for I thought that someone was blackberrying, and depreciating the value of the

[1] A *stone* is a British unit of weight equaling fourteen pounds.

undergrowth. On coming nearer, I saw it was not a man who had trodden on the twig and snapped it, but a bird, and I felt pleased. My bird. The bird was not equally pleased. Ignoring the relation between us, it took fright as soon as it saw the shape of my face, and flew straight over the boundary hedge into a field, the property of Mrs. Henessy, where it sat down with a loud squawk. It had become Mrs. Henessy's bird. Something seemed grossly amiss here, something that would not have occurred had the wood been larger. I could not afford to buy Mrs. Henessy out, I dared not murder her, and limitations of this sort beset me on every side. Ahab did not want that vineyard—he only needed it to round off his property, preparatory to plotting a new curve—and all the land around my wood has become necessary to me in order to round off the wood. A boundary protects. But—poor little thing—the boundary ought in its turn to be protected. Noises on the edge of it. Children throw stones. A little more, and then a little more, until we reach the sea. Happy Canute! Happier Alexander! And after all, why should even the world be the limit of possession? A rocket containing a Union Jack will, it is hoped, be shortly fired at the moon. Mars. Sirius. Beyond which . . . . But these immensities ended by saddening me. I could not suppose that my wood was the destined nucleus of universal dominion—it is so very small and contains no mineral wealth beyond the blackberries. Nor was I comforted when Mrs. Henessy's bird took alarm for the second time and flew clean away from us all, under the belief that it belonged to itself.

In the third place, property makes its owner feel that he ought to do something to it. Yet he isn't sure what. A restlessness comes over him, a vague sense that he has a personality to express—the same sense which, without any vagueness, leads the artist to an act of creation. Sometimes I think I will cut down such trees as remain in the wood, at other times I want to fill up the gaps between them with new trees. Both impulses are pretentious and empty. They are not honest movements towards money-making or beauty. They spring from a foolish desire to express myself and from an inability to enjoy what I have got. Creation and enjoyment are both very, very good, yet they are often unattainable without a material basis, and at such moments property pushes itself in as a substitute, saying, "Accept me instead—I'm good enough for all three." It is not enough. It is, as Shakespeare said of lust, "The expense of spirit in a waste of shame": it is "Before, a joy proposed; behind, a dream." Yet we don't know how to shun it. It is forced on us by our economic system as the alternative to starvation. It is also forced on us by an internal defect in the soul, by the feeling that in property may lie the germs of self-development and of exquisite or heroic deeds. Our life on earth is, and ought to be, material

29

and carnal. But we have not yet learned to manage our materialism and carnality properly; they are still entangled with the desire for ownership, where (in the words of Dante) "Possession is one with loss."

And this brings us to our fourth and final point: the blackberries.

Blackberries are not plentiful in this meagre grove, but they are easily seen from the public footpath which traverses it, and all too easily gathered. Foxgloves, too—people will pull up the foxgloves, and ladies of an educational tendency even grub for toadstools to show them on the Monday in class. Other ladies, less educated, roll down the bracken in the arms of their gentlemen friends. There is paper, there are tins. Pray, does my wood belong to me or doesn't it? And, if it does, should I not own it best by allowing no one else to walk there? There is a wood near Lyme Regis, also cursed by a public footpath, where the owner has not hesitated on this point. He had built high stone walls each side of the path, and has spanned it by bridges, so that the public circulate like termites while he gorges on the blackberries unseen. He really does own his wood, this able chap. Dives in Hell did pretty well, but the gulf dividing him from Lazarus could be traversed by vision, and nothing traverses it here. And perhaps I shall come to this in time. I shall wall in and fence out until I really taste the sweets of property. Enormously stout, endlessly avaricious, pseudo-creative, intensely selfish, I shall weave upon my forehead the quadruple crown of possession until those nasty Bolshies come and take it off again and thrust me aside into the outer darkness.

—E. M. FORSTER*

V. The student essays reprinted below are structurally weak. Analyze them following the instructions for exercise III. List and comment on major faults. Write a revised outline for each, using as much of the original material as possible but improving the structure. Compare the first outline with the revision.

A.   *"THE GOLDEN YEARS"*

After living on a college campus for three years, you begin to realize that certain axioms about college are just not true. One phrase that comes to my

* From ABINGER HARVEST, copyright, 1936, 1964, by E. M. Forster. Reprinted by permission of Harcourt, Brace & World, Inc. Published in England by Edward Arnold (Publishers) Ltd.

mind, for instance, is not about college in particular but about the years spent in college, the so-called "golden years." From the moment of his departure to the university, the student is faced by well-meaning older friends who sagely advise, "Enjoy yourself, these are the freest and best years of your life." This is like telling someone you want him to meet so-and-so, whom you know he will just love! When a friend of the family, well past the age of fifty, tells you that the next four years will be the best of your life, you cannot help but wonder if he has been on a constant decline since his own student days some thirty-odd years ago. The older people who are so optimistic about youth must be suffering from an exaggerated case of hindsight which has lost its knowledge of how things really were.

I would present two main arguments to such optimists. They are practically saying that after twenty-four life does not get better and usually gets worse. If this be true, what is the purpose of the medical research that is trying to keep us alive forever? They are also under the false impression that colleges and universities offer nothing more than luxurious weekends spent in well-carpeted fraternity houses, all-night beer parties and jam sessions. Unfortunately, it is not hard to understand how this latter opinion might be formed. There are students who consider social life the principal advantage of college. But there are just as many who take education seriously and try to spend their time wisely. For instance, there are YWCA chapters on campuses whose members take care of children in orphanages as well as in homes for the mentally retarded. The Phi Beta Kappa chapters on campuses prove that there are some students who are academically alert. Summer resort areas are usually filled with college students who have become maids, waitresses, dishwashers and menial laborers for the summer, in order to give their college expenses a boost.

When the adults who harp on the "golden years of youth" are shown these hard-working young people, they say that the kids do not really have to work hard. Besides, when everyone else is working, it is not that distasteful. But this is not the point. The students do not mind the summer jobs which give them three months of financial independence from parents and a feeling of doing something practical. What they want these retrospective viewers to understand about youth is that it isn't all bantering good times and thoughtless activity. These young men and women are finding out things that they have been sheltered from for twenty years. They are meeting new people. For every new friend there are fifty who might have been friends but who were discarded. These "would be" friends are the most valuable, though sometimes the most painful experiences.

I once knew a young co-ed who thought she had fallen in love with the

31

ideal man. Unfortunately, someone else had felt the same way two years earlier, his wife. He neglected to mention his wife to his new friend as he told her of his personal glories. She found out about his marriage through friends who already knew.

A liberal college sophomore was deeply concerned with liberty and "freedom for mankind." He indiscriminately joined as many "racial equality" movements as he could. After actively campaigning and working closely with this group for a year, he discovered they were a Communist-front organization. The young man was a political science major who had hoped for a top job in the National Security Agency after graduation.

Perhaps these situations are unfortunate, but sometimes they help build character. These students are finding out what it is to make an accurate judgment and how to make wise decisions. They usually find out these things through their own mistakes during the "golden years." They've reached a time when they no longer believe something true because they are told it is so. Chemistry labs have taught them critical thinking. Hopefully, their studies in philosophy have given them a reasonable firm mattress, philosophy, which will absorb the shock of some of their analytical observations. For instance, a student discovers that the ideas he formed about people when he was captain of the football team no longer seem important when he is in chair number 125 in the biology lecture room. What keeps him from completely giving up and going back to Jonestown when the first D comes back on a mid-term exam? God only knows what it is that gets students through the first two years of college while they take the uninteresting required courses in order to get into a major field. It may be blind perseverance, a sort of ramming-your-head-against-the-wall type of thing that deadens sensitivity. Perhaps this intensive pace forces them to forget they are no longer Randolph Lewis Marshall IV who was president of the student body at Bobville High, but who is now student no. P-5663-2159 in a class of two thousand in a school of twelve thousand. Lots of students do not make it; they cannot fight the upstream struggle, so they swim back home and take that comfortable little job in their dad's store. Are these the potential "golden years" advocates? How could they be when they have been so rudely and roughly shaken by a very ungolden world?

There are those who do graduate, who stick it out, and take their college degrees to well-salaried positions. Can these be the "golden years" preachers of the future? They know what it has been. The grueling all-night sessions before examinations, the D on the lab report that required a week's worth of research have all been a part of their college experience. But somewhere between the ages of twenty-four and forty-four they seem to change into a Frankenstein of forgetfulness. They no longer remember the broken friendships, bad grades, and sharp, first-experience disappointments of twenty years ago.

Does no one ever approach a middle-aged business executive or college professor and say to him that he is in the prime of life? Well, someone should. These are men who are doing something with the degree they got years ago. Not only have they passed the pain of growing up, but they have also the pleasure of seeing the theories they learned in business school being practically applied. The literature and languages the professor spent years learning and perfecting are now made alive for new students. These men have developed the very small bit of learning they got in college until now it has become a major interest in their life. Why won't a professor ever walk up to his students and say, "You won't know what life really is until you've reached forty. Forget the 'golden years' of your early twenties, they are simply the years when you equip yourself with enough knowledge to finish your education once you've left college. These last years are the 'golden years.' "

B.   *"THE PROHIBITION ERA"*

Early in 1920 when prohibition was just beginning to be felt, Johnny Torrio, a Chicago underworld figure, realized that bootlegging was a very lucrative business, but in order to take full advantage of the situation, he had to dispose of his competition. To do this, he brought in a New York hoodlum, Al Capone.

Capone was a very capable man for this type of work. He quickly and efficiently organized a well-disciplined gang of men handy with their fists and their guns who, by intimidating rival bootleggers and persuading proprietors that life might not be too happy for them unless they bought Torrio liquor, soon controlled the bootlegging business of the Chicago area. Capone was smart and vicious, as his many killings indicate, and soon acquired "finesse in the management of politics and politicians."[1] It was not long before Capone had developed into the most feared gangster of all time.

From Capone's bootlegging gangs, racketeering developed and spread tentacles as the sale and distribution of liquor increased. The racket was a scheme for collecting cash from businessmen to protect them from damage, and it prospered because the victim soon learned that if he did not pay,

[1] Frederick Lewis Allen, *Only Yesterday* (New York: Harper and Brothers, 1931), p. 260. The remaining ideas in these first two paragraphs are from the same source, pp. 259-260.

his shop would be bombed, or his trucks wrecked, or he himself might be shot in cold blood—and never a chance to appeal to the authorities for aid, because the authorities were frightened or fixed.[2]

Thus, big time crime spread even further.

For many years the United States has been recognized as the most progressive and most prosperous nation the world has ever known. If this is true, it makes one wonder how anything as terrible and degenerative to mankind as the development of big time crime could have possibly taken place. The answer to this question is found in the fact that the United States is also one of the most highly industrialized nations the world has ever known. This is, however, somewhat misleading, for the development of big time crime could have taken place in any large industrial country.

The rise of modern industry greatly benefited mankind in some ways, but on the other hand, it increased the rate of degeneration of mankind. Man lost his individuality; he became just another screw in the massive machine of industry. Man became dependent on industry for everything; he no longer raised his own food or spun the cloth for his clothes. He was dependent on industry for a place to live and, more likely than not, he ended up living in crowded industrial housing areas where sanitation, recreation facilities, and police and fire protection were very bad.

When the labor force was small wages were fairly good and people overlooked some of these disadvantages, but with the increase in the labor force wages fell. As wages continued to fall poverty increased and man's life was thrown into a turmoil. Man was confused and lacked both the knowledge and experience necessary to cope with the situation.

As conditions grew worse man began looking for a way to escape from his problems; many started drinking. Alcohol consumption increased greatly and resulted in much trouble for man. Finally, the government passed a law prohibiting the sale of alcoholic beverages, but the law had little effect. People were going to drink no matter what; they were even willing to break the law in order to drink. This defying the law set the stage for big time crime to develop. The opportunity was present, and it was just a matter of time before someone with enough insight such as Johnny Torrio, would take advantage of this opportunity.

The effects of industry that made it possible for big time crime to become a reality are just a few of the ways in which industry has adversely affected man. One can only guess as to how many of the factors in the world today which are considered harmful and degenerative to mankind can trace their causes to the rise of modern industry. One must not think, however, that the rise of industry has been entirely bad for man, for that is not true.

[2] *Ibid.*

Industry has also had many good and worthwhile effects on man; the point here is that industry has not been entirely good for man.

VI. Select a subject that interests you and that you know well. Decide on the kind of reader you would like to reach. Write a "working outline" and then an essay based on the outline and adapted to the anticipated reader. When you have finished, write a more formal outline of the essay *as written.* Comment on the differences between the two outlines. Be prepared to hand in the outlines and the comment together with the essay itself. The list given in exercise I will suggest a few possibilities, but feel free to depart from it.

The Paragraph

Like essays, paragraphs need to be planned. A good paragraph does not "just happen," it is the result of several factors working together to create the impression that we sum up with the word "good." The qualities that an author emphasizes vary with his purpose. At one time he may give logical rigor first priority; at another, emotional appeal; at another, vividness and at still another, variety. To achieve the desired effect, he must have the general purpose of his essay firmly in mind as well as the special requirements of the section for which the paragraph is written.

Good paragraphing begins with careful thought and a knowledge of the principles of paragraphing. With practice, it becomes habitual, often unconscious. On the other hand, no writer, from the novice to the most seasoned professional, reaches the point where all paragraphs come without effort. Some paragraphs seem to write themselves. Others require tinkering or revision or out-and-out deletion. Beyond this, some paragraphs are "right" whether from luck or hard work or inspiration, while others defy the writer's efforts to revise. While weak paragraphs are usually caused by errors that can be corrected when pointed out by an instructor, editor or friendly critic, at times they resist analysis. There are occasions when "It doesn't seem right" is the best comment possible.

2.1 TOPIC SENTENCE

A paragraph is a unit of thought. This is the most important rule of paragraphing. Indentation is simply a means of giving visual definition to the unity of the material within the paragraph.

Since a paragraph is a unit of thought, all material in the paragraph must be related to a dominant theme or idea. This is usually expressed in the topic sentence. **A topic sentence is a sentence stating the dominant theme or idea of the paragraph. A paragraph for which no topic sentence can be formulated lacks unity.** If two or more different topic sentences are needed for a paragraph, the paragraph is two or more thought units and should be divided accordingly. When a paragraph lacks unity, it is **incoherent.** The reader has no way of knowing what is dominant and what is subordinate. He has the impression of aimless jumping from one thought to the next like the travels of a monkey swinging from branch to branch of a tree.

The requirement that a topic sentence exist for every unified paragraph does not mean that a topic sentence must *appear* in every paragraph. The unity of the paragraph may be sufficiently obvious to allow omission of the topic sentence. An author mentioning vivid colors, balmy air, sunlight on water and the musical sound of the wind does not have to begin with the statement "Several aspects of the scene were delightful." In fact, if, for his own convenience, he begins his paragraph with a sentence like this, he will probably delete it when revising.

A paragraph containing a topic sentence has **explicit unity,** and a paragraph without one has **implied unity.** Although both types are common, explicit unity is more frequent than implied unity. Expository paragraphs which aim first at clarity almost always include a topic sentence. When included, the topic sentence should be in a position of emphasis. The beginning of the paragraph is the most common position for the topic sentence because it is the most emphatic.

2.2 SUBJECT MATTER

The subject matter of the paragraph is the material presented by the author to illustrate, make vivid, explain, qualify or otherwise develop the topic sentence. Paragraphs vary widely in length because some topic sentences need a great deal of development, others, little or none. There is no "standard length" for paragraphs. The average English paragraph is about 150 words. In newspapers the average is 50 words or less; and in philosophical and scientific writing, paragraphs of over 300 words are common. When used with discretion, short paragraphs are effective for emphasis and for marking transitions between major sections of an essay. They are, of course, regularly used in direct quotation. Long paragraphs are often necessary for adequate presentation of complex ideas.

With due allowance for variation, paragraph length can be used as a test for adequacy of thought. If an essay consists mostly of two- and three-sentence paragraphs the author has probably not given his subject matter the consideration it deserves. The reader has the impression of superficiality. Conversely, an essay consisting entirely of very long paragraphs probably suffers from inadequate analysis. The purpose statement may need additional subdivisions and the paragraphs themselves may lack unity.

39

2.3   PARAGRAPH DEVELOPMENT

There are many methods for developing a topic sentence. The common ones are development by (1) detail, (2) example, (3) comparison-contrast, (4) definition and (5) logical methods, especially cause-and-effect. Each of these methods will be discussed at length in later chapters. For the present we will limit ourselves to a few comments on use of details and examples and on paragraphs employing a combination of methods.

The object of pure description is to reproduce the object or event described as accurately as possible. This is done through citing specific details. In pure description the basis for selecting details is the fact that they are necessary for accuracy. Relevant details must be included and irrelevant or trivial ones omitted. To select details the writer must train himself to observe. When he realizes that several hundred words may be necessary to describe an object as commonplace and simple as a dining room chair, he will recognize that his problem is not so much discovering detail as selecting from the many details that *might* be cited. Pure description is common in technical and scientific writing. The following paragraph, from a popular "field guide" to insects, is an example.

Adult cicadas are large, robust insects of rather uniform appearance, with broad heads and protruding eyes. The wings, the fore pair much the larger, are usually transparent, with few cross veins, and are held roof-like over the body. There are 3 ocelli in a triangle between the eyes, and the antennae are short, consisting of a stout basal segment and a 5- or 6-segmented filament. The male "harvestflies," as these insects are often called, are responsible for the sad, sustained whirring sound which fills the air on late summer days. The sound-producing and amplifying organs are internal, concealed beneath 2 large plates below the third thoracic segment. A pair of vibrating membranes operated by powerful muscles make the sounds— really a type of drumming. The legs are short, the femora of the first pair heavy and usually armed with spines below. Cicadas insert their eggs in the branches of broad-leaved trees, in the stems of various weeds, and in grass stems.

—RALPH B. SWAIN*

*From *The Insect Guide* (Garden City, N.Y.: Doubleday & Co., 1948), p. 50.

Notice that the purpose of the description is to permit identification of the cicada. The first sentence is the topic sentence. It states the subject of the paragraph and gives five details indicating "general appearance." These are *large, robust, uniform appearance, broad heads, protruding eyes.* The following sentences are more technical. They enable the reader to confirm the identification made on the basis of first impressions. They are grouped in five main categories: wings, eyes and head, sound and sound organs, legs and breeding habits. Several specific details are given in each category. List them. Comment on the author's selection of detail. To do this you may find it useful to refer to an encyclopedia article on the cicada.

When a writer wants to create an impression or illustrate a point, his details become **examples.** The impression to be created or point to be illustrated determines the choice of examples. The author must use enough examples to be convincing, but not so many as to be long-winded. He should also avoid examples that are trite or uninteresting. In the following paragraph Mark Twain uses a great many vivid details to convey his impression of the effect of the arrival of the daily steamboat on a small Southern town. Sentence two is the topic sentence.

Once a day a cheap, gaudy packet arrived upward from St. Louis, and another downward from Keokuk. Before these events, the day was glorious with expectancy; after them, the day was a dead and empty thing. Not only the boys, but the whole village, felt this. After all these years I can picture that old time to myself now, just as it was then: the white town drowsing in the sunshine of a summer's morning; the streets empty, or pretty nearly so; one or two clerks sitting in front of the Water Street stores, with their splint-bottomed chairs tilted back against the walls, chins on breasts, hats slouched over their faces, asleep—with shingle-shavings enough around to show what broke them down; a sow and a litter of pigs loafing along the sidewalk, doing a good business in watermelon rinds and seeds; two or three lonely little freight piles scattered about the levee; a pile of skids on the slope of the stone-paved wharf, and the fragrant town drunkard asleep in the shadow of them; two or three wood flats at the head of the wharf, but nobody to listen to the peaceful lapping of the wavelets against them; the great Mississippi, rolling its mile-wide tide along, shining in the sun; the dense forest away on the other side; the point above the town and the point below, bounding the river-glimpse and turning it into a sort of sea, and withal a very still and brilliant and lonely one. Presently a film of dark smoke appears above one of these remote points; instantly

41

a Negro drayman, famous for his quick eye and prodigious voice, lifts up the cry, "S-t-e-a-m-boat a-comin'!" and the scene changes! The town drunkard stirs, the clerks wake up, a furious clatter of drays follows, every house and store pours out a human contribution, and all in a twinkling the dead town is alive and moving. Drays, carts, men, boys, all go hurrying from many quarters to a common center, the wharf. Assembled there, the people fasten their eyes upon the coming boat as upon a wonder they are seeing for the first time. And the boat *is* rather a handsome sight, too. She is long and sharp and trim and pretty; she has two tall, fancy-topped chimneys, with a gilded device of some sort swung between them; a fanciful pilot-house, all glass and gingerbread, perched on top of the Texas deck behind them; the paddle-boxes are gorgeous with a picture or with gilded rays above the boat's name; the boiler-deck, the hurricane-deck and the Texas deck are fenced and ornamented with clean white railings; there is a flag gallantly flying from the jack-staff; the furnace doors are open and the fires glaring bravely; the upper decks are black with passengers; the captain stands by the big bell, calm, imposing, the envy of all; great volumes of blackest smoke are rolling and tumbling out of the chimneys—a husbanded grandeur created with a bit of pitch-pine just before arriving at a town; the crew are groups on the forecastle; the broad stage is run far out over the port bow, and an envied deck-hand stands picturesquely on the end of it with a coil of rope in his hand; the pent steam is screaming through the gauge-cocks; the captain lifts his hand, a bell rings, the wheels stop; then they turn back, churning the water to foam, and the steamer is at rest. Then such a scramble as there is to get aboard, and to get ashore, and to take in freight and to discharge freight, all at one and the same time; and such a yelling and cursing as the mates facilitate it all with! Ten minutes later the steamer is under way again, with no flag on the jack-staff and no black smoke issuing from the chimneys. After ten more minutes the town is dead again, and the town drunkard asleep by the skids once more.

—Mark Twain*

It is unnecessary to make a distinction here between **examples** and **evidence**. The difference is a matter of emphasis. Mark Twain does not need to *prove* that before the riverboat arrives the town is "glorious with expectancy." The reader is willing to accept the idea. The examples fill in the picture, allowing the reader to share the experience. As long as they are colorful and entertaining, the reader's demands are satisfied. Often, however, the topic sentence of a paragraph is an assertion that must

* From *Life on the Mississippi* (1883).

be demonstrated. The assertion may be one that is unfamiliar or unexpected. If the reader's reaction is likely to be "Show me," the author should select details with an eye to persuading him that the assertion is valid. In a recent essay, the critic Philip Durham wished to show that Raymond Chandler (writing from the point of view of his detective hero, Philip Marlow) had an exceptionally vivid style. Since Chandler is usually considered a rather uninteresting author by critics, Durham cited many instances of the use of striking details in the novels to prove his point. The reader who says "Show me" as he begins the paragraph will probably say "I'm convinced" at the end.

> Wherever the hero went he vividly described what he saw—the streets, houses, yards, weather, and people—and no detail was too small to escape his observant eye. He never saw merely a car but a four-door, grey, '36 Plymouth sedan; not an ice cream truck but the Good Humor man in his blue and white wagon, playing "Turkey in the Straw" on his music box; not a butterfly landing on a flower but a large black and gold butterfly fish-tailing in and landing on a hydrangea bush, moving its wings slowly up and down a few times and then taking off heavily and staggering away through the motionless hot scented air; not simply rain but rain that hit the window, flattened out, and slid down in a thick wave like melted gelatine; not merely a girl but one sitting stiffly erect, with knees close together, chin level, bright teeth shining between parted lips, mad eyes wide open as she sat on a fringed orange shawl on a teakwood chair, and wore nothing but a pair of long jade earrings which probably cost a couple of hundred dollars. As Marlow moved back and forth across the city, its suburbs, and adjacent towns, his reaction to each area depended largely on his relationship to, or feeling about, a section of humanity. The fact that the hero appeared really to care about the people and their plights, to be sensitive to each little detail of their lives and surrounding, provided an intimacy between the reader and the city.
>
> —PHILIP DURHAM*

Often paragraphs use a variety of methods. A single paragraph may include details, examples, comparisons and definitions. In addition it may have sentences that explain, restate and qualify. Paragraphs using a combination of methods are **composite paragraphs.** In a composite paragraph

* From *Down These Mean Streets a Man Must Go* (Chapel Hill, N.C.: University of North Carolina Press, 1963), pp. 51-2.

the author uses several techniques to develop the thought of the topic sentence. The general rule is that all material and all techniques be related to the topic sentence. Since the relation between the topic sentence and any later sentence may be indirect, composite paragraphs demand special care. When the historian Vernon Louis Parrington wrote a paragraph showing that "General Grant was no conventional military hero," he relied chiefly on examples. However, he also felt the need to define Grant's qualities and to explain briefly why Northerners of the Civil War period considered Grant "heroic." The paragraph begins with the topic sentence. It then gives (1) *explanation* of Northern attitudes; (2) *definition* of qualities: "plainness" and "pungent phrase"; (3) *example* of Vicksburg; (4) *restatement*: he was "least imposing of heroes"; (5) additional *examples*: unimposing appearance, dullness of mind, fatalistic acceptance of war. There is no simple formula for such a paragraph. It succeeds because of the author's skill in relating all of his materials and techniques to the unifying idea.

> General Grant was no conventional military hero. It was not the gold stars on his epaulets that dazzled his generation. The people of the North had seen too many gold stars rise and set on the military horizon, they had been stricken too sorely by the bitter struggle, to be caught by military popinjays. They had gone through the fire and any hero of theirs must himself have passed through the fire. It was something veracious in the man, something solid and unyielding in the soldier, something plain as an old shoe in the field marshal of bloody battles, that caught the imagination of the North and made Grant a hero—this together with a certain gift of pungent phrase, befitting the leader of democratic hosts, that served to spread his fame amongst the common people. Vicksburg did much for his reputation, but the demand for "unconditional surrender," sent to a Confederate leader, did far more. The words fixed his character in the popular mind. Here at last was a fighting man who instead of planning how to fall back, as other generals did, thought only of going ahead; so the popular judgment shut its eyes to his dull plebeian character and set a wreath on his brows. It rested there somewhat grotesquely. In spite of a deep unconscious integrity and a stubborn will that drove him forward along whatever path his feet were set on, he was the least imposing of military heroes. Short, stooped, lumpish in mind and body, unintellectual and unimaginative, devoid of ideas and with no tongue to express the incoherent emotions that surged dully in his heart, he was a commonplace fellow that no gold braid could

set off. He hated war and disliked soldiering; yet accepting life with a stolid fatalism he fought his bloody way to ultimate victory.

—VERNON LOUIS PARRINGTON*

Composite paragraphs are found in all types of writing. The more complex the subject, the more frequent they become. In writing dealing primarily with ideas and their relationships—philosophy, political science, criticism and the like—they appear regularly. The following paragraph, from John Stuart Mill's essay *On Liberty*, is fairly typical.

When we consider either the history of opinion, or the ordinary conduct of human life, to what is it to be ascribed that the one and the other are no worse than they are? Not certainly to the inherent force of the human understanding; for, on any matter not self-evident, there are ninety-nine persons totally incapable of judging of it for one who is capable; and the capacity of the hundredth person is only comparative: for the majority of the eminent men of every past generation held many opinions now known to be erroneous, and did or approved numerous things which no one will now justify. Why is it, then, that there is on the whole a preponderance among mankind of rational opinions and rational conduct? If there really is this preponderance—which there must be unless human affairs are, and have always been, in an almost desperate state—it is owing to a quality of the human mind, the source of everything respectable in man either as an intellectual or as a moral being, namely, that his errors are corrigible. He is capable of rectifying his mistakes, by discussion and experience. Not by experience alone. There must be discussion to show how experience is to be interpreted. Wrong opinions and practices gradually yield to fact and argument; but facts and arguments, to produce any effect on the mind, must be brought before it. Very few facts are able to tell their own story, without comments to bring out their meaning. The whole strength and value, then, of human judgment, depending on the one property, that it can be set right when it is wrong, reliance can be placed on it only when the means of setting it right are kept constantly at hand. In the case of any person whose judgment is really deserving of confidence, how has it become so? Because he has kept his mind open to criticism of his opinions and conduct. Because it has been his practice to listen to all that could be said against

* From *The Beginnings of Critical Realism in America* (New York: Harcourt, Brace & Co., Inc., 1930), pp. 27-8.

him; to profit by as much of it as was just, and expound to himself, and upon occasion to others, the fallacy of what was fallacious. Because he has felt that the only way in which a human being can make some approach to knowing the whole of a subject, is by hearing what can be said about it by persons of every variety of opinion, and studying all modes in which it can be looked at by every character of mind. No wise man ever acquired his wisdom in any mode but this; nor is it in the nature of human intellect to become wise in any other manner. . . .

—John Stuart Mill*

 ## 2.4   COHERENCE

Even when all sentences in a paragraph are logically related to the topic sentence, the paragraph may seem obscure to the reader. To avoid this impression the writer uses techniques for emphasizing **coherence.** These are **arrangement, verbal links** and **transitions.**

The simplest method of arranging details within the paragraphs is **random listing.** It is occasionally necessary but is unemphatic. Usually it is a sign of missed opportunities. The author has collected his materials, but has not taken the trouble to present them in an emphatic order. Coherence is increased when the materials in the paragraph are arranged according to a definite method. The methods available are the same as those for the essay as a whole (see chapter 1; 1.7). They include the **inherent orders of time, space and process; and the logical orders such as general to specific, least to most important, cause and effect and climax.**

Each of the five paragraphs already cited to illustrate subject matter uses a different method of arrangement. The paragraph about the cicada presents its details in terms of an order based on steps of identification. Mark Twain's paragraph uses chronological order. Philip Durham's comment on Chandler begins with a list of details and then draws conclusions from them. It thus moves from evidence to conclusion. Parring-

* From *On Liberty* (1859).

ton's description of Grant moves from general to specific. The paragraph from *On Liberty*, although complex in content, relies on the simple order of question and answer.

Verbal links are devices that clarify and emphasize relationships within the paragraph. At times they are simply a convenience to the reader, but often they are necessary for comprehension. Consider the following two sentences: "I finished the job as rapidly as possible. Afterwards, I went home." *Afterwards* is a verbal link emphasizing the time relation between "finishing the job" and "going home." It is not essential since it can be deleted without ambiguity, but it assists comprehension. Now consider another example: "The desk was large and deeply scarred from years of hard use. Behind it Mr. Wallace sat, gazing into space." *Behind it* is a verbal link emphasizing a space relation. If *behind it* were deleted the passage would be ambiguous. In this case the verbal link is necessary.

Words and phrases like *moreover, in addition to, however, on the other hand, for example* and *therefore* emphasize relationships that are not inherent. The first two indicate **continuity** between one sentence and the next. *However* and *on the other hand* indicate **qualification** or **contrast.** *For example* and *therefore* emphasize **logical relationships.**

Many verbal links act as **connectives.** *Pronouns* are particularly important in this respect. When used as a verbal link, a pronoun connects the sentence in which it is used with the sentence containing its antecedent. In the same way, **repetition** of a key word or phrase can be used to connect two sentences. **Parallelism**—the use of like grammatical structure in two or more sentences—is a particularly useful kind of repetition.

2.5 TRANSITIONS

Transitions have already been mentioned in connection with organization (1.10). Paragraphs often begin with **transition sentences** that smooth the movement between one paragraph and the next. Transition sentences are also often useful within longer paragraphs. **Verbal links**

can act as **transition phrases,** but so can any word or phrase that helps to bridge the gap between two sentences or units of thought.

2.6 ANNOTATED EXAMPLES

The following paragraphs contain several devices of coherence. Words and phrases contributing to coherence are italicized; other devices are noted in the margin.

1. Narration; emphasis on chronology and space:

TRANSITION BE-
TWEEN PARAGRAPHS

There was some foundation for *such an idea,* for the ground was none of the best for a race, and grew worse continually *as we proceeded*; indeed *it* soon became desperately bad, consisting of abrupt hills and deep hollows, cut by frequent ravines not easy to pass. *At length, a mile in advance,* we saw a band of bulls. *Some* were scattered over a green declivity, while *the rest* were crowded together in the wide hollow below. *Making a circuit,* to keep out of sight, we rode toward them, *until we ascended a hill within a furlong of them,* beyond which nothing intervened that could possibly screen us from their view. *We* dismounted *behind the ridge,* just out of sight, drew our saddle-girths, examined our pistols, and mounting again, rode over the hill, and descended at a canter toward *them,*

NOTE PARALLELISM

bending close to our horses' necks. *Instantly they* took the alarm: *those* on the hill descended, *those* below gathered into a mass, and the *whole* got into motion, shouldering each other along at a clumsy gallop. *We* followed, spurring our horses to full speed; and *as the herd rushed,* crowding and trampling in terror through an opening in the hills, *we* were close at their heels, half suffocated by the clouds of dust. *But as we drew near,* their alarm and speed increased; *our* horses, being new to the work, showed signs of the utmost fear, bounding violently aside *as we approached,* and refusing to enter *among the herd. . . .*

—FRANCIS PARKMAN*

* From *The Oregon Trail* (1849).

2. Exposition; emphasis on logical relationships:

TRANSITION BE-
TWEEN PARAGRAPHS

Our previous discussion indicates the general algebraic background of geometrical constructions. Every ruler and compass *construction* consists of a sequence of steps, each of which is one of the following: *1*) connecting two points by a straight line, *2*) finding the point of intersection of two lines, *3*) drawing a circle with a given radius about a point, *4*) finding the points of intersection of a circle with another circle or with a line. An element (*point, line, or circle*) is considered to be known if it was given at the outset or if it has been constructed in some previous step. *For a theoretical analysis we* may refer *the whole construction* to a coordinated system x, y. *The given elements* will then be represented by points or segments in the *x, y* plane. *If only one segment is given* at the outset, we may take this as the unit length, which fixes the point *x 1, y O. Some-times* there appear "arbitrary" *elements: arbitrary lines* are drawn, *arbitrary points* or *radii* are chosen. (*An example* of *such an arbitrary element* appears in constructing the midpoint of a segment; *we* draw two circles of equal but *arbitrary* radius from each endpoint of the segment, and join their intersections.) *In such cases we* may choose the element to be rational. . . .

PARALLELISM (NOTE
THE USE OF NUM-
BERS FOR COHER-
ENCE.)

—Richard Courant
and Henry Robbins*

Examine the paragraphs on subject matter given above in section 2.3. Underline or write out examples of each type of verbal link. As an experiment, cross out verbal links that are not necessary to the thought of the sentences in which they appear. Which are essential to the coherence of the paragraph? Are all useful, or could some be deleted without loss? Examine the first sentence of each paragraph. Which sentences contain transitions?

► 2.7 A NOTE ON UNCONVENTIONAL PARAGRAPHS

We have observed that paragraphs do not always have to contain topic sentences. Omission of the topic sentence is possible when the dominant idea is sufficiently obvious from the subject matter itself.

* From *What Is Mathematics?* (New York: Oxford University Press, 1941), p. 127.

With or without topic sentence, the normal paragraph must have unity. Two exceptions to this rule are impressionistic and stream-of-consciousness paragraphs. In both types the details are intended to have the effect of a series of impressions recorded *as they occur* in the mind. The details need not have either unity or order so long as they all occurred at the same time or in association with the same event. Verbal links may be supplied or they may be suppressed in order to intensify the reader's illusion of sharing directly in the author's mental world. Since the impressions are undifferentiated there is no logical basis for separating them into paragraph units. Impressionistic paragraphing tends to be arbitrary, giving the reader a chance to catch his breath rather than marking logical divisions; and individual paragraphs tend to be long. The most famous example of stream-of-consciousness technique in English is the monologue of Molly Bloom at the end of Joyce's novel, *Ulysses*, which is a single paragraph fifty pages long. A more manageable example is Dylan Thomas's impressionistic description of the plight of the lecturer in America.

There they go, every spring, from New York to Los Angeles: exhibitionists, polemicists, histrionic publicists, theological rhetoricians, historical hoddy-doddies, balletomanes, ulterior decorators, in love with steaks, men after millionaires' widows, men with elephantiasis of the reputation (huge trunks and teeny minds), authorities on gas, bishops, best sellers, editors looking for collars, existentialists, serious physicists with nuclear missions, men from the B.B.C. who speak as though they had the Elgin Marbles in their mouths, potboiling philosophers, professional Irishmen (very lepri-corny), and I am afraid, fat poets with slim volumes.

And see, too, in that linguaceous stream, the tall monocled men, smelling of saddle soap and club arm-chairs, their breath a nice blending of whisky and fox's blood, with big protruding upper-class tusks and county moustaches, presumably invented in England and sent abroad to advertise *Punch*, who lecture to women's clubs on such unlikely subjects as "The History of Etching in the Shetland Islands." And the brassy-bossy men-women, with corrugated-iron perms,[1] and hippo hides, who come, self-announced, as "ordinary British housewives," to talk to rich minked chunks of American matronhood about the iniquity of the Health Services, the criminal sloth of the miners, the visible tail and horns of Mr. Aneurin Bevan, and the fear of everyone in England to go out alone at night because of the organized

[1] Permanent waves—British slang.

legions of cosh boys[2] against whom the police are powerless owing to the refusal of those in power to equip them with revolvers and to flog to ribbons every adolescent offender on any charge at all.

And there shiver and teeter also, meek and driven, those British authors unfortunate enough to have written, after years of unadventurous forgotten work, one bad novel which became enormously popular on both sides of the Atlantic. At home, when success first hit them, they were mildly delighted; a couple of literary luncheons went sugar-tipsy to their heads, like the washing sherry served before those luncheons; and perhaps, as the lovely money rolled lushly in, they began to dream in their moony writers' way, of being able to retire to the country, keep wasps (or was it bees?), and never write another lousy word. But in come the literary agent's triggermen and the publisher's armed narks.[3] "You must go to the States and make a Personal Appearance. Your novel is killing them over there, and we're not surprised either. You must go round the States lecturing to women." And the inoffensive writers, who've never dared lecture anyone, let alone women—they are frightened of women, they do not understand women, they write about women as creatures that never existed, and the women lap it up —these sensitive plants cry out: "But what shall we lecture about?"

—DYLAN THOMAS*

Novice writers sometimes assume that because it lacks obvious order impressionistic writing is totally disorganized. The alert reader will notice that beneath the artfully helter-skelter surface of Dylan Thomas's prose there is a good deal of order. In fact, it is easy to produce tenth-rate imitations of impressionistic writing, but it is extremely hard to use the impressionistic method successfully.

TERMS TO BE LEARNED

▶ Paragraph
▶ Topic sentence
▶ Subject matter (definition and three types)

[2] Club-carrying juvenile delinquents—British slang.
[3] Henchmen, especially informers—British slang.
* From QUITE EARLY ONE MORNING by Dylan Thomas. Copyright 1954 by New Directions. Reprinted by permission of the publishers, New Directions, New York; and by permission of the Literary Executors of the Dylan Thomas Estate. Published in England by J. M. Dent & Sons Ltd: Publishers.

▸ Arrangement (two methods of securing coherence)
▸ Devices of coherence (definition and four types)
▸ Transition

Exercises & Theme Topics

I. Write out the topic sentence for each of the following paragraphs. If the author has not included a topic sentence, write one that indicates the unifying idea of the paragraph. Then indicate subject matter, method of arrangement, verbal links and transitions. Select one paragraph and be prepared to comment on the author's reasons for using the techniques observed.

A.

A couple of hours' march brought us to LaCrosse, the great city whose wonders I had longed to confront. It stood on the bank of a wide river and had all the value of a seaport to me, for in summer-time great hoarsely bellowing steamboats came and went from its quay, and all about it rose high wooded hills. Halting there, we overlooked a wide expanse of snow-covered ice in the midst of which a dark, swift, threatening current of open water ran. Across this chasm stretching from one ice-field to another lay a flexible narrow bridge over which my father led the way toward hills of the western shore. There was something especially terrifying in the boiling heave of that black flood, and I shivered with terror as I passed it, having vividly in my mind certain grim stories of men whose teams had broken through and been swept beneath the ice never to reappear.

—HAMLIN GARLAND*

* From *A Son of the Middle Border* (New York: The Macmillan Company, 1934), pp. 71-2.

B.

At five o'clock on the morning of Thursday, the 12th of May, from his bedroom on the corner of the Rue des Poullies, Don Bernardino de Mendoza heard the tramp of many armed men coming down the Rue Saint-Honoré. Even to the ambassador's purblind eyes there was no mistaking these burly figures looking, in their padded doublets and voluminous pantaloons, even bigger than they were. They were the king's Swiss, the regiments from Lagny. They filled the Rue Saint-Honoré from side to side and for most of its length, marching as they might have marched entering a captured city, colors uncased, pikes and halberds at the ready, the slow matches of the arquebusiers and musketmen alight. Behind them the regiments of the French Guard were coming through the Porte Saint-Honoré, and the early sun was beginning to glint on morions and pike heads, gold lace and gun barrels. Mendoza watched the column hold on past the narrow streets that led to the Louvre and angle left towards the Cemetery of the Holy Innocents. As they did so, there came the rolling thunder of twenty tambours and the shrill squealing of a score of fifes. From the direction of the gate, the music of the French Guard took up the defiant rhythm.

—Garrett Mattingly*

C.

Even in its earliest manifestations the Newcomen engine was simple enough so that observers could understand its operating principle and cyclical sequence of events as soon as an explanation was provided. A vertical steam cylinder, fitted with a piston, was located under one end of the large, pivoted working beam; the piston rod was hung on a flat chain secured to the top of the arch-shaped head of the beam. Steam was supplied to the cylinder by the boiler directly below it. A verticle lift pump was located under the other end of the beam and the pump rod hung on a flat chain secured to the arch head just above it. Thus both the piston rod and the pump rod moved vertically, always tangent to a circle whose center was at the pivot of the beam.

A working stroke began after the steam cylinder had been filled with steam, at a pressure just slightly above atmospheric, from the boiler. The pump end of the working beam was held down by the weight of the re-

* From *The Armada* (Boston: Houghton Mifflin Company, 1959), p. 218.

ciprocating pump parts, which extended down into the mine. The steam-admission cock was closed, and water was then injected into the cylinder in order to condense the steam and produce a vacuum. The atmosphere, acting on the top of the piston, pushed the piston down into the evacuated cylinder, which caused the pump rod to be lifted by the other end of the beam. The cycle of operation was completed by again admitting steam to the cylinder in order to allow the pump end of the working beam to go down. As soon as the cylinder pressure reached atmospheric, the spent injection water was discharged into a sump.

—EUGENE S. FERGUSON*

D.

When Webster debated Hayne, the clash was not just of views but of styles—of language as much as of law. But today's New England Yankee inheritors of the Webster mantle stand mute. The region's best orator is probably Senator John Pastore of Rhode Island, an Italian-American who brings a Mediterranean passion to debate. Similarly, the great Southern oratorical tradition is being juggled precariously between generations. Young Russell Long of Louisiana may inherit it from Georgia's Richard Russell, but many question whether he has the intellect and the temperament to carry it well. Sam Ervin of North Carolina and Thruston Morton of Kentucky are almost in the late Alben Barkley's class as storytellers, but who is there in the West or the Midwest who can turn a thought to poetry, as William Jennings Bryan did in this speech on Prohibition?

—DAVID S. BRODER†

E.

The worship of the oak tree or of the oak god appears to have been shared by all the branches of the Aryan stock in Europe. Both Greeks and Italians associated the tree with their highest god, Zeus or Jupiter, the divinity of the sky, the rain, and the thunder. Perhaps the oldest and certainly one of the most famous sanctuaries in Greece was that of Dodona,

---

* From "The Origins of the Steam Engine," *Scientific American* (January, 1964), 102-3.
† From "Great Speeches Aren't Necessarily Good Politics," *New York Times Magazine*, May 29, 1964, p. 22.

where Zeus was revered in the oracular oak. The thunderstorms which are said to rage at Dodona more frequently than anywhere else in Europe, would render the spot a fitting home for the god whose voice was heard alike in the rustling of the oak leaves and in the crash of thunder. Perhaps the bronze gongs which kept up a humming in the wind round the sanctuary were meant to mimick the thunder that might so often be heard rolling and rumbling in the coombs of the stern and barren mountains which shut in the gloomy valley. In Boeotia, as we have seen, the sacred marriage of Zeus and Hera, the oak god and the oak goddess, appears to have been celebrated with much pomp by a religious federation of states. And on Mount Lycaeus in Arcadia the character of Zeus as god both of the oak and of the rain comes out clearly in the rain charm practised by the priest of Zeus, who dipped an oak branch in a sacred spring. In his latter capacity Zeus was the god to whom the Greeks regularly prayed for rain. Nothing could be more natural; for often, though not always, he had his seat on the mountains where the clouds gather and the oaks grow. On the Acropolis at Athens there was an image of Earth praying to Zeus for rain. And in time of drought the Athenians themselves prayed, "Rain, rain, O dear Zeus, on the cornland of the Athenians and on the plains."

—James George Frazer*

F.

Reason, according to the simplest view of it, is the faculty of gaining knowledge without direct perception, or of ascertaining one thing by means of another. In this way it is able, from small beginnings, to create to itself a world of ideas, which do or do not correspond to the things themselves for which they stand, or are true or not, according as it is exercised soundly or otherwise. One fact may suffice for a whole theory; one principle may create and sustain a system; one minute token is a clue to a discovery. The mind ranges to and fro, and spreads out, and advances forward with a quickness which has become a proverb, and a subtlety and versatility which baffle investigation. It passes on from point to point, gaining one by some indication; another on a probability; then availing itself of an association; then falling back on some received law; next seizing on testimony; then committing itself to some popular impression or some inward instinct, or some obscure memory; and thus it makes progress not unlike a clamberer

* From "The Worship of the Oak," *The Golden Bough* (New York: The Macmillan Company, 1944) , p. 159.

on a steep cliff, who, by quick eye, prompt hand, and firm foot, ascends how he knows not himself, by personal endowments and by practice, rather than by rule, leaving no track behind him, and unable to teach another. It is not too much to say that the stepping by which great geniuses scale the mountains of truth is as unsafe and precarious to men in general, as the ascent of a skilful mountaineer up a literal crag. It is a way which they alone can take; and its justification lies in their success. And such mainly is the way in which all men, gifted or not gifted, reason—not by rule, but by an inward faculty.

—John Henry Newman*

G.

This small lake was of most value as a neighbor in the intervals of a gentle rain storm in August, when both air and water being perfectly still, but the sky overcast, midafternoon had all the serenity of evening, and the wood-thrush sang around, and was heard from shore to shore. A lake like this is never smoother than at such a time; and the clear portion of the air above it being shallow and darkened by clouds, the water, full of light and reflections, becomes a lower heaven itself so much the more important. From a hilltop near by, where the wood had been recently cut off, there was a pleasing vista southward across the pond, through a wide indentation in the hills which form the shore there, where their opposite sides sloping toward each other suggested a stream flowing out in that direction through a wooded valley, but stream there was none. That way I looked between and over the near green hills to some distant and higher ones in the horizon, tinged with blue. Indeed, by standing on tiptoe I could catch a glimpse of some of the peaks of the still bluer and more distant mountain ranges in the northwest, those true-blue coins from heaven's own mint, and also of some portion of the village. But in other directions, even from this point, I could not see over or beyond the woods which surrounded me. . . .

—Henry David Thoreau†

II. Each of the following passages from student essays needs improvement. Identify the principal faults and rewrite, correcting them. Where necessary, add material of your own.

* From *The Idea of a University* (1852).
† From *Walden* (1854).

A.

The view from my room this morning was dismal. The trees were soaked with rain. There were dead leaves and fallen branches everywhere. Cars were proceeding at a snail's pace. The window panes were smudged with brown soot and grime. An emaciated squirrel was looking disconsolately for acorns. The air was hot from the steam radiator, and I noticed that my roommate had left his toothbrush on the desk. The flowers in the quadrangle had been beaten down into the dirt. Most of the blossoms had been broken off, and the ones that remained were the color of mud. The sky was slate gray. I felt like going back to bed. But before I did, I noticed the wind whipping the branches of the trees. From the distance, the chimes in the bell tower announced that it was time for class.

B.

There were various reasons for the popularity of canasta. It could be played by different numbers of players. Bridge, of course, required no more and no less than four. Many people naturally continued to like bridge. Some players found canasta more dramatic than bridge. They liked the appeal of the different combinations of cards. Canasta became popular about 1950. Many card players liked the freedom of personal choice and independence from a partner's decisions.

C.

Many people who use the word *Fascism* in discussing current world problems confuse it with *Communism*. Both Fascism and Communism are totalitarian, but Fascism is the economic antithesis of Communism. Fascism uses military force to sustain capitalism. Obviously, no two systems of government could be more different. But there has never been a clear explanation of the two systems. The popular mediums of information—nwspapers, radio and movies—refer indiscriminately at times to Communism and Fascism in the same terms.

D.

One of the books I read in high school English was Dickens' *Tale of Two Cities*. In it the author tells of some of the horrors of the French

Revolution. He spent several pages telling about how the French aristocrats suffered. The climax part of the book tells how a n'er-do-well who had failed in life sacrifices himself for another. He took his place in a prison and went stoically to the guillotine for him.

E.

It is estimated that well over 500 million people use English as a native or secondary language. The inventions that make communication possible— radio, telephone, telegraph, the motion picture—are largely controlled by English-speaking peoples. English has replaced French as the language of diplomacy. Various corrupt forms of English, like Pidgin English, are widely spoken in the Pacific area. English is made up largely of words from both Teutonic and Romance languages; a good part of its vocabulary is already familiar to those who speak a European language. The 400 million who speak Chinese are separated in innumerable and mutually unintelligible dialectal groups.

F.

According to Charles Darwin, as one or more individuals are born than can possibly survive, there must in every case be a struggle for existence. This statement applied to the eighteenth century class struggle between the proletarian and the bourgeois. In the eighteenth century the focus of industrialization created a middle class, the bourgeoisie. This class composed the high-ranking members of industry: merchants, businessmen, and shopkeepers. The proletarians, the workingmen, composed the majority of the population, in spite of the bad working conditions and poor sanitation practices that existed. The demand of the proletarian for improvements in working conditions and sanitation practices was recognized as a struggle—a struggle for the survival of the proletarian. . . .

G.

Many people ask if freshman English courses are worth the time spent in them. Since the course is mandatory in most all colleges, one would think that freshman English is beneficial. But the course is little more than a waste of time and effort.

First, the freshman student has had twelve years of schooling before college. Strictly speaking the grade school stressed grammar while the high school followed up with rhetoric. Freshman English is nothing but a repeat course.

Second, the freshman receives most elements of rhetoric in his other courses. In college, most exams are of the essay type. The professors of the other courses mark off for grammatical or rhetorical errors. In this way the student learns and corrects his mistakes, making an English course entirely unnecessary. . . .

H.

I have taken two criticisms by Tom F. Driver and one by Robert Coleman for my discussion. In presenting these, I shall offer a few comments of my own concerning the book of Job and the play, but not always exactly on the criticism.

I believe that the "meat" of the story has been left out in the play to a degree. I believe my thinking is somewhat along the line of Tom F. Driver's. Job is not actually seeking an answer for the cause of his misfortunes. He knows from living a Christian life that God does not answer to man, but that man answers to God.

God does not promise us a good, wealthy life if we are faithful to Him. . . .

III. Write a paragraph on one or more of the following subjects.

A. A pure description based on direct observation. For example, a chair, your classroom, a campus building, a textbook, the person sitting next to you in class.

B. A description of an event based on direct observation, emphasizing its dominant quality. For example, a fraternity initiation, a speech or lecture, an interview, an automobile accident.

C. A paragraph illustrating or demonstrating a general point. For example, "Democrats (or Republicans) are unpopular in my family"; "Everyone should own a station wagon"; "Othello has a noble character"; "Most cities are overcrowded"; "Benjamin Franklin was a practical philosopher."

D. A paragraph explaining a process or giving instructions. For example, the operation of a spark plug; freezing vegetables; taking notes; voter registration; the dissection of a frog; making a budget.

IV. Write an essay on one of the following topics. Plan it carefully and submit your outline with the finished essay. When the draft is completed, underline each topic sentence once and each important verbal link and transition twice. In the lefthand margin indicate the method of arrangement for each paragraph.

A. A newspaper report, based on direct observation, of a recent campus event.

B. An analysis of a current political or social problem, or an essay advocating a needed change or reform.

C. An essay-review of a movie, play or book that has interested you, designed to recommend it to the general public.

D. A description of a person whom you know well and you find interesting, colorful or significant; or a description of a building or locale.

Style (I)

Style is one of the most elusive terms in rhetoric. To a certain extent style is a reflection of the personality, taste and experience of the author; hence the saying "style is the man." However, to define style only in terms of personality is to miss an important point. An author has only one personality, but he has several styles from which he selects the one best suited to his immediate purpose. We can therefore define style rhetorically as **the way in which an author adapts his expression to his purpose.** Style in this sense may be improved by practice in the same way as skill in tennis or playing the piano. The present chapter is an introduction to the principles of good style. The student should study these principles with the aim of applying them to his own writing.

Style has sometimes been thought of as "fancy decoration" found chiefly in poetry and other consciously artistic forms of writing. Nothing could be more false. Since style arises from the use of language, any discourse, written or spoken, has style. A child's one-paragraph essay, a business letter, a laboratory report, all have style just as surely as a novel by Dickens or a poem by Milton. The writer cannot choose between using style or leaving it out. His only choice is whether to control his style by adapting it to the work at hand or to leave it to chance in the vain hope that it will turn out all right in the end.

One excellent way to develop a sense of style is by reading. Through contact with professional writers the student will become familiar with the various kinds of style which have been used in the past. Sometimes direct imitation is helpful to the beginner. Benjamin Franklin, for example, tells in his *Autobiography* how he taught himself to write effectively by deliberate imitation of the essays of Addison and Steele in *The Spectator*. He would read an essay in *The Spectator*, write one of his own, and then compare the two. The contemporary novelist Somerset Maugham used the essays of Jonathan Swift in a similar way. The student need not go so far as Franklin or Maugham, but he will find that the broader and more attentive his reading, the better his style will become.

3.1 TONE

Style may be considered descriptively or functionally. When a critic points out an author's fondness for certain words or images, his characteristic sentence structure or his tendency to avoid adjectives or use them frequently, the critic is *describing* his style. The functional approach is different. It assumes that the author uses a particular device because he decides it contributes to the passage in which it occurs and, ultimately, to his purpose. For example, in *The Fall of the House of Usher* Edgar Allan Poe describes the ancestral mansion of the Ushers by using words which suggest melancholy and fear. This is appropriate to the purpose of the story as a whole, because it is a tale of terror and the supernatural. On the other hand, a real-estate prospectus attempting to sell the same mansion would probably describe it with words suggesting its quaint charm, in order to make it seem attractive to a purchaser. Notice that each description would be correct. The difference in style reflects the different purposes of the two writers.

It is useful to have a term for the effect of a passage on the reader. The most common one, and the one that will be used here, is **tone. Tone is the quality that controls the response of the reader to the subject matter.** In Poe's story, the subject matter is a country mansion. Since Poe's description is calculated to frighten or mystify, its **tone** is fear or melancholy. Likewise, the **tone** of the hypothetical real-estate prospectus would be charm. An appropriate tone is one that contributes to the larger purpose of the author. An inappropriate tone, on the other hand, is one that conflicts with his purpose, as though, for example, the real-estate prospectus described the mansion in such a way as to make it seem unattractive to the buyer.

The following three passages illustrate tone. They describe the same scene, the entrance of the Cathedral of St. Mark in Venice. Yet each has a unique tone reflecting the personality and purpose of its author. The first is by Mark Twain. Its tone is satirical, almost contemptuous, reflecting Twain's doubts about the value of European traditions. The second is from a travel sketch by Henry James. Its tone is one of admiration for the beauty and age of the cathedral, in keeping with James's deep respect for European traditions. The third is from a guidebook. Its tone is objective and reflects the author's desire to relate precise information in relatively few words.

> Everything was worn out—every block of stone was smooth and almost shapeless with the polishing hands and shoulders of loungers who devoutly idled her in bygone centuries.
>
> —MARK TWAIN

> The pavement was dark, rich, cracked, uneven, spotted with porphyry and time-blackened malachite, polished by the knees of innumerable worshippers.
>
> —HENRY JAMES

63

The pavement (walk with care!) shows irregularities resulting from the continual settling of the building on its pilings. . . . It is in mosaic formed of colored pieces of marble and arranged in an extreme variety of designs (XII century), based on *opus sectile* and *opus tessellatum*, but in large part restored. The most interesting areas are indicated in the choice of the description of the church (see below).

—Tourist Guide to Venice

Although they are brief, the preceding examples illustrate the fact that tone is the result of several factors working together. The three most important are word choice, imagery and sentence structure. For the present, we will consider only the first two. The third, which is perhaps the most difficult, will be treated separately in chapter 9.

3.2 WORD CHOICE; DENOTATION AND CONNOTATION

Word choice is a major factor in creating tone. The words an author uses betray the extent of his vocabulary, his mastery of it and his attitudes, both conscious and unconscious.

To control word choice it is necessary to distinguish between two aspects of language. The first is **denotation** and the second **connotation**. A thorough analysis of denotation and connotation would lead into the fields of linguistics and semantics and cannot be undertaken here. **For present purposes, the following working definitions are adequate: Denotation is the literal or dictionary meaning of a word. Connotation is the implied overtone of meaning of the word as determined by use—the coloration or shade of meaning that the word suggests.** For example, a man who donates generously to charity could be called either a philanthropist or a do-gooder. Both words have the same **denotation** (here the literal meaning as determined by their common referent—that is, a person who makes an effort to promote human welfare). However, they have opposite **connotations**. *Philanthropist* has a favorable connotation suggesting admiration. *Do-gooder* has an unfavorable (pejorative) connotation suggesting contempt. In the same manner, a man with a cheerful

64

disposition could be called either an *optimist* or a *Pollyanna*; and a man without a job, either an *unemployed worker* or a *bum*. Most words have both connotation and denotation, and it is wrong to think of one element as less important than the other. This can be illustrated by listing several adjectives that might be used in the phrase "a beautiful picture." Among these are *beautiful, pretty, elegant, attractive, voluptuous, breathtaking, ornate, flashy* and *dazzling*. Each of these words has a different connotation. *Flashy,* for example, is unfavorable; it connotes a false or tasteless beauty. *Ornate* suggests too much ornament. *Voluptuous* suggests sensual, especially erotic appeal, and could be either favorable or unfavorable. *Pretty* and *attractive* are favorable but suggest mediocrity. *Beautiful* and *elegant* are somewhat more favorable; and *dazzling* and *breathtaking* are words of unqualified praise.

3.3 LEVELS OF USAGE

Level of usage is such an important aspect of language that it needs special treatment. Everyone knows that many words that are perfectly appropriate in conversation would be out of place in a formal essay such as a research report or a legal brief. This is because many words are restricted to one level of usage. We will here recognize four levels of usage:

1. Technical and formal:

Some words are technical or formal. They are used where precise denotation is necessary for the accurate expression of ideas. A lawyer uses terms like *tort, probate* and *habeas corpus,* not to mystify the layman, but to convey an exact idea to a trained reader. A historian speaks of the *enlightenment* or the *baroque;* a stockbroker of *preferred stock, marginal buying* or the *Dow-Jones average;* and a mathematician of *parameters, functions* and *prime numbers.* All of these are technical expressions. In general, the **technical vocabulary** tends to merge with the **formal vocabulary,** made up of words that are not common in standard writing such as nonfiction articles in popular magazines. Both technical and formal words are extremely useful when employed properly. They create a tone of precision and objectivity and help convince the reader that the author knows his subject well. On the other hand, they can be misused. When employed unnecessarily or in an informal passage, they create a bad effect. They make the author seem pretentious and suggest that he wishes to confuse rather than inform his reader. In this case they are called **jargon.**

2. Standard:

Most words are appropriate in both formal and informal writing. They form the **standard vocabulary** of English. Most nonfiction magazine articles, newspaper features and student essays employ the standard vocabulary.

3. Colloquial:

Many words in common use are colloquial. They are perfectly correct in everyday speech, but they are out of place in formal and standard writing, unless used occasionally for emphasis or in dialogue. When used they create a racy, familiar tone that has some of the immediacy of direct conversation. Colloquialisms are common in fiction and certain kinds of nonfiction where the author's main purpose is to stimulate or amuse, but they should generally be avoided in writing that is meant primarily to convey information.

4. Slang:

The colloquial vocabulary shades into slang, which should be avoided except where the author is transcribing someone's speech *verbatim.*

Levels of usage may be illustrated by listing some of the terms that could be used to describe an emotionally disturbed person. *Psychoneurotic, manic-depressive* and *schizoid* are **technical.** They not only indicate emotional disturbance, but define the precise kind of disturbance exhibited. *Maladjusted* and *neurotic* are **formal** but are used so often that they are gradually becoming **standard.** *Nervous, tense, excitable, irritable* and *unstable* are all **standard.** *Jumpy, touchy, flighty, edgy* and *tensed up* are **colloquial,** with the last word on the border between colloquial and **slang.** *Screwy, batty, nutty* and *hopped up* are **slang.** As these words make clear, there is no neat dividing line between one level and the next. Levels of usage blend into one another. Many words are extremely difficult to classify, and words often migrate from one level to another.

3.4 PRECISE USE OF LANGUAGE; EXAMPLES

Precision arises from using words in a way that is both exact and appropriate. Obviously, an author must use words exactly; that is, in accordance with their denotative meanings. *Imply* and *infer,* for example, have different denotative meanings. An author who writes, "Marx's theory of history *infers* that man does not have free will" is using inexact language since *infer* means "to draw a conclusion from previously established facts or premises." What the author means is, "Marx's theory *implies* that man does not have free will."

In addition to using words exactly, the author must select words that contribute to an appropriate tone. This is not a matter of being careful with one or two words and forgetting the rest. It is a requirement that must be observed throughout the essay or story. If it is neglected, the writing will become vague, ambiguous or even self-contradictory. Conversely, the more carefully it is observed, the more clear and emphatic the final product.

The following passage uses words in a way that is both exact and appropriate. It is from the *Columbia Encyclopedia* entry for "hydrogen bomb." The purpose is to inform. Exactness is essential, and the appropriate tone is one of objectivity. Therefore the words are from the standard vocabulary, with several key terms added from the technical and formal vocabulary. The use of these terms is limited, because the article is for the intelligent layman rather than the specialist. Several typical instances are italicized.

HYDROGEN BOMB, weapon *deriving* its energy from the *union* of atoms of *low atomic weight.* In the atomic bomb, which employs the *elements uranium* and *plutonium,* the *explosive conversion of mass into energy* is achieved by *fission* or splitting of the *nuclei* of these *heavy elements.* In a hydrogen bomb, on the other hand, a *fusion* of extremely *light elements* must be accomplished. It has been estimated that a temperature of more than *20,000,000°C.* would be required to bring about such a *fusion.* To produce heat of such intensity an atomic bomb would probably have to be used as a *detonator;* the most likely materials to be used as *bomb ingredients* seem to be *tritium* (the *nucleus* of which is *triton*) and *deuterium* (the *nucleus* of which is *deuteron,*) both *isotopes* of *hydrogen.*

—*The Columbia Encyclopedia**

The preceding example is typical of writing that conveys information. Similar passages can be found in almost any textbook or manual, in scholarly essays and in research papers and reports.

In much writing, including informal essays and works of fiction, the desire to inform is coupled with or even secondary to the desire to stimulate emotions such as admiration, amusement, friendship, greed and fear. The following paragraph from Washington Irving's *Legend of Sleepy Hollow* uses words from the standard and colloquial vocabulary to stimulate a feeling of delight in the scene being described. Understood in terms of Irving's purpose, his use of language has as much precision as that in the encyclopedia entry on the hydrogen bomb. Again, typical instances are italicized.

As Ichabod *jogged* slowly on his way, his eye, ever open to every symptom of culinary *abundance*, ranged with *delight* over the *treasures* of *jolly* autumn. On all sides he beheld *vast stores* of apples; some hanging in oppressive *opulence* on the trees; some gathered into baskets and barrels for the market; others heaped up in rich piles for the cider press. Further on he beheld *great* fields of Indian corn, with its *golden* ears *peeping* from their leafy coverts, and holding out the *promise* of *cakes* and *hasty pudding*; and the yellow pumpkins lying beneath them, turning up their *fair round bellies* to the sun, and giving *ample* prospects of the *most luxurious of pies*; and anon he passed the *fragrant* buckwheat fields, breathing the odor of the bee-hive, and as he beheld them, *soft anticipations* stole over his mind of dainty flap-jacks, well buttered, and garnished with *honey* or *treacle* by the *delicate* little hand of Katrina Van Tassel.

—WASHINGTON IRVING†

* From *The Columbia Encyclopedia*, eds. William Bridgwater and Seymour Kurtz (New York: Columbia University Press, 1963), p. 996.
† From *The Legend of Sleepy Hollow* (1820).

Here no single word or phrase stands out. The tone is created by repetition of words that connote delight. *Jogged, abundance, delight, treasures, jolly, opulence, rich, golden*—these and the rest work together, and their effect is cumulative. To test the paragraph the student can make the experiment of substituting different words. What would be the effect of using *walked* in place of *jogged* in the first sentence? Of *autumn harvest* in place of *treasures of jolly autumn*? Of *yellow ears visible* in place of *golden ears peeping*? None of these substitutions would destroy the paragraph, but each one would rob it of its effect. If the whole paragraph were treated in this way, it would become flat and fail to achieve its purpose.

The test applied to Irving's paragraph can be applied to any writing. The writer should choose words that create a clearly defined tone while composing his first draft. No one can be entirely successful on first try. Therefore, during revision he should test his word choice. Has he missed opportunities to emphasize tone? Equally important, has he used any word that is inconsistent with the dominant tone?

▶ ## 3.5 IMAGERY

Imagery is another important factor in tone. An ability to use imagery is necessary to all writers—not merely to poets. Imagery can explain, emphasize and stimulate emotion; and it can serve as an indirect comment on what is being said. Some of these functions will be explained here. Others which depend on the structure of comparison will be considered in chapter 7.

In the broadest sense, imagery is any device of emphasis, ornament or sense appeal. It includes such varied devices as simile, metaphor, pun, irony, personification, repetition, onomatopoeia and antithesis. Even words used literally can become imagery in the broad sense, as when we speak of the "imagery of darkness" in *Macbeth,* or the "sun-imagery" in *Henry IV, Part 1.* Although the word **image** suggests a *picture,* much **imagery** is nonvisual.

To avoid complication the present discussion of imagery will be limited to **simile** and **metaphor.**

69

3.6   SIMILE AND METAPHOR

Simile is a comparison made explicit by the use of "like" or "as." Metaphor is an implied comparison without "like" or "as." The phrase, "the snow lay like a blanket on the ground," is a **simile** comparing the appearance of new-fallen snow to a blanket on a bed. If we say, "the snow blanketed the ground," we have changed the simile into a **metaphor.** The *comparison* is identical, but in the first example it is explicit, and in the second, implicit. This explains why metaphor is far more common in everyday speech than simile. In metaphor the speaker need not be aware he is making a comparison. Simile is more literary. The speaker usually knows he is making a comparison when he uses it.

The largest class of images is **buried imagery,** and buried images are all metaphors. They are expressions that at one time were conscious images, but have been used in their nonliteral sense so long that their original meaning has been forgotten. *Run,* for example, refers to an action performed by the legs; yet no one thinks of the phrase "running water" as an image. *Define* is used almost exclusively in connection with words, but it comes from the Latin root *finis,* which originally meant a physical boundary, limit or end.

Buried imagery is so extensive that some authorities believe all words were originally metaphors. Whether or not this is true, it is clear that language evolves by images. As man discovers more about himself and his world, he constantly needs new words to express new concepts. Occasionally he invents new words (for example, *cola* and *plutonium*), but for the most part he gains new words by extending the meanings of old ones; that is, by using old words as images. This is easy to show in connection with words related to thinking. Most of the terms we use today began their careers as metaphors. An intelligent man is said to have "insight" or "perspicuity" (from Latin *per-spicere, to see through*); he can be "introspective" (from *intro-spicere, to see within*), or "keen" or "sharp" or "imaginative" (from *image*) or "brilliant," "lucid," "clear," or "obscure." *Reason* is from Latin *ratio,* originally meaning a *reckoning* or *account; intellect* is from Latin *inter-legere, to choose between*; and *ponder* is from Latin *ponderare, to weigh.* Each of these words was originally a metaphor, although today the literal meaning has been all but forgotten.

Colloquial imagery is imagery that is clearly figurative, but so commonplace that it is often (though by no means always) used unconsciously. Slang and everyday speech abound in colloquial images. They are often trite, but they can also be vivid and emphatic. They are usually employed as substitutes for more precise, formal expressions, and because of their frequency they are very difficult to avoid. Professional authors from Chaucer to Mark Twain have used them to give their writing (especially dialogue) a realistic flavor. On the other hand, colloquial images are usually too imprecise for formal writing and should always be used with caution. The list below illustrates colloquial imagery. The student can easily make a list twice as long by thinking back over expressions he uses frequently.

Similes	*Metaphors*
like a ton of bricks	feeling blue
like something the cat dragged in	hot jazz
as high as a kite	stuck-up
like a bull in a china shop	production target
as cool as a cucumber	flat broke
as poor as a churchmouse	an icy stare
as easy as falling off a log	green thumb
like a chicken with its head cut off	a ratty garment

Deliberate imagery is imagery used consciously for a desired effect and is often invented by the author. Its two most important effects are clarity and emotional stimulation. In formal exposition, the author generally avoids imagery that appeals to the emotions, since it would be inconsistent with an objective tone. Formal exposition, however, regularly uses images that clarify. These images are called **analogies**. One example, familiar to all students of physics, is the analogy comparing the flow of electricity through a wire to the flow of water through a pipe. The analogy is usually expanded to explain the various factors affecting the flow of current. Thus electrical resistance is compared to friction in the pipe, voltage to water pressure and amperage to the volume of water flow. Often analogies are visual, as when a tepee is said to resemble

71

an ice cream cone turned upside down, or the organization of a novel is said to be like a wheel with all of its "spokes" leading back to the central theme.

Imagery that stimulates emotion is more common than analogy. It is used widely by popular essayists, news reporters, fiction writers and poets, because it is a powerful means of controlling the response of the reader to the subject. Consider the variety of responses stimulated by the following images associated with dawn.

the dawn was pale pink, like apple blossoms
the blushing dawn
a bloody gash in the sky indicated the approach of dawn
the dawn rose like thunder
the dawn rose a sullen red
the dawn was like a fire searing the edges of the horizon
the dawn was like a bright red fire engine racing back and forth over my
    head with five firemen singing "Rosie O'Grady" on the tailgate

Any typical dawn could be described by any one of these images. To select the best image, the author must ask himself which will contribute most to the desired tone. He may, of course, decide not to use an image; but if he consistently avoids imagery, he will be in the same position as a mechanic who arbitrarily decides to give up using pliers. He will fail to achieve the best possible effect, and he will create unnecessary difficulties for himself.

Any number of poems, stories and passages from novels could be cited to illustrate the effective use of imagery. However, it is important to understand that imagery is useful in all forms of writing. The following example, taken from a newspaper reporter's account of a World War II battle, is an account that makes no pretense of being "literary" in the popular sense of the word, but it abounds in effective images.

The first huge flight passed directly overhead and others followed. We spread our feet and leaned far back trying to look straight up, until our steel helmets fell off. We'd *cup* our fingers around our eyes, *like field glasses,* for a clearer view. And then the bombs came. They began *like the crackle of popcorn* and almost instantly swelled into a *monstrous fury of noise* that seemed surely to destroy all the world ahead of us. From then on for an hour and a half that had in it the *agonies of centuries,* the bombs came down. *A wall of smoke and dust* erected by them grew high in the sky. It *filtered* along the ground back and through our orchards. It sifted around us and into our noses. The bright day grew slowly dark from it. By now everything was *an indescribable cauldron of sounds.* Individual noises did not exist. The *thundering* of the motors in the sky and the *roar* of the bombs ahead filled all the space for noise on earth. Our own heavy artillery was *crashing* all around us, yet we could hardly hear it.

—ERNIE PYLE*

This passage was written to appeal to a mass audience. It is informal, and the effect is created by the use of colloquial and deliberate images. The writer's purpose is to inform and at the same time make the reader share the experience. Therefore, part of the imagery is analogy (for example, *cup, like the crackle of popcorn, wall of smoke*); and part is intended to create a tone of awe or shock (for example, *monstrous fury of noise, agonies of centuries, indescribable cauldron of sound, thundering, roar, crashing*). The two kinds of imagery reinforce each other. The more vividly the reader sees the action, the more he feels its impact. It should be noted also that the effect is cumulative. No single image is so striking that it, alone, creates the tone. The tone is deliberately built up by several images working together. Remove one and the paragraph is still forceful; remove all of them and the paragraph becomes lifeless.

Style is not something that can be learned in two or three "easy lessons." The beginning writer should consciously experiment with word choice and imagery, recognizing that his skill will develop gradually, over a series of essays. Because style reflects the personality, education and attitudes of the author as well as writing skill, it will continue to evolve as long as he continues to respond to new experiences.

TERMS TO BE LEARNED

▸ Tone
▸ Denotation
▸ Connotation

* From *Brave Men* (New York: Henry Holt & Company, 1945), p. 298.

> ▸ Usage
> ▸ Precision
> ▸ Imagery
> ▸ Metaphor
> ▸ Simile

Exercises & Theme Topics

I. The paragraphs below are selected from a variety of works, some fictional, some scientific, some journalistic. For each paragraph assigned, list the words and images that contribute emphatically to the tone. Write a single-sentence definition of the tone. Then answer these questions: (1) Is the paragraph formal, informal or colloquial? (2) Are there words or images in the paragraph which are inconsistent with the dominant tone? (3) Are there words or images that should be changed to make the tone more emphatic?

A.

The most important applications of calculus are to the physical sciences and to geometry. It enables us to study effectively many of the phenomena of physics: the velocity, acceleration, and general character of the motion of objects acted upon by known forces; the work done by an impounded fluid upon the walls of its container; the gravitational attraction due to material objects of various shapes and composition. It enables us to compute or measure many important things: areas; volumes; the masses of bodies of variable density; the location of the center of gravity of a body; the moment of inertia of a body when it is revolved about an axis. The laws of electricity and magnetism and all of the modern developments of atomic physics require calculus for their elaboration.

—George E. Sherwood
and Angus E. Taylor*

* From *Calculus* (New York: Prentice-Hall, Inc., 1954), p. iii.

B.

Walking about the streets of the summer capital once more, walking by spring sunlight, and a cloudless skirmishing blue sea—half-asleep and half-awake—I felt like the Adam of the mediaeval legends: the world-compounded body of a man whose flesh was soil, whose bones were stones, whose blood water, whose hair was grass, whose eyesight sunlight, whose breath was wind, and whose thoughts were clouds. And weightless now, as if after some long wasting illness, I found myself turned adrift again to float upon the shallows of Mareotis with its old tide-marks of appetites and desires refunded into the history of the place: an ancient city with all its cruelties intact, pitched upon a desert and a lake. Walking down with remembered grooves of streets which extended on every side, radiating out like the arms of a starfish from the axis of its founder's tomb. Footfalls echoing in the memory, forgotten scenes and conversations springing up at me from the walls, the cafe tables, the shuttered rooms with cracked and peeling ceilings. Alexandria, princess and whore. The royal city and the *anus mundi*. She would never change so long as the races continued to seethe here like must in a vat; so long as the streets and squares still gushed and spouted with the fermentation of these diverse passions and spites, rages and sudden calms. A fecund desert of human loves littered with the whitening bones of its exiles. Tall palms and minarets marrying in the sky. A hive of white mansions flanking those narrow and abandoned streets of mud which were racked all night by Arab music and the cries of girls who so easily disposed of their body's wearisome baggage (which galled them) and offered to the night the passionate kisses which money could not disflavour. The sadness and beatitude of this human conjunction which perpetuated itself to eternity, an endless cycle of rebirth and annihilation which alone could teach and reform by its destructive power. . . . A great honeycomb of faces and gestures.

—LAWRENCE DURRELL*

C.

The President, as usual, began to play with ideas about places for the conference and suggested a wide variety of locations, none of which included Russia. I told the President, as soon as the discussion started, that there was not a chance of getting Stalin out of Russia at this time in the light of the military situation on Germany's eastern front and that if he did not look out we would wind up with a lot of long-winded, irritating

* From *Clea* (New York: E. P. Dutton & Co., Inc., 1960), pp. 63-4.

cables back and forth getting exactly nowhere and that we might as well make up our minds first at least to go to some convenient point—preferably in the Crimea.

—HARRY HOPKINS on the Yalta
Conference, quoted by ROBERT SHERWOOD*

D.

The uncritical acceptance of a simple equation between security and armaments can only lead us into an accelerating arms race, mounting international tensions, and diminishing security. It is quite possible for us to possess overwhelming military superiority and still be confronted with the erosion of our power and influence in the world—if our alliance system is allowed to weaken, if confidence in our resolution is called into question, if our judgment is too often doubted, if our political and economic policies are ineffective, or if by ill-considered unilateral measures we provoke our adversaries into hostile countermeasures. We must therefore avoid giving undue weight to the political views of highly specialized technical experts whose experience and knowledge have only very limited relevance to the complexities of international relations. War, said Clemenceau, is too serious a business to be left to the generals. It is also too serious a business to be left to the nuclear physicists or, indeed, to anyone except an elected political leadership whose experience and competence is not in the specific technical fields but in understanding the generality of the nation's problems, their effects upon each other, and the relative importance of one as against another.

—J. W. FULBRIGHT†

E.

His very person and appearance were such as to strike the attention of the most casual observer. In height he was rather over six feet, and so excessively lean that he seemed to be considerably taller. His eyes were sharp and piercing, save during those intervals of torpor to which I have alluded; and his thin, hawk-like nose gave his whole expression an air of alertness and decision. His chin, too, had the prominence and squareness which mark the man of determination. His hands were invariably blotted with ink and stained with chemicals, yet he was possessed of extraordinary

* From *Roosevelt and Hopkins* (New York: Harper and Brothers, 1948), p. 844.
† From *Old Myths and New Realities* (New York: Random House, 1964), pp. 49-50.

delicacy of touch, as I frequently had occasion to observe when I watched him manipulating his fragile philosophical instruments.

—A. CONAN DOYLE*

F.

That time of year thou mayst in me behold
When yellow leaves, or none, or few, do hang
Upon those boughs which shake against the cold,
Bare ruin'd choirs, where late the sweet birds sang.
In me thou see'st the twilight of such day   5
As after sunset fadeth in the west,
Which by and by black night doth take away,
Death's second self, that seals up all in rest.
In me thou see'st the glowing of such fire
That on the ashes of his youth doth lie,   10
As the death-bed whereon it must expire,
Consum'd with that which it was nourish'd by.
   This thou perceiv'st, which makes thy love more strong,
   To love that well which thou must leave ere long.

—WILLIAM SHAKESPEARE†

II. Each of the following lists contains words that are similar (though not always identical) in denotation, and differ in connotation. Classify the words according to positive and negative connotation. Then differentiate between the words in each category. Note also which words are formal, standard and colloquial.

A. desire, wish, fancy, inclination, urge, bent, whim, partiality, predilection, liking, love, longing, yearning, mania, passion, hankering, compulsion, obsession

B. boldness, courage, fortitude, rashness, temerity, imprudence, audacity, desperation, precipitancy, bravery, resolution, nerve, pluck, heroism, fierceness, manliness, fool-hardiness, grit, impetuousness, gumption, zip, drive

C. prodigy, marvel, wonder, miracle, freak, sport, monstrosity, curiosity, sight, spectacle, knockout, remarkable phenomenon

* From *A Study in Scarlet* (1905).
† From *Sonnets*, Sonnet 73 (1609).

III. Make a list similar to the list on page 71 of colloquial images. Classify them as similes and metaphors. Do the same for the images in the Shakespeare sonnet in exercise I.

IV. Compose five similes and/or metaphors on one of the following subjects.

a library, an old car, a dog, a political speaker, a fire, a meal, a hot day

V. Read Poe's description of the house of Usher. Then write a real-estate prospectus offering the house for sale.

VI. Write a descriptive paragraph on one of the topics in exercise IV or a topic of your own choosing. Define the tone you have tried to create. Then rewrite the paragraph in two different versions, each with a different tone. After each version write a single-sentence definition of the tone.

VII. Essay topics:

A campus meeting
A well-known building
The campus cafeteria at noon
A local hangout on Saturday night
A vivid incident (the opening of a store, a campus election, a fire, a wedding, the crowd at a foreign movie)

After you have decided on a topic, take notes based on first-hand observation. Then write a single-sentence statement of what you want to say *about* the topic. This will be your purpose statement as defined in chapter 1. On the basis of your purpose statement, write a sentence defining the tone appropriate to your purpose. Having done this, complete your outline and write the essay (400-600 words). Hand in your preliminary material with your essay. It is part of the assignment, and you will be graded on it.

Development
by Detail

Organization, paragraphing and style are the most general categories of rhetoric. They are involved in all writing, and more specialized rhetorical subjects depend on them. For the beginning writer, the most important of these more specialized subjects is **development.** No matter how long the essay, its quality depends primarily on its developing section. The common methods of development have been mentioned in connection with organization and paragraphing. They are development by detail, by example, by comparison, by definition and by logical methods. At times it may suit a writer's purpose to use one method throughout his developing section; at other times he may use a combination of methods. For convenience the methods will be treated separately, beginning with development by detail.

4.1 DEVELOPMENT BY DETAIL

Development by detail is a fundamental writing technique. It is used by professionals as well as beginners, scientists as well as novelists and for the most complex as well as the most commonplace subjects. It is used instinctively by people who have no formal training in writing, and it is also used by writers of the stature of Chaucer, Shakespeare, Hemingway and James Joyce. In the work of these writers it becomes art. It is also used routinely for such workaday purposes as lab reports, instruction booklets, advertisements, lectures and familiar letters. Whenever it is used it poses two problems. First, the writer must present enough details to create the desired effect. Second, he must avoid details that are unnecessary or irrelevant. Solving these problems requires knowledge of the subject, a clearly formulated purpose and an understanding of the audience addressed.

4.2 USE OF DETAIL

An experience is the result of a large number of separate but related impressions. When we describe the experience, these impressions become **details** of the description. Our minds record details automatically. In recalling the experience we may forget details or remember only one or two of the most vivid. Yet details are essential to adequate communication of the experience. They are the writer's means of introducing reality—or the illusion of reality—into his work. They define and clarify,

80

they explain and they add vividness and credibility to what would otherwise be a pallid series of generalizations.

We use detail as a matter of course whenever we wish to communicate. Suppose Mr. Jones has narrowly escaped being hit by a car and wants to tell his friend Mr. Smith about the experience. He may begin by saying, "I had a narrow escape yesterday." The sentence states a fact, but it says nothing about the experience. Having caught Mr. Smith's attention, Mr. Jones adds two details: "I was crossing Tenth Street and a car almost ran me down." If Mr. Jones stops here, Mr. Smith is likely to begin asking questions: "Tell me about it. How did it happen? Were you frightened? Was the car speeding? Did you see the license plate?" What Mr. Smith is really asking for is more detail. He does not doubt Mr. Jones' word, but he wants to be able to share the experience— to recreate it in his own mind by removing it from the abstract and placing it in the real world.

Whether he knows it or not, Mr. Smith is acting as an impromptu literary critic. He is telling Mr. Jones that the account needs to be developed, and he is suggesting details that should be included in the development.

The writer usually does not have a friendly critic like Mr. Smith to suggest details to him while he is composing. His job therefore requires a certain amount of imagination. He must be able to anticipate the reader's questions and answer them before they occur. Obviously, he cannot answer every question that can be asked. He must therefore select details in terms of his purpose and the sort of reader he expects to have.

Suppose that after his conversation with Mr. Smith, Mr. Jones writes two accounts of the near-accident, the first for a police complaint form and the second for a letter to a former neighbor. The police form will require details specifying place, time and sequence of events, and the details should be as exact as possible. In the section of the form labeled "Describe the incident in your own words" Mr. Jones might write the following:

> The incident occurred on Monday, March 19, at the intersection of Tenth Street and Maple Avenue, at 8:40 A.M. I am sure about the time because I always leave my house at 8:30 in order to catch the 8:50 bus on Tenth Street. There is no traffic light at the intersection, but Maple has a stop

81

sign. I checked for traffic both ways, and when I was sure that it was safe to cross, I entered the intersection. When I was about half way across Tenth, I heard the sound of a car moving rapidly toward Tenth on Maple. The area is a residential zone with a 20 mile-an-hour speed limit, but the car was going at least 35. It did not stop at the intersection but turned left into Tenth and seemed to be heading straight toward me. The driver did not sound his horn or attempt to stop. I jumped back, and the car missed me by less than a foot. It continued on Tenth Street without slowing down.

The license number was LA 703-42. Since the car was a convertible and the top was down, I could see the driver. He was a young man, about seventeen, with dark hair and a crew cut. Although I do not wish to bring charges, I urge that he be reprimanded by the police before he causes a serious accident.

This is a reasonably detailed report, but it obviously represents a selection from a great many details that might have been included. Mr. Jones does not mention the weather or the color of the tie he was wearing. Obviously, these details are irrelevant and should be omitted. On the other hand, at least one detail has been omitted that *is* relevant. There is no mention of witnesses. Yet whether or not the police act on Mr. Jones's complaint may depend on this detail. Presence or absence of witnesses is a **necessary detail** and to omit it is an error.

Throughout the report, Mr. Jones quite properly limits himself to details that would help the police decide on the seriousness of the offense and identify the driver. When he writes to his former neighbor, he is likely to place greater emphasis on his personal feelings.

Dear Fred,

It's been several weeks since my last letter, but there just hasn't been much to report. The kids are fine, the job is the same as ever, and the people who moved into your old house continue to neglect your rose bushes.

Yesterday I had quite a shock. Do you remember that petition we circulated to have a stoplight put on Maple and Tenth Street? Well, nothing was ever done about it. I hadn't thought about it for almost a year, but on the way to work yesterday morning I was almost run down. I was about halfway across Tenth when I heard a car coming up behind me like an express train. I hardly had time to think before it was on top of me. I don't know how fast it was going. Thirty-five or forty at least, and I'm sure it was more like fifty. The tires squealed when it took the corner. For a second I was afraid that it was going to skid right into me, but I was lucky.

I managed to jump back—at least I must have jumped back since when I had time to think I found myself next to the curb. When I looked up, the car was a half a block down Tenth.

I didn't feel much at first, but when I reached the sidewalk my legs were rubbery and I was covered with sweat. I had to sit down on Bill Stevens' front steps for ten minutes, and after that I rode a taxi to work. Now I'm just angry. The car was driven by a kid. He didn't look more than seventeen. I know he saw me. For a second just before I jumped I was looking right into his eyes. And Fred, I'll swear he was smiling! He *meant* to frighten me. It's lucky he didn't kill me.

I was able to take down the license number, and you can bet that I've reported the incident to the police. I've already located an old copy of our traffic-light petition and intend to try circulating it again. There are too many children in the neighborhood to take any more chances. The next time could be really serious.

Now that you have the latest news about the Jones's, let me know what you're doing. Mary sends her regards to all the family. She is just as sorry as I am about your roses.

Best wishes,
Karl

Mr. Jones's report and his letter illustrate the fact that details are necessary even in the most unpretentious kinds of writing. If Mr. Jones planned to write an account of his near-accident for publication or for use in a formal speech, he would need to do a good deal of polishing. The development is clear enough in both versions, but the details are rather obvious and lack color. In the letter, for example, the scene could be made more specific. A few details suggesting a quiet, unexciting residential area where "nothing ever happens" would provide an effective contrast to the sudden, unexpected danger represented by the car. The reference to the smiling driver is good but needs supporting detail. "He didn't look more than seventeen" is both vague and unemphatic.

4.3 EFFECTIVE DETAIL

A few simple rules can be used to select details and evaluate them during revision. Development by detail is used most frequently in **literary description, narrative** and **exposition. Literary description and narrative** seek to entertain as well as inform and are usually intended for the general reader. In exposition, the primary object is to inform, and frequently (as in technical writing) the reader is assumed to be a specialist in the subject treated. The qualities sought in literary description and narrative are **concreteness, immediacy** and **economy**. The most important qualities of expository detail are **precision** and **necessity**.

Concreteness is the use of specific details rather than general ones. A reporter writes, "the big C-37 lumbered off the field," not "the plane took off." **Immediacy comes from using details that are meaningful to the reader.** A science-fiction writer describing an experiment with crystals mentions that they were heated—but not that they were heated to exactly 185°—and adds that while they cooled, the hero thoughtfully puffed on his old briar pipe. **Economy is the result of using the smallest number of details consistent with the desired effect.** One picture may be worth a thousand words, but if a writer used a thousand words to describe each scene and character in a story, the reader would soon fall asleep. In literary description and narrative, details should suggest as well as spell out.

The greater the writer's emphasis on conveying exact information, the greater his emphasis on precision and necessity. **Precision comes from exactness of detail.** A financial report refers to "the Standard and Poore Industrial Average," not to the "stock market average." A cookbook calls for "½ tablespoon of butter," not "a small lump of butter." **Necessity is the quality achieved when each detail adds something essential and no detail can be deleted without loss of meaning.** A lab report notes that "after being heated to 185° the crystals were allowed to cool gradually at room temperature to 70° and then washed in dilute sulphuric acid." It does not mention that while the crystals were cooling the experimenter smoked his pipe.

4.4 EXAMPLES OF EFFECTIVE DETAIL

1. Literary description:

In the pair of selections that follow, two distinguished novelists, one American, the other British, deal with a similar theme: the passing of time as revealed in the decaying shell of a human dwelling. In the first example, the subject is not a particular house but the homes of Oklahoma farmers which were involuntarily abandoned during The Great Depression. In the second example, the house is an English summer place near the sea, the retreat of a particular family that was well-endowed with education, intelligence and income. Granted the differences in length and locale, consider the kinds of detail used and the reasons why each passage is successful in its own terms.

The doors of the empty houses swung open, and drifted back and forth in the wind. Bands of little boys came out from the towns to break the windows and to pick over the debris, looking for treasures. And here's a knife with half the blade gone. That's a good thing. And—smells like a rat died here. And look what Whitey wrote on the wall. He wrote that in the toilet in school, too, an' teacher made 'im wash it off.

When the folks first left, and the evening of the first day came, the hunting cats slouched in from the fields and mewed on the porch. And when no one came out, the cats crept through the open doors and walked mewing through the empty rooms. And then they went back to the fields and were wild-cats from then on, hunting gophers and field mice, and sleeping in ditches in the daytime. When the night came, the bats, which had stopped at the doors for fear of light, swooped into the houses and sailed about through the empty rooms, and in a little while they stayed in dark room corners during the day, folded their wings high, and hung head-down among the rafters, and the smell of their droppings was in the empty houses.

And the mice moved in and stored weed seeds in corners, in boxes, in the backs of drawers in the kitchens. And weasels came in to hunt the mice, and the brown owls flew shrieking in and out again.

Now there came a little shower. The weeds sprang up in front of the doorstep, where they had not been allowed, and grass grew up through the porch boards. The houses were vacant, and a vacant house falls quickly apart. Splits started up the sheathing from the rusted nails. A dust settled on the floors, and only mouse and weasel and cat tracks disturbed it.

On a night the wind loosened a shingle and flipped it to the ground. The next wind pried into the hole where the shingle had been, lifted off three, and the next, a dozen. The midday sun burned through the hole and threw a glaring spot on the floor. The wild cats crept in from the fields at night, but they did not mew at the doorstep any more. They moved like shadows of a cloud across the moon, into the rooms to hunt

85

the mice. And on windy nights the doors banged, and the ragged curtains fluttered in the broken windows.

—JOHN STEINBECK*

The house was left; the house was deserted. It was left like a shell on a sandhill to fill with dry salt grains now that life had left it. The long night seemed to have set in; the trifling airs, nibbling, the clammy breaths, fumbling, seemed to have triumphed. The saucepan had rusted and the mat decayed. Toads had nosed their way in. Idly, aimlessly, the swaying shawl swung to and fro. A thistle thrust itself between the tiles in the larder. The swallows nested in the drawing-room; the floor was strewn with straw; the plaster fell in shovelfuls; rafters were laid bare; rats carried off this and that to gnaw behind the wainscots. Tortoise-shell butterflies burst from the chrysalis and pattered their life out on the window-pane. Poppies sowed themselves among the dahlias; the lawn waved with long grass; giant artichokes towered among roses; a fringed carnation flowered among the cabbages; while the gentle tapping of a weed at the window had become, on winters' nights, a drumming from sturdy trees and thorned briars which made the whole room green in summer.

—VIRGINIA WOOLF†

2. Narration:

As an example of the use of detail in a narrative intended for the general reader, consider the following account of a trip along the old Inca road in Peru. Note that the paragraphs, while brief, are never abstract. Each presents one or more specific, highly colorful detail. The details have concreteness, immediacy and economy. Underline several and comment on them. What qualities are most obvious? Has the author selected his details carefully? Are there important questions left unanswered or details that are irrelevant?

THE INCA ROAD

The mountain highway north and south of Ayacucho follows roughly the old Inca imperial road from Quito to Cuzco. It is so narrow in places that traffic goes one way on Monday, the other on Tuesday. So it was Tues-

* From *The Grapes of Wrath* (New York: Viking Press, Inc., 1939), pp. 158-9.
† From *To the Lighthouse* (New York: The Modern Library, 1937), pp. 206-7.

day before our party could set out in the Bells' station wagon to traverse the interlocking valleys and ridges and high plateaus of the sierra that lay between us and the coast. In our luggage we carried a bottle of oxygen in case of altitude sickness.

Our way was bright with yellow blossoms of retama, as glowing as the bonfires the night before. Sunlight shimmered on eucalyptus trees, which came, Peruvians assured me, from Australia by way of California.

"Those blue flowers in the meadow are *chamicos*—if a gringo drinks a love potion made from them, he will never leave Peru," Elena told us with a mischievous smile.

Agricultural terraces built by Inca engineers climbed some of the valley walls. In other places, farms clung to impossible slopes. On one hillside we watched a farmer tilling an incredibly steep potato patch. We measured it: only 35 degrees from vertical.

Why were his rows up and down? I wondered about this as I saw vertical rows all over Peru. An agricultural expert finally explained that as the Indians chop or hoe, they can back down the hill more easily than they can move sideways. Most of them know little about erosion and contour planting.

Llamas Limit Loads to 100 Pounds

Flocks of goats and sheep occasionally blocked our road; or arrogant llamas with little red tassels in their ears and sacks of potatoes carried like saddlebags.

"The llama is stubborn," Elena remarked. "He will carry no more than a hundred pounds, and if you load on more he will lie down."

Serrano women hurried along the road in a shuffling little trot, invariably bent beneath a load. Mantas, or shawls slung over the back served as cradles and carryalls. Spindles twirled ceaselessly at their sides as the women spun the wool of alpaca and sheep. Some of the girls wore flowers in their hats—sign meaning "Husband wanted!"

And such colors! The sierra woman prides herself on bright-hued homespun skirts flaring like square-dance dresses.

In the isolated colonial town of Huancavelica, by contrast, a few women wore solid black. Elena explained that here Inca tradition remains strong; these women still mourn the last Inca emperor, who died more than four centuries ago.

By following the stewardess's advice on mountain sickness, I was able to avoid symptoms until we climbed to 14,000 feet to visit the Santa Barbara mercury mine near Huancavelica. There we all found ourselves sleepy and lethargic. Even taking out my notebook to scratch a few notes was an effort; my pen moved with annoying slowness.

"That's all right," the mine manager said with a grin. "It takes me five days to recuperate when I come up from sea level."

Santa Barbara was prized by the Spanish kings of the 17th century because its mercury was useful to amalgamate, or "pick up," silver and gold from ore. Today this mine is the largest producer of mercury in South America.

We watched hard-hatted miners in an open pit digging out lumps of reddish ore. Workmen wearing masks against poisonous fumes heated the ore in furnaces to vaporize the mercury, then condensed it to the familiar silvery liquid. I undertook to lift a gallon-and-a-half bucket of the stuff. It didn't look like much, but the bucket felt bolted down. I checked the scales—77 kilograms, or 169 pounds. Exactly my own weight.

Santa Barbara is but a drop in Peru's vast mineral riches. The gold that the conquistadors sought so greedily has been superseded by copper, silver, iron ore, lead, and zinc. Peru, in fact, produces nearly all the major metals. Her enormous new pits at Toquepala in the far south tap one of the world's largest deposits of copper.

Still climbing beyond Huancavelica, with our ears popping, we left soft green valleys behind and passed for miles through treeless plateau country known as puna, reaching a height of 16,000 feet. Nowhere in the United States does a road go above 14,500.

Llamas grazed by the thousands on pastures of bunch grass called *ichu*, watered by melt streams from snowfields. An Andean goose flew over, white with black wings. Flamingos waded in a little lake. They are called *peruanos*, Dona Elena told us, because the red wings and white chest suggest the Peruvian flag.

Alpaca's Weak Spot: Tender Ears

Within an easy climb of the snowline, we came across men shearing alpacas in a stone corral. The alpacas—shaggy cousins of the llama—squealed viciously and spat at the shepherds as they were lassoed. But as soon as one of the women seized their tender ears, they lay quiet. The shearers hacked away the fleece with broad-bladed knives. All the while a murmur of unrest, almost a moan, swept over the flock of 150 beasts.

Dropping toward the coast, we skirted precipices hundreds of feet above rushing mountain streams. At one curve, a truck coming from the opposite direction failed to honk, and we skidded to a dusty halt hardly a bumper's width apart. Slowly we scraped by each other, with our outside wheels crumbling away the very lip of the cliff.

Peruvians give their trucks fancy names. This one—"The Friend of Death" —did no good for my peace of mind.

A day later we encountered the terror of the Peruvian highlands—a landslide. Near Castrovirreyna we rounded a curve to find our narrow ledge above the Sinto River blocked for a hundred yards where the side of a hill, lubricated by the seasonal rains, had come crashing down. Buses and trucks waited on both sides as a bulldozer and a score of workmen strained to clear the way.

After a cold night in a miners' rest house, we returned to watch under a sun that burned with special ferocity through the thin air. Boulders were sent flying into the ravine, but new cracks kept appearing in the slope, and rivulets of sand slithered down beside us.

Women from the puna came down to sell food: a dish of sheep liver, onions, and rice for three soles; three small potatoes for a sol (about four cents). The potatoes had purple flesh. They were one of a hundred or more varieties grown in this land where the "Irish" potato originated.

Finally, near sundown on the third day, a one-way passage was cleared. A countryman in a brown poncho, with a sack of rockets for a fiesta, came leaping across like a frightened deer. *"Dios es grande!* (God is great!) " he gasped as he reached safety.

—KENNETH F. WEAVER*

3. Technical exposition:

If details are important in reporting, they are essential in expository writing intended to convey precise information. An executive writing a memorandum advocating a change in his company's administrative procedure must be specific about methods to be used, costs and personnel involved. A scientist writing up an experiment must describe his equipment, the conditions of the experiment, the steps followed, conclusions reached and possible errors. Exact description of process also involves detail. The following selection, from a biology textbook, describes cell division. The details are arranged in order of process.

CELL DIVISION

The division of a cell is a complicated process. Fairly satisfactory observations of it may be made in living tissues, but for many of the finer

* From "The Five Worlds of Peru," *The National Geographic*, Vol. 125 (February, 1964), 226-32. © National Geographic Magazine. Reprinted by permission.

points it is necessary to kill the cells, to stop divisions at various places, and then cut thin sections and bring out details by applying suitable stains. A favorite tissue for the study of this process is the growing tip of a root.

When the cell is in the metabolic state, that is, not in process of division, the nucleus contains one or more conspicuous, spherical *nucleoli* and the granular *chromatin* in the form of a series of irregular, knotty threads whose details can be observed only by careful manipulation of a good microscope.

When the time for the division of the cell approaches, these thread-like units of chromatin shorten and condense to form definite, elongated, rod-like bodies, the *chromosomes*. Under favorable conditions it can be seen that each chromosome is really double in nature, as if it were composed of two threads united side by side. It has not thus far been possible to determine exactly when and how this double structure of the chromosomes develops.

While the chromosomes are assuming this form, there appear in the cytoplasm, on opposite sides of the nucleus, certain differentiations which appear in stained preparations as two masses of fibers growing toward the nucleus. The nuclear membrane and nucleoli disappear, and the two masses of fibers meet among the chromosomes and form a structure which, because of its shape, is known as the spindle.

The nature of these fibers and the part which they play in the division of the nucleus have long been matters of controversy. Some of them become attached to the chromosomes, while others extend from end to end of the spindle and remain free from the chromosomes.

The chromosomes now move to definite positions so that they come to lie approximately in a plane, their position with reference to the spindle being like that of spokes of a wheel around the hub. The two halves of each chromosome next separate and move toward the opposite ends of the spindle.

Some investigators have thought that the chromosomes were pulled into their new positions by the contraction of the fibers attached to them, but carefully performed micro-dissections indicate that there are probably no true fibers in the living cell. There is no entirely satisfactory explanation as to what causes the chromosomes to move during cell division.

When the two groups of new chromosomes reach their respective poles of the spindle, a nuclear membrane appears around each group, and the nucleolus reappears. At the same time, the chromosomes become longer and less compact, and the chromatin gradually resumes the condition in which it was found before division began. This marks the end of the division of the *nucleus*. The cell is not yet divided.

In the meantime, the spindle fibers which extend from pole to pole, without being attached to chromosomes, are engaging in an activity which leads to the final step in the division of the cell. At first they increase in number, and the spindle broadens out until it reaches the lateral walls of the cell. Then the material of which the fibers are made begins to move toward a plane midway between the two new nuclei and to form there a layer of cytoplasm known as the *cell plate.*

This plate now splits into two layers, the surface layers of which become the plasma membranes of the two new bodies of protoplasm and join the older plasma membranes at the sides of each cell. This step marks the actual division of the cell because henceforth the two bodies of protoplasm act as separate units. Between these two membranes the *primary wall* separating the two new cells is now secreted. It is, in reality, a double wall, one layer being produced by one of the new cells and the other layer by the other. A secondary layer of wall material is usually soon formed by each cell on its respective side of the primary wall.

The method of cell division here described is technically known as *mitosis*. It consists of the division of the nucleus involving a systematic division of the chromatin, followed by a division of the cell itself. It is by far the most prevalent type of division, but other kinds occur occasionally as exceptions or quite regularly in some plants.

—PAUL WEATHERWAX*

This description is technical. It is intended for readers with prior training in biology. Beginning writers sometimes assume that this kind of writing is "for experts only" and is therefore irrelevant to their own interests and needs. Actually, it is an extremely common type. College students need it for term papers, reports and examinations, and they continue to use it regularly after graduation. A lawyer writes legal briefs; a doctor, case histories; an economist, economic reports; a financial expert, stock market analyses; a historian, technical studies of men and events. Such writing is a by-product of the author's professional activities and not intended for popular consumption. It is writing "by a specialist for specialists" and the demand for it constantly increases throughout a successful career.

4. Nontechnical exposition:

When the author writes exposition intended for the general reader, he must compromise between the need for accuracy and the need to

* From *Plant Biology* (Philadelphia: W. B. Saunders Company, 1942), pp. 154-6. Reprinted by permission.

91

express himself in a way that does not require extensive technical knowledge of the subject treated. Details must be selected with a view to their interest as well as to their intrinsic importance. The author must ask himself "How much knowledge can I expect my audience to have?" and "How can I introduce essential details without boring or confusing the reader?" The answers to these questions will vary widely. John Audubon's descriptions of American birds, although written over a hundred years ago, remain classic examples of nontechnical exposition. The following description of the red-headed woodpecker assumes that the reader is well-educated and mature, but it avoids details that would interest only the professional ornithologist. Note how Audubon introduces "human interest" through the details selected. The passage is informative but never ignores the need for concreteness and immediacy. The paragraphs follow logical rather than inherent order. In paragraphs two and three the details are presented by the simple method of listing; in paragraph four the details are presented chronologically.

"THE RED-HEADED WOODPECKER"

You have now, kind reader, under consideration a family of woodpeckers, the general habits of which are so well known in our United States, that, were I assured of your having traversed the woods of America, I should feel disposed to say little about them.

The *red-heads* (by which name this species is usually designated) may be considered as residents of the United States, inasmuch as many of them remain in the Southern Districts during the whole winter, and breed there in summer. The greater number, however, pass to countries farther south. Their migration takes place under night, is commenced in the middle of September, and continues for a month or six weeks. They then fly very high above the trees, far apart, like a disbanded army, propelling themselves by reiterated flaps of the wings, at the end of each successive curve which they describe in their flight. The note which they emit at this time is different from the usual one, sharp and easily heard from the ground, although the birds may be out of sight. This note is continued, as if it were necessary for keeping the straggling party in good humour. At dawn of day, the whole alight on the tops of the dead trees about the plantations, and remain in search of food until the approach of sunset, when they again, one after another, mount the air and continue their journey.

With the exception of the mocking bird, I know no species so gay and frolicksome. Indeed, their whole life is one of pleasure. They find a super-abundance of food everywhere, as well as the best facilities for raising their broods. The little labour which they perform is itself a source of enjoyment, for it is undertaken either with an assurance of procuring the nicest dainties, or for the purpose of excavating a hole for the reception of themselves, their eggs, or their families. They do not seem to be much afraid of man, although they have scarcely a more dangerous enemy. When alighted on a fence-stake by the road, or in a field, and one approaches them, they gradually move sidewise out of sight, peeping now and then to discover your intention; and when you are quite close and opposite, lie still until you are past, when they hop to the top of the stake, and rattle upon it with their bill, as if to congratulate themselves on the success of their cunning. Should you approach within arm's length, which may frequently be done, the woodpecker flies to the next stake or the second from you, bends his head to peep, and rattles again, as if to provoke you to a continuance of what seems to him excellent sport. He alights on the roof of the house, hops along it, beats the shingles, utters a cry, and dives into your garden to pick the finest strawberries which he can discover.

I would not recommend to any one to trust his fruit to the red-heads; for they not only feed on all kinds as they ripen, but destroy an immense quantity besides. No sooner are the cherries seen to redden, than these birds attack them. They arrive on all sides, coming from a distance of miles and seem the while to care little about the satisfaction you might feel in eating some also. Trees of this kind are stripped clean by them. When one has alighted and tasted the first cherry, he utters his call note, jerks his tail, nods his head, and is at it again in an instant. When fatigued, he loads his bill with one or two, and away to his nest to supply his young.

—John J. Audubon*

4.5   INADEQUATE DEVELOPMENT AND FILLER

To a beginner an essay of 300 words may be an effort, 500 a major challenge, and 2,000 unthinkable. The struggle simply to fill a blank page with words frequently causes two complementary errors: inadequate development and filler. **Inadequate development is the inadequate "filling out" of the topics of the outline.** The essay becomes a series of short, choppy, abstract paragraphs. The writer either does not know how to

* From *Ornithological Biography* (1831).

develop his ideas or he is so ill-equipped that he has not tried. An inadequately developed descriptive passage will lack **concreteness** and **immediacy;** an expository passage will be deficient in **precision** and **necessity.** At the opposite extreme we have **filler. Filler is material added to the essay for the sole purpose of increasing word length.** Repetition, jargon, flowery language, dwelling on the obvious, unnecessary qualification and digression are examples of filler. An essay with a large amount of filler violates the principle of **economy.** It remains empty no matter how many words it has.

TERMS TO BE LEARNED

▸ Three qualities of detail used in narrative and literary description: concreteness; immediacy; economy
▸ Two qualities of detail used in expository and technical writing: precision; necessity
▸ Inadequate development
▸ Filler

Exercises & Theme Topics

I. The following selections range from literary description to exposition intended for the general reader. Comment on their use of detail. Which of the qualities discussed in this chapter are most prominent? Comment. The last three selections all deal with the same topic. Compare them. What details are used in all three accounts? What details are used in only one or two? Is one account better than the others? Comment.

A.

Forthwith a change came over the waters, and the serenity became less brilliant but more profound. The old river in its broad reaches rested unruffled at the decline of day, after ages of good service done to the race that peopled its banks, spread out in the tranquil dignity of a waterway leading to the uttermost ends of the earth. We looked at the venerable stream not in the vivid flush of a short day that comes and departs forever, but in the august light of abiding memories. And indeed nothing is easier for a man who has, as the phrase goes, "followed the sea" with reverence and affection, than to evoke the great spirit of the past upon the lower reaches of the Thames. The tidal current runs to and fro in its unceasing service, crowded with memories of men and ships it had borne to the rest of home or to the battle of the sea. It had known and served all the men of whom the nation is proud, from Sir Francis Drake to Sir John Frankling, knights all, titled and untitled—the knights-errant of the sea. It had borne all the ships whose names are like jewels flashing in the night of time, from the *Golden Hind* returning with her round flanks full of treasure, to be visited by the Queen's Highness and thus pass out of the gigantic tale, to the *Erebus* and *Terror*, bound on other conquests—and that never returned. It had known the ships and the men. They had sailed from Deptford, from Greenwich, from Erith—the adventurers and the settlers; kings' ships and the ships of men on 'Change; captains, admirals, the dark "interlopers" of the Eastern trade, and the commissioned "generals" of East India fleets. Hunters for gold or pursuers of fame, they all had gone out on that stream, bearing the sword, and often the torch, messengers of the might within the land, bearers of a spark from the sacred fire. What greatness had not floated on the ebb of that river into the mystery of an unknown earth! . . . The dreams of men, the seed of commonwealths, the germs of empires.

—JOSEPH CONRAD*

B.

	Notes
Ther was also a nonne, a PRIORESSE,	
That of hir smylyng was ful symple and coy.	
Hir grettest ooth was but by Seint Loy;	(A VERY MILD OATH)
And she was cleped Madame Eglentyne.	(CLEPED: CALLED)
Ful wel she soong the servyce dyvyne, 5	
Entuned in hir nose ful semely,	
And Frenssh she spak ful faire and fetisly	(FETISLY: ELEGANTLY)
After the scole of Stratford atte Bowe,	(TOWN NEAR LONDON)
For Frenssh of Parys was to hire unknowe.	

* From "The Heart of Darkness," in *Tales of Land and Sea* (New York: Hanover House, 1953), pp. 34-5.

10 At mete wel y-taught was she with alle;
She leet no morsel from hir lippes falle,
Ne wette hir fyngres in hir sauce depe;
Wel koude she carie a morsel, and wel kepe   (KEPE: TAKE CARE)
That no drope ne fille upon hir brest.
15 In curteisie was set ful muchel hir lest.   (MUCHEL HIR LEST: MUCH HER CONCERN)
Hir over lippe wyped she so clene
That in hir coppe ther was no ferthyng sene   (FERTHYNG: MORSEL)
Of grece whan she dronken hadde hir draughte.
Ful semely after hir mete she raughte,   (RAUGHTE: REACHED)
20 And sikerly she was of greet desport,   (SIKERLY: CERTAINLY; DESPORT: FUN)
And ful plesaunt and amyable of port,
And peyned hire to counterfete cheere   (CHEERE: MANNERS)
Of court, and to been estatlich of manere,   (ESTATLICH: COURTLY)
And to been holden digne of reverence.   (DIGNE: WORTHY)
25   But for to speken of hir conscience,
She was so charitable and so pitous,
She wolde wepe if that she sawe a mous
Caughte in a trappe, if it were deed or bledde.
Of smale houndes hadde she that she fedde
30 With rosted flessh, or mylk and wastel breed;   (WASTEL BREED: FINE WHITE BREAD)
But soore wepte she if oon of hem were deed,
Or if men smoot it with a yerde smerte.   (YERDE SMERTE: STICK SHARPLY)
And al was conscience and tendre herte.
   Ful semely hir wympel pynched was,   (HER HEADDRESS WAS GRACEFULLY PLEATED)
35 Hir nose tretys, hir eyen greye as glas,   (TRETYS: SHAPELY)
Hir mouth ful smal, and ther-to softe and reed,
But sikerly she hadde a fair forheed;
It was almost a spanne brood, I trowe,   (TROWE: BELIEVE)
For hardily she was nat undergrowe.   (HARDILY: INDEED!)
40 Ful fetys was hir cloke, as I was war;   (FETYS: ELEGANT)
Of smal coral aboute hir arm she bar
A peyre of bedes, gauded al with grene,   (PEYRE: STRING)
And ther-on heng a brooch of gold ful shene,   (SHENE: SHINING)
On which ther was first writen a crowned A,
45 And after *Amor vincit omnia.*   ("LOVE CONQUERS ALL")

—GEOFFREY CHAUCER*

* From *General Prologue of The Canterbury Tales* (1400?).

96

C. "BRAZIL'S REBEL CHIEFTAINS CLAIM CONTROL OF COUNTRY; FLEEING GOULART DEFIANT"

RIO DE JANEIRO, Brazil—Brazilian rebel forces drove leftist President João Goulart out of Rio de Janiero Wednesday, but he scoffed at their victory claims and flew early Thursday into Brazil's deep south, vowing a fight to the death.

Goulart, accused by rebel leaders of planning to turn Latin America's largest country into a Cuban-type Communist satellite, fled first to Brasilia, the inland capital 600 miles northwest of Rio de Janeiro.

Then, late Wednesday night, he took off for Porto Alegre in his home state of Rio Grande do Sul where his brother-in-law, former Gov. Leonel Brizola was reported in control of the 3rd Army.

A Goulart spokesman said his wife and two children had flown with him but planned to continue to a foreign country to await the outcome of the crisis.

Victory Proclaimed

Goulart's dramatic flight and vow to wage last-ditch warfare climaxed a day in which rebel chiefs proclaimed Goulart's fall and installed a new president, Paschoal Ranieri Mazzilli, president of the Chamber of Deputies and constitutionally in line for the job.

Loyal staff members were with Goulart and his family in the Viscount turboprop airliner that took off from Brasilia shortly before midnight. The group had been forced to Brasilia in a Coronado jetliner which developed engine trouble in a first attempt to reach Porto Alegre.

Hectic victory demonstrations under clouds of confetti and ticker tape had erupted in Rio de Janeiro and São Paulo at the first broadcast word that Goulart had been ousted.

Then came a broadcast from Brasilia that Goulart would make a stand there.

The departure for the south apparently changed that decision.

A Porto Alegre broadcast heard in Buenos Aires said Brazilian navy ships with a destroyer in the lead had left Rio de Janeiro for Porto Alegre with "orders to mobilize," presumably in support of Goulart.

Strongest Army

The Third Army in Rio Grande do Sul is by far the strongest of Brazil's four armies. However, rebel leaders here reported that one of its strongest units, garrisoned at a rail center near the Uruguayan border, had revolted against Brizola and was moving on Porto Alegre.

97

Brizola, former governor of Rio Grande do Sul, is a member of the National Congress and a power in the deep south.

A Goulart spokesman said Goulart would address the nation from Porto Alegre at 3 a.m. (1 a.m. Eastern Standard Time.)

One of Goulart's first acts on arriving in Brasilia was to sign a decree nationalizing all gasoline distributing firms. This evidently was done to show that he considered himself still president and in full exercise of his authority.

When Goulart fled to Brasilia two rebellious armies were moving on Rio. At least eight states were lined up against him.

Bloodshed was apparently light in the two-day revolt that broke out in the neighboring state of Minas Gerais Tuesday and spread rapidly.

Two pro-Goulart students were reported killed in a clash with troops at Recife.

Gov. Carlos Lacerda of Rio's state of Guanabara, a bitter foe of Goulart and believed a mastermind of the revolt, declared in an interview: "We conquered in this immense territory of Brazil the force of Russia which suffers thereby a defeat in the revolutionary war. I hope that all the people of the continent understand the value of this democratic effort of Brazil."

The revolt broke out only a day after a high State Department official in Washington had said the situation in Brazil had "steadily deteriorated" recently and the Brazilian government was becoming increasingly subject to Communist influence.

The official had expressed deep concern over the future of political developments in Brazil.

Goulart had said he was not a Communist but had sought to legalize the Communist party and pushed for sweeping economic reforms.

Goulart left before rebels, charging that he was leading Brazil down the road to Communism, could deliver an ultimatum for him to resign or be ousted.

Crowds in Street

Thousands of people poured into the streets of Rio waving Brazilian flags and white handkerchiefs. A huge crowd gathered outside the palace of Gov. Carlos Lacerda of Guanabara State in which Rio is located. They cheered Lacerda, a bitter foe of Goulart.

Ticker tape cascaded from the skyscrapers of São Paulo. Cars raced down the streets with horns blaring. Radio announcers shouted over and over, "Long live democracy, long live Brazil."

—Associated Press*

* April 2, 1964. Reprinted by permission.

D. "GOULART BELIEVED IN EXILE; BRAZIL SWEARS NEW CHIEF; JOHNSON WELCOMES MOVE"

Rio Hails Victory; Million Turn Parade, Set Before Revolt, Into Celebration

RIO DE JANEIRO, April 2. — João Goulart, deposed yesterday as Brazil's President, was reported to have fled into exile today.

The Uruguayan chargé d'affaires, Manuel Areosa, said he believed Mr. Goulart was accompanied by his brother-in-law, Federal Deputy Leonel Brizola, and a military aide, Gen. Assis Brasil.

Mr. Goulart's flight from Brazil was the result of a revolt that broke out Tuesday. Most of the military leaders turned against the President, charging that he was leading the country toward Communism.

In Brasilia last night, where he had flown from Rio de Janeiro when troops in Rio joined the rebels, Mr. Goulart declared that he intended to defend his office "until I die."

A few hours later he took off for his home state of Rio Grande do Sul to join Mr. Brizola, ostensibly to make a last-ditch fight.

Mazzilli Is President

After Mr. Goulart left Brasilia, the President of the Senate, Auro Moura Andrade, declared the Presidency of Brazil vacant and called on the next in line to assume the post. He is a man who has been Acting President of Brazil four times—Ranieri Mazzilli, President of the Chamber of Deputies.

A "march of the family for God and liberty," which had been scheduled before the revolution as a demonstration against Communism and the Goulart Administration, turned into a victory celebration here today.

Almost a million men, women and children marched soberly but triumphantly.

The march had been organized by a number of religious and democratic anti-Communist groups that sprang up as the Goulart Government intensified its leftist programs, with Mr. Goulart demanding changes in Brazil's social, economic and constitutional structure.

The celebration was larger but soberer than those that marked the return of Brazil's World War II expeditionary force from Italy and the homecoming of Brazil's soccer team after it had won the world championship in Europe.

Tons of torn paper fluttered down from windows. Marchers carried Brazilian flags and waved handkerchiefs. Their banners called for "liberty, democracy, and reforms without agitation."

99

The marchers sang the national anthem and "Marvelous City," Rio's official song, which is associated with Gov. Carlos Lacerda of Guanabara who was a leader of the nearly bloodless revolt against the Goulart Government.

Guanabara state consists almost entirely of Rio de Janeiro.

Before his departure for Uruguay, Mr. Goulart appeared determined to make a stand in Porto Alegre, capital of his home state of Rio Grande do Sul in the far South of Brazil.

Armies Line Up

At first Mr. Goulart appeared to be getting support from the powerful Third Army, which has its headquarters in Rio Grande do Sul and is reported to be the strongest of Brazil's four armies. However, both the Second Army, in São Paulo and Mato Grosso, and the Fourth Army, based in the northeast, lined up against Mr. Goulart. Then most of the First Army, situated in the important states of Minas Gerais, Rio de Janeiro and Guanabara, turned against Mr. Goulart.

Units were reported ready to march on Porto Alegre, and the navy dispatched a task force there to oppose pro-Goulart forces. Even part of the Third Army failed to support Mr. Goulart.

Mr. Goulart apparently had hoped for significant popular and military support in Rio Grande do Sul, where Mr. Brizola, a fiery leftist, was once governor.

In a broadcast last night, Mr. Brizola denounced three of Brazil's prominent governors as "traitors" and "cowards."

Mr. Brizola's language was indicative of the bitterness between the opposing force that carried Brazil to the brink of civil war. He called on "sergeants" in the army and "workers" to join forces to beat back the threat to the Goulart Government.

However, despite a welter of conflicting reports on army movements and the stands of various unit commanders, no significant popular support for Mr. Goulart's cause developed and his military supporters were greatly outnumbered by his opponents. So it was that this afternoon he flew off to exile in Uruguay.

The governors of Brazil's most important states had denounced the Goulart regime and announced their support of the military-political revolt that started in the large and influential state of Minas Gerais.

Among the prominent governors who took part in the rebellion were Mr. Lacerda, Jose Magalhaes Pinto of Minas Gerais, Adhemar de Barros of São Paulo and Ilda Meneghetti of Rio Grande do Sul. It was Governors

Magalhaes Pinto, de Barros and Lacerda whom Mr. Brizola called "traitors" and "cowards."

—The New York Times*

E. *"GOODBYE TO JANGO"*

If ever there was a popular revolution, it was the one that last week toppled Brazilian President João ("Jango") Goulart. In São Paulo, samba dancers whirled through the streets, singing, shouting and kicking. In Rio, some 300,000 cariocas pranced and danced along the Avenida Presidente Vargas beneath a storm of confetti, tootling carnival horns, waving handkerchiefs, clapping every back within reach. At a Copacabana restaurant, three tired, rain-drenched college boys tramped in off the street, plopped down at a table and lovingly draped a damp green, blue and yellow Brazilian flag over the fourth chair. "We are wet and dirty but not ashamed," said one dramatically. "The Communists threatened our right to carry this beautiful flag. Now we are fighting for our liberty." The man at the piano struck up the national anthem: all joined in.

President Johnson was almost as enthusiastic, and forthwith sent his "warmest good wishes" to the new President Paschoal Ranieri Mazzilli. In Peru, Lima's La Prensa called the revolution a "healthy action"; in Argentina, former President Pedro Aramburu said that "democracy has won out." But despite all the enthusiasm, getting rid of Goulart was only a first and far-from-conclusive step. He had mismanaged Brazil so badly that his downfall became inevitable, but the fruits of that mismanagement remain for his successors to cope with.

Post-Mortem

Brazil has been on the road to trouble for years. Under the spend-build, spend-build administration of Juscelino Kubitschek (1956-61), the country lavished millions on massive public works projects, including the construction of the nation's $600 million capital of Brasilia. Erratic Janio Quadros, who took office in 1961, slapped on rigid austerity measures. But he stuck around only seven months before resigning in a fit of pique, and then Goulart—his Vice President—moved into the palace.

A wealthy rancher from Rio Grande do Sul state, Goulart learned his

* April 2, 1964, p. 12, col. 1. © 1964 by The New York Times Company. Reprinted by permission.

politics at the knee of a ranching neighbor, old-time Brazilian Strongman Getulio Vargas, swept back into the presidency in 1950. Jango immediately began buying labor's votes with promises of pay boosts, was finally pressured out of the ministry by the military when he tried to double Brazil's minimum wage. With Vargas' suicide in 1954, Goulart inherited the leadership of the Brazilian Labor Party, became Vice President under Kubitschek, then under Quadros, thanks to a system that permits the election of a President from one party, a Veep from another.

As President, Goulart continued wooing labor at all costs. When he needed money, he just printed it—and Jango needed plenty, as the economy began flying apart. During his 31 months in office, the country's cost of living soared 300%. The value of the cruzeiro dropped 83%. The country ran up a staggering $3.7 billion foreign debt, with almost no hope of repaying it. Foreign investors kept their capital safely at home, or sent it anywhere but to Brazil.

As ruin approached, Goulart turned desperately to the far left for political support, threatened to rewrite the constitution, which prevents a President from succeeding himself, and entrench himself in power. A left-run nation of permanent chaos loomed as an all too real prospect. And Brazil, of course, is no island; the largest and most important nation in Latin America, it could conceivably drag the rest of the continent down with it.

This prospect finally alarmed not only Brazil's conservatives but middle-roaders and liberals as well. Even the radical groups Jango had tried to organize—unions, peasants, non-commissioned officers—in the end did not follow him. It was practically everybody against Jango and his ambitions, his ineptness, his phony reforms. At a party meeting in Rio, even the Communists turned on him. "As far as we are concerned," said one Communist leader, "Jango is dead. He was a stupid man."

Slow Groundwork

Spontaneous it seemed, but last week's revolt was actually hatched in October. At first, only half a dozen colonels were involved, and their plan was purely defensive; only if Goulart actually tried to seize dictatorial powers would they act. But as Goulart turned farther and farther left, as more and more of the demagogue came out in him, as fiscal madness multiplied, his opponents at last decided that they must act before he did, not after.

General Artur da Costa e Silva, 61, the army's senior ranking officer and one of Brazil's ablest tacticians, began organizing and planning. The plan was twofold. First, troops at Juiz de Fora, in Minas Gerais state, would rise up in rebellion. Then would follow a pause until Goulart's loyal forces were fully committed to crushing the trouble in Minas Gerais. Then a main force would march on Rio, and other commands would join the revolt. Costa e Silva's emissaries began crisscrossing the country, discreetly lining up support. "In the final days before the revolt," said Goulart's rebelling air force chief of staff, "we knew that if pilots in Rio were ordered to fly against us, they would refuse to go up."

Civilian political backing was hardly a problem. São Paulo's militantly anti-Communist Governor Adhemar de Barros had been plotting his own revolt for three months, and was in secret contact with the governors of several other Brazilian states. Carlos Lacerdo, governor of pivotal Guanbara state, which consists mostly of the city of Rio de Janeiro, was Jango's declared enemy and would surely go along.

Planned Pause

A fortnight ago, the plot came to a boil when pro-Goulart navy and marine enlisted men rebelled against their officers and staged a sit-in strike in a Rio union hall, demanding passage of Goulart's broad and sweeping social and economic "reforms." Far from cracking down on the mutineers for insubordination, Goulart's leftist Navy Minister gave them all weekend passes and full pardons. Newspapers, middle-road and right-wing politicians sensed that Goulart was bent on the swift formation of a socialist regime, and began a clamor of public protest.

Up to then, ex-President Juscelino Kubitschek (1956-61) had never publicly criticized Goulart. But now his patience had run out. He warned angrily: "Goulart has gone too far." Instead of falling back, Goulart last week went before a meeting of military police noncoms to accuse the army and navy brass of "carrying out intrigues" against him, and to label the opposition "a minority of privileged ones who live with eyes turned toward the past." So worked up was Goulart that his worried aides summoned his private physician and the doctor stayed by his side through the rest of his speech, lest he overdo it.

The morning after Goulart's speech, the troops rose in Minas Gerais; a force of 10,000 soldiers marched off toward Rio. Then came the pause planned by the plotters, and with it a gap in the news that set all of Brazil speculation: had the revolt failed? Was it all a false alarm? The next morning, Goulart responded by ordering the 1st Infantry Division, supposedly loyal to him, to put down the Minas Gerais revolt.

Once Goulart's troops were committed and on the road, however, all doubt ended. Suddenly, 14 Brazilian states stood in open rebellion; two of the country's four armies had risen, and the other two were wavering. When

Goulart's 1st Infantry Division met the Minas Gerais troops, it promptly switched sides. The outlawed Communist-controlled General Labor Command tried to stage a general strike in Goulart's favor, with only spotty success. Goulart's leftist, Yankee-hating brother-in-law, Congressman Leonel Brizola, tried to mobilize peasant and Gaucho guerrillas he had armed, but they just stayed home.

Back to Brasilia

The turning point came as rebel troops, led by anti-Jango General Amaury Kruel, flew from São Paulo over the defense lines Goulart had set up outside Rio and took over the city behind them. Within the city, Goulart's archenemy, Carlos Lacerda, had manned the governor's palace with 500 state troopers and barricaded it with 20 city garbage trucks still bearing an anti-litter slogan: "HELP US. WE ARE CLEANING UP THE CITY." When the tide turned against Jango, Lacerda went on television to proclaim emotionally, "God has taken pity on the people. God is good."

Jango fled, ironically enough, to the nation's capital—the remote, grandiose inland city of Brasilia. But even Brasilia threatened to become too hotly rebellious for comfort. Still spouting defiance, Jango flew south to still loyal Porto Alegre, homeground of his firebrand brother-in-law and capital of his home state of Rio Grande do Sul. From there, Goulart hoped to lead a counterattack of the legalist forces. Vowed Jango: "I will not resign. I will not put a bullet through my chest. I will resist."

Within four hours after Jango left Brasilia, the Senate president gaveled a special joint session of Congress to order and announced that Goulart "had abandoned the site of the republic" and "left the presidency vacant." Mazzilli, president of the Chamber of Deputies and next in line of succession, thereupon became chief of state automatically—even though it took Goulart one more day to accept the inevitable and follow his lovely wife, Maria Tereza, and his two children to exile in Uruguay. Only a few scattered shots were ever fired in his defense. Those who saw him just before his plane took off from the airport said he was a beaten man, verging on tears.

Within 30 days, Congress must elect a "permanent temporary" President to fill out the rest of Goulart's term which runs until January 1966. No real presidential candidate will want to jeopardize his chances in next year's elections by becoming an interim President legally forbidden to succeed himself. At week's end seven of Brazil's key states had already endorsed General Humberto Castelo Branco for the temporary job. One of the key plotters and Goulart's army chief of staff, General Branco handled many of the top contacts before the revolt. Behind the scenes, real power will be held by the civilian leaders of the revolt—the governors of several states, including Carlos Lacerda. Other potentially powerful men, such as ex-President Kubitschek, wait in the wings.

A Start

In the first flush of revolutionary fervor, Brazil's right and center went after the left. Crowds burned out the headquarters of the left-dominated National Students Union. The left-leaning governor of Pernambucco was packed off to exile on a lonely island in the Atlantic, along with a passel of Communists and other assorted leftists. Brother-in-law Brizola was last seen gunning up the highway out of Porto Alegre in a borrowed green Volkswagen. Moscow recalled its ambassador; the Cuban ambassador braced for a diplomatic break any moment. The U.S. promised sympathy and aid.

But Brazil itself still has an uphill fight ahead. It will have to re-create a business climate that will appeal anew to foreign investors long ago disenchanted. It must assure the U.S. that solid economic aid will not just be fed, greenback by greenback, onto a fire of inflation. It must inspire a sense of national responsibility among its people. That means that labor must forgo any more of those massive 75% and 100% raises long demanded —and won—under Jango. The government will have to slow down the money presses and cut back overloaded federal payrolls. Manufacturers will have to hold the line on prices. But at least by dumping Goulart, Brazil has made a start along the road to confidence in itself. Over one 24-hour period during the revolution, Rio's black-market exchange rate for cruzeiros dropped from 2,200 to the dollar to 1,300.

—Time*

II. The following selections are in differing degrees specialized and technical. Comment on each. Are the details adequate for the author's purpose? Is the exposition too technical or too simple? Is the arrangement of details clear? Do the details have precision and necessity?

A.   *MRS. ATHAS' CHOCOLATE CAKE*

Melt ¼ cup of butter; break 2 eggs in it and fill up cup with milk. Add 1 cup of sugar and beat together. Sift in 1 heaping cup flour with 1 heaping teaspoon baking powder. Add a little vanilla. Add 2 squares of chocolate melted, (or 3 tablespoons of cocoa). Bake in oven at 350°.

* April 10, 1964, pp. 26-7. Courtesy TIME; copyright Time Inc. 1964.

B. OPERATION OF COLDSPOT THERMO-DEFROST REFRIGERATOR

The Thermo-Matic model provides completely automatic defrosting. Each time your refrigerator door is opened, warm-moist air enters, causing a coat of frost on the surface of the Freezer Chest. The accumulated length of time your door is open directly controls the initiation and frequency of the defrost cycle. When defrosting is completed, your Coldspot automatically returns to the refrigerating cycle. The Thermo-Defrost model operates in the same manner except that defrosting occurs only when you push the defrost button to initiate a defrost cycle.

1. The Thermo-Matic Knob and the Thermo-Defrost Button are both located just above the top of the Freezer Chest. If you have the Thermo-Matic model, "Matic" lights up when the defrost cycle is in operation. This light turns off automatically when the defrost cycle is completed.

2. IF YOU HAVE THE THERMO-MATIC MODEL, defrost water is collected in a water evaporation tray which is placed in slides under the refrigerator. The tray need not be emptied under normal operating conditions since the amount of water collected from each defrosting cycle is small and will evaporate between defrost cycles. IF YOU HAVE THE THERMO-DEFROST MODEL, defrost water collects in a tray which slides on tracks attached to the bottom of the Humiderator. It is suggested that this container be emptied daily after each defrosting.

3. After a defrost cycle is completed and your Coldspot resumes operation, a slightly different sound pitch may be noted. This will continue for only a short time.

4. The refrigerating unit produces freezing temperatures immediately after the completion of a defrost cycle. The last small droplets of defrost water will freeze to the bottom of the Freezer Chest. This condition is normal and it is not necessary that these droplets be wiped from the Freezer.

5. IF YOU HAVE THE THERMO-MATIC MODEL and want to start the defrost cycle manually (without waiting for the defrost cycle to start automatically), simply turn the Defrost Knob clockwise until "Matic" lights up. NOTE: Defrost cycle should not be initiated unless there is frost on the Freezer Chest. This extra defrost cycle will end automatically at the proper time. IF YOU HAVE THE THERMO-DEFROST MODEL, it is suggested that you make a habit of initiating a defrost cycle at a regular time each day by simply pushing the Defrost Control Button.

6. IF YOU HAVE THE THERMO-MATIC MODEL, you can also delay the defrost cycle. Simply turn the Defrost Knob clockwise until

"Matic" lights up. Then continue to turn the knob approximately ⅛ of a turn past the point where the light goes off. Your Coldspot is now operating on its normal refrigerating cycle.

*—Coldspot Owner's Manual**

C. *NEW YORK TIMES STOCK MARKET ANALYSIS—APRIL 2, 1964*

N.Y. Stock Exchange. Stocks closed sharply up with key market averages climbing to record levels in the heaviest trading since late November; volume 684 million shares.

Bonds were mostly higher in active trading; transactions, $10.28 million.

American Exchange. Stocks advanced; 2,406,915 shares traded.

Bonds were mixed; sales $415,000

Foreign Exchange. Pound Sterling rose; Canadian dollar was steady.

Commodity Futures. Grain and soybeans mixed; cotton mostly up.

D. *SOUTHERN FELLOWSHIPS FUND REPORT*

Four types of grants have been made available: one, the faculty fellowship already described, with stipends ranging from $1700 to $2500, plus supplements for dependents and to cover tuition costs; second, summer grants-in-aid ranging from $300 to $750, open to faculty members in accredited four-year southern colleges offering degrees not higher than the master's; third, the three-year college teaching career fellowship, for which carefully selected college seniors of high qualification who intend to become college professors have been eligible to apply, with stipends from $1200 to $2000, plus supplements for tuition and dependents. Effective during 1961-62 and 1962-63, dissertation year fellowships only, with stipends ranging from $2500 to $3600, were made available. The dissertation year fellowships were open only to persons who at the time of application had completed all doctoral requirements except dissertation research, writing, and defense. Awards were not offered for 1963-64, since the residue of the grant made in 1954 to the Council by the General Education Board was not sufficient to finance another series.

* Published by Sears, Roebuck and Co.

The terms of award which governed a fellowship once it was made, and which explained clearly the relationship of the Fund to the recipient and to the university selected for graduate study by the recipient, were sent to each recipient at the time of notification of award; written agreement with these by the recipient was a required part of his letter of acceptance.

Although these terms varied slightly from year to year in light of experience, they were substantially the same for each type of grant. In Part II are shown typical statements of terms: one, for faculty awards, 1960-61; one for dissertation year grants, 1962-63; one for college teaching career fellowships, 1960-61.

The faculty fellowships were made on a one-year basis, with possible renewal for an additional year. The summer grants-in-aid offered during six summers were limited to two separate awards to a person. College teaching career fellowships were offered in 1957, 1958, 1959, and 1960, for three successive years of graduate study, subject to termination if graduate performance was reported by graduate professors to be of less than distinguished quality.

Of the recipients, 532 have reported, up to this writing, the attainment of the doctorate since receiving a Fund grant. The degrees have been awarded by 84 universities, North, South, East, West, and abroad. One hundred fifty (150) other recipients report that they expect to complete all doctoral requirements before the year 1965. Other faculty members have completed a second, third, or fourth year of graduate work under a Fund fellowship and are now back in their teaching positions carrying on research and writing, preliminary to completing their degree requirements.

The awards in the different types of fellowships have been as follows:

	Awards	Used
Summer Grants-in-Aid	402	377
Faculty Fellowships	648	582
Dissertation Year Fellowships	83	77
College Teaching Career Fellowships	292	187
	1425	1223[1]

[1] This total represents 1115 persons.

It now seems probable that by the end of 1965, unless unfavorable conditions arise, more than 750 persons will have attained the doctorate after having been aided by the Fund.

—ROBERT H. LESTER*

* From *The Southern Fellowships Fund; A Summing Up, 1954-1964* (Chapel Hill, N.C.: The Southern Fellowships Fund, 1964), pp. 10-1.

E.   *EGYPTIAN COSMOLOGY*

The Egyptian conceived of the earth as a flat platter with a corrugated rim. The inside bottom of this platter was the flat, alluvial plain of Egypt, and the corrugated rim was the rim of mountain countries which were the foreign lands. This platter floated in water. There were the abysmal waters below, on which the platter rested, called by the Egyptian 'Nun.' Nun was the waters of the underworld, and, according to one continuing concept, Nun was the primordial waters out of which life first issued. Life still issued from these underworld waters, for the sun was reborn every day out of Nun, and the Nile came pouring forth from caverns which were fed from Nun. In addition to being the underworld waters, Nun was the waters encircling the world, the Okeanos which formed the outermost boundary, also called the 'Great Circuit' or the 'Great Green.' Thus it was clear that the sun, after its nightly journey under the world, must be reborn beyond the eastern horizon out of those encircling waters, just as all the gods had originally come forth out of Nun.

Above the earth was the inverted pan of the sky, setting the outer limit to the universe. As we have already said, the craving for symmetry, as well as a sense that space is limited, called forth a counterheaven under the earth, bounding the limits of the underworld. This was the universe within which man and the gods and the heavenly bodies operated.

Various qualifications to this picture are immediately necessary. Our picture gives the vault of heaven as suspended by apparent levitation above the earth. That would appeal to the ancient Egyptian as dangerous, and he would ask for some visible means of support. As we have already said, he provided various means of support in various concepts, the incompatibility of which he cheerfully ignored. The simplest mechanism was four posts set on earth to carry the weight of heaven. These were at the outer limits of the earth, as is indicated by such texts as: 'I have set . . . the terror of thee as far as the four pillars of heaven,' and the number four suggests that they were placed at the four points of the compass. Fortunately, this arrangement appealed to the Egyptian as being both strong and permanent: '(As firm) as heaven resting upon its four posts' is a simile used more than once.

—JOHN A. WILSON*

* From "Egypt: The Nature of the Universe," in *Before Philosophy* by Henri Frankfort and others (Harmondsworth, England: Penguin Books, 1949), pp. 54-5.

F.   *"SAMUEL PEPYS (1633-1703)"*

Samuel Pepys has become the best-known character of his time; in his famous diary we can relive the life of a citizen of Restoration London. He was an ordinary man in some ways—a busy, inquisitive government clerk recording for nine years everything that he thought and did, but a genius too, in his quick response to the many aspects of life, his aptitude for catching the salient detail of every moment. "I staid up till the bellman came by with his bell under my window, as I was writing of this very line, and cried 'Past one of the clock, and a cold, frosty, windy morning.'" His hopes and fears and discomforts, his love of music and the theater, his domestic pleasures and troubles, his casual amours—all are set down without reserve, and with such enthusiasm and vividness as to give distinction to the commonplace.

These details stand out against the great historical events which Pepys saw and in which he had a share. The son of a London tailor, he was well educated at St. Paul's and Cambridge, and appears as a protégé of Edward Montagu, afterwards first Earl of Sandwich. At the Restoration he was made Clerk of the King's ships and of the Acts of the Navy, and became an efficient and indispensable administrator of naval affairs at a crucial period. Though he took perquisites and presents, he was far superior to the typical office-holder of his time; the history of the Navy during these years was inglorious, but Pepys did what he could. He was President of the Royal Society in 1684 and 1685, and Secretary of the Admiralty from 1684 to 1688. Through his career he was closely associated with the Duke of York, afterwards James II, and went out of office after the Revolution of 1688. He left his collections of books, broadside ballads, and manuscripts, including the famous diary, to his own college, Magdalene, Cambridge, where the visitor to the Pepsian Library may still see them in bindings and cases of Pepys' own design. He accumulated large masses of letters and official documents which have been used by recent biographers to reconstruct his important career as a public official.

His later years are well described in Evelyn's *Diary*, May 26, 1703:

> This day died Mr. Samuel Pepys, a very worthy, industrious and curious person, none in England exceeding him in knowledge of the navy, in which he had passed through all the most considerable offices, Clerk of the Acts and Secretary of the Admiralty, all which he performed with great integrity. When King James II went out of England, he laid down his office and would serve no more; but withdrawing himself from all public affairs, he lived at Clapham with his partner, Mr.

Hewer, formerly his clerk, in a very noble house and sweet place, where he enjoyed the fruit of his labors in great prosperity. He was universally beloved, hospitable, generous, learned in many things, skilled in music, a very great cherisher of learned men of whom he had the conversation. His library and collection of other curiosities were of the most considerable, the models of ships especially. Besides what he published of an account of the navy, as he found and left it, he had for divers years under his hand the History of the Navy, or *Navalia*, as he called it.

Pepys kept his diary from New Year's, 1660, to May 31, 1669, when he gave it up because of failing eyesight. It consists of about three thousand pages written in Shelton's shorthand, a well-known system of the time. This can hardly be called a secret code, but the diary was thus made inaccessible to the ordinary reader, and evidently Pepys wrote only for himself. The diary was first transcribed early in the nineteenth century by a Cambridge student named John Smith; Lord Braybrooke published about a quarter of the text in 1825, Mynors Bright published much more in 1875, and Henry B. Wheatley published the whole, except for some expurgations, in 1893-99. Pepys' method obviously contrasts with John Evelyn's, who wrote more formal entries and carefully revised his text. Indeed, most diarists, like all letter-writers, have a reader in mind; the complete spontaneity and frankness of Pepys are so rare as to give him a unique place in literature.

—ALAN DUGALD MCKILLOP*

III. Comment on the strong and weak points in the use of detail in the following student essay.

"THE MISSISSIPPI RIVER—A SYMBOL OF FREEDOM"

The wide, fast-moving Mississippi River can be more than just a mass of water or raw force. It can have significant meaning in many other areas, but I am going to deal with only two of these meanings, which are as a symbol of freedom and as a route of escape in the novel *Huckleberry Finn*.

Mark Twain, who created Huckleberry Finn, spent several years working on a riverboat on the Mississippi River. Knowing this, one understands

* From *English Literature from Dryden to Burns* (New York: Appleton-Century-Crofts, 1948), pp. 57-9.

111

Huck's knowledge of the river. It is very possible for Huck to acquire this knowledge from his father and others in the novel.

When a person was traveling on a raft on this large river, he did not have the social restrictions to contend with that prevailed in town. It was not necessary to wash before meals, or for that matter, wash at all, wear clean clothes, eat with manners, or the like. He was in a situation where other people would not be offended by his lack of etiquette. I do not mean everyone who traveled on a raft did not use any manners, but that the atmosphere was, generally, a lazy one.

A person who traveled by raft was seldom, if ever, approached on the water by other people who wanted to engage in long conversations. He might have someone check his raft for runaway slaves, but they would be only passing by. There were so many rafts on the river that most people did not pay any attention to them. I expect that people on the large riverboats might observe the rafts, but only out of curiosity. Huck did not want to take this chance, however, and rode at night most of the time.

The river life was very leisurely. The meals were mostly fish caught while traveling. The raft Huck Finn possessed had a raised section for living quarters. In normal weather he could lie around and fish or sleep without ever getting wet. About the only work involved was tying up the raft at night and fixing meals, neither of which required much work. Over all, it is easy to see why this life can be called a leisurely one. To the people like Huck Finn, who traveled on the river, all these freedoms were taken for granted. To Jim, the runaway Negro with Huck, the river had a different meaning. It was a way to freedom from slavery to him.

To both Huck and Jim, the river was a route of escape. To Huck it was a getaway from "civilized" things and from his father, who had been treating him very roughly. However, as I have said, it was a getaway to a new life for Jim. In this escape, Jim needed Huck to keep the runaway-slave catchers away. Huck needed Jim for his ability to build things, such as a shelter on the raft. Having Huck along made life easier for Jim in another way, too. Jim had not planned his escape, but Huck had planned his, and had brought along a few things that made the trip easier for them, such as a gun and corn meal to cook with.

They had little trouble finding a raft for their trip, but they were in luck to find one large enough to build a shelter on. People using rafts to haul supplies on probably let them go when the job was done, and the current tore a good many of them loose from their moorings. This accounted for the many rafts on the river.

Huck knew the river very well. Therefore, it was a logical route for their escape. The river also offered many places in which to hide. The many coves, the places where the trees hung out over the river and the thick undergrowth along the banks of the river made hiding the canoe and raft little trouble.

Although in the book, only Jim's need for escape was evident, I do not believe either Huck's or Jim's escape was necessary. If Huck had gone to the authorities about his father, they could have helped him. He also said that he wanted to get away from "civilized" places, which was impossible to do in the complete sense of the word. He could have stayed on the raft traveling, but I do not believe he really wanted that for himself.

As long as Jim and Huck were on the river, their freedom and escape were the only important things to them. However, Jim was already a free slave and did not have to be running away, but he did not know this until the end of the book.

IV. Assume you are a reporter. Write a news story of 150-200 words based on direct observation of an event, character or process. For example: "New Freshman Dormitory Nears Completion"; "Campus YMCA Holds Dance"; "Chemistry Students Perform First Quantitative Analysis"; "College Players Stage *J.B.*" Then use the same event, character or process in a different context—for example, a feature article, a short story or a report. Develop your material in an essay of about 500 words. Include as part of your assignment the notes that you took while observing.

Development by Example

5

When details are used to support a general point, they become examples. Development by example is an extension of development by detail and there is no need to draw a fine distinction between the two forms. In practice the distinction is a matter of emphasis. When details are presented for their own sake, as in a manual giving the steps for lubricating a Volkswagen, an enumeration of the characteristics of acrylic

115

paint or a list of facts in the entry for Ulysses S. Grant in a biographical dictionary, the method is clearly development by detail. If the details are selected and arranged to illustrate a general point such as "Lubricating a VW is easy" or "General Grant was a weak President," they begin to function as examples. The greater the emphasis on the general point, the more obvious this function. In argumentation, details functioning as examples are called evidence.

5.1 GENERALIZATION AND INSTANCE

Two elements are involved in every use of example, a **generalization** and one or more **instances. A generalization is an assertion about a group or class of instances. An instance is a specific member of the group or class referred to.** In normal usage **example** is a synonym for **instance.** Hence, "Most bricks are made of clay" is a *generalization,* and a clay brick is an *example.* "Today was my lucky day" is a generalization, and "At lunchtime I found a quarter under my chair" is an example. "Low margin requirements contribute to extreme fluctuations in the stock market" is a generalization, and "low margin requirements characterized the period 1925 to 1930" is an example.

5.2 USE OF EXAMPLES

Examples are used for illustration, clarification and proof. **In illustration, examples suggest a dominant impression or inform by giving instances of a general point. In clarification, examples explain a statement that might otherwise be unclear. In proof, examples are used to convince.**

These distinctions are not absolute, but they help the writer decide on his selection of examples and his method of presenting them. In general, the qualities that make for effective use of **detail** also apply to example. In informal writing, **concreteness, immediacy and economy**

116

receive emphasis. The more formal the writing, the more stress is placed on **precision and necessity.** In formal proof, footnotes and other techniques of **documentation** contribute to the **precision** of examples.*

5.3   ILLUSTRATION

When describing a scene, person or event, an author necessarily uses details. If his object is simply to convey information or to create a "sense of reality," he uses the method of development by detail. If, on the other hand, he wishes to create a dominant impression, the impression begins to function as a **generalization** and the details as **illustration.** Thus "The movie was exciting" is a generalization and "The heroine was captured by Indians after a wild chase" is an example. Assuming that "The movie was exciting" is not obscure or controversial, the example functions as an illustration. The author is not using it to explain the meaning of "exciting" or to change the mind of someone who found the movie boring; he is using it simply to convey his impression. By the same token, the author of an essay on American government may write "The executive branch has wide powers. The President can initiate legislation and veto undesirable bills, killing them or sending them back to Congress for further debate." The first sentence is a generalization. *Initiate 'legislation* and *veto* function as illustrations. The author is not seeking to prove the generalization but to convey information.

Illustration is a standard method for literary description and narration. The author selects details that convey the impression desired and omits details that do not contribute to the impression. If the details are carefully selected and their significance emphasized through stylistic techniques, the generalization may not need to be stated explicitly. When Mark Twain wrote the following description of a day on the Mississippi River, he wished, of course, to create a "sense of reality." He also wished to convey a distinct impression—an impression of pleasant, relaxed idling.

---

* The use of examples to **define** is a special case of **clarification** and will be considered in the chapter on definition (chapter 8).

PRACTICAL RHETORIC

Style plays an important part in the passage—notice, for example, the repetition of the word *lazy*. The most important element, however, is the use of details illustrating the impression: fishing and hot breakfast; gazing at the river; dozing off; watching a steamboat in the distance; doing nothing for an hour; watching a raft; listening to the sound of an ax; hearing boats go by in the fog.

> A little smoke couldn't be noticed now, so we would take some fish off of the lines and cook up a hot breakfast. And afterwards we would watch the lonesomeness of the river, and kind of lazy along, and by and by lazy off to sleep. Wake up by and by, and look to see what done it, and maybe see a steamboat coughing along up-stream, so far off towards the other side you couldn't tell nothing about her only whether she was a stern-wheel or side-wheel; then for about an hour there wouldn't be nothing to hear nor nothing to see—just solid lonesomeness. Next you'd see a raft sliding by, away off yonder, and maybe a galoot on it chopping, because they're most always doing it on a raft; you'd see the ax flash and come down—you don't hear nothing; you see that ax go up again, and by the time it's above the man's head then you hear the k'chunk!—it had took all that time to come over the water. So we would put in the day, lazying around, listening to the stillness. Once there was a thick fog, and the rafts and things that went by was beating tin pans so the steamboats wouldn't run over them. A scow or a raft went by so close we could hear them talking and cussing and laughing—heard them plain; but we couldn't see no sign of them; it made you feel crawly; it was like spirits carrying on that way in the air. Jim said he believed it was spirits; but I says:
> "No; spirits wouldn't say, 'Dern the dern fog.'"

> —MARK TWAIN*

To the reader, the passage is an effortless and pleasantly haphazard collection of observations. It definitely "works." A little analysis will show that it "works" because of the skill with which it has been put together. The details are arranged in simple chronological order from early morning to dusk and all illustrate "pleasant relaxation." If Huck and Jim burned their catfish, the detail is omitted; if Huck was bothered by mosquitos, we never learn of it. More important, no detail suggests "effort" or "activity with purpose." We know that the breakfast fire did

* From *The Adventures of Huckleberry Finn* (1884).

118

not build itself, but we are not told how the wood was collected or that it was wet and had to be kindled several times before burning. If there were chores to do—scouring the frying pan, for instance—they are not mentioned. In place of such purposeful activity, we have dozing, gazing, and listening. The working world is only introduced for contrast: the steamboat is presumably going someplace; and unlike Huck and Jim the man on the raft has to chop *his* wood. The total effect is so definite— the selection of details so expert—that a topic sentence would be superfluous.

For a more workaday instance of details used for illustration we can turn to a history textbook, where the author's purpose is to inform rather than entertain. The generalization—"clerical students had worldly interests"—is spelled out in the topic sentence of the first paragraph. It is followed by several illustrations. The use of footnotes and the fact that the illustrations are direct quotations give the passage the tone of formal proof. It is not proof, however. The generalization is offered as an accepted point of medieval history, not a topic for debate. To prove a generalization of this kind to the satisfaction of the professional historian would require more evidence, more systematic presentation, discussion of negative instances and the paraphernalia of scholarly argument— qualifications, additional footnotes and the like. The passage is expository, not argumentative.

Naturally the clerical students were far more exuberant in their lives and more outspoken in their writings than were the professors. Although technically classed as a clergyman, the average student seems to have had a pagan attitude in morals and poetry. He could laud Bacchus as the god of drunkenness and admire the man who "carried his liquor best."

> If there's here a fellow lurking Who his proper share is shirking
> Let the door to him be shown . . .
> When your heart is set on drinking, Drink on without stay or thinking,
> Till you cannot stand up straight, Nor one word articulate![1]

In the twelfth century one of these students wrote "The Contest between Wine and Water," in which he related how water accused wine of being a curse to mankind.

[1] J. A. Symonds, *Wine, Women and Song* (London: Chatto and Windus), p. 174.

119

All thy life is foul and sordid, Sunk in misery, steeped in vice;
Those who drink thee lose their morals, Waste their time in sloth and
quarrels
Rolling down sin's precipice.
Thou dost teach man's tongue to stutter; He goes reeling in the gutter
Who hath deigned to kiss thy lips; Hears men speak without discerning,
Sees a hundred tapers burning When there are but two poor dips.

But wine finally wins the debate by expatiating as follows on the danger of drinking infected water.

Thou of things the scum and rotten, Sewer, where odures best forgotten
And unmentioned still descend!
Filth and garbage, Stench and poison, Thou dost bear in fetid foison!
Here I stop lest words offend . . .
Many a man and oft who swallowed Thine infected potion, followed
After death in one day's time.[2]

Toward women the student attitude was frankly sensual, and student poetry reveals none of the romantic chivalry of troubador literature. From as early a period as the tenth century comes a poem in which a young roué is represented as inviting his mistress to his room for dinner. He promises her cushions, "flowers of sweetest scent," "meats and drinks of rare delight"; there too "wine flows sparkling free"; there she shall have servants to wait on her, a flutist and a lyre player to entertain her; and love. From the twelfth century comes an interesting poem which opens with prayers to the Virgin Mary, continues with references to Venus, and closes with a passionate love scene:

What more? Around the maiden's neck My arms I flung with yearning;
Upon her lips I gave and took A thousand kisses burning . . .
Who is the man that does not know The sweets that followed after?[3]

There were also many other love lyrics dedicated to Phyllis, or Flora, some of them written in the most sensually descriptive detail. All of this, it should be remembered, was by clerical students.

—LOREN C. MACKINNEY*

[2] *Ibid.*, pp. 167ff.
[3] *Ibid.*, pp. 122f.
* From *The Medieval World* (New York: Farrar & Rinehart, 1938), pp. 686-7.

5.4   CLARIFICATION

Clarification is an aid to comprehension. We all know how confusing abstract statements can be. If we cannot relate them to familiar situations, we have trouble understanding them. When used for clarification, examples bridge the gap between the abstract and the concrete. Because they assist understanding, they are especially common in writing intended to explain or instruct. If a point is sufficiently complex, clarification by example may be necessary, but even when an example is not essential it can be helpful. A writer who asserts "Energy can be stored in a great many forms" will probably not be misunderstood, but he can make the reader's job easier if he adds "as, for example, in the raised weight of a clock, in the coiled spring of a watch, in the chemicals in the cells of the body, in the coal we burn in our furnaces and in the gasoline we burn in our cars." For an instance of examples that are necessary for comprehension, consider the following two versions of a discussion of Immanuel Kant's theory of knowledge. In the first version the examples used by the author have been deleted; the second is printed as the author originally wrote it.

> Not every judgment is knowledge; in an *analytical judgment* the predicate merely elucidates what is already contained in the subject. The judgment must be synthetic; that is, add something to the predicate, *extend* our knowledge, not merely elucidate it. Not all synthetic judgments, however, give us knowledge; some are derived from experience. In other words, such judgments are lacking in *necessity.*

Even a trained philosopher would have difficulty following this. Now consider the passage as originally written:

> Not every judgment is knowledge; in an *analytical judgment* the predicate merely elucidates what is already contained in the subject: *e.g.,* "Body is an extended thing." The judgment must be synthetic; that is, add something to the predicate, *extend* our knowledge, not merely elucidate it: *e.g.,* "All bodies have specific gravity." Not all synthetic judgments, however, give us knowledge; some are derived from experience; they inform us, for example, that an object has such and such properties or behaves thus or

so, but not that it *must* have these qualities, or behave so. In other words, such judgments are lacking in *necessity*.

—FRANK THILLY*

In the preceding passage, the author clarifies his statements with three **brief examples** that do not interrupt the flow of his thought. Frequently an **extended example** is helpful. The following selection is an excerpt, as the first sentence clearly shows. If the first sentence were revised to "Classical mechanics conspicuously failed to solve the problem of radiation," the passage would resemble a short essay on "The Failure of Classical Mechanics." Its most important element is an extended example. Notice that the whole second paragraph is devoted to the example. Within this paragraph the development is by a series of details about the energy of billiard balls.

Another conspicuous failure of the classical mechanics was with one aspect of the problem of radiation. Here it predicted very general and particularly clear-cut results, which observation was found to negate completely. A simple illustration will explain the nature of the conflict.

Imagine a crowd of steel balls set rolling about on a steel floor. If two balls bump into one another, their individual speeds and directions of motion will change, but the incident will not alter the total energy of motion of the balls. There must, however, be a steady leakage of energy from other causes, such as air resistance and the friction of the floor, so that the balls continually lose energy and, after no great length of time, will be found standing at rest on the floor. The energy of their motion seems to have been lost, although we know that actually most of it has been transformed into heat. The classical mechanics predicts that this must happen; it shows that all energy of motion, except possibly a minute fraction of the whole, must be transformed into heat whenever such a transformation is physically possible. It is because of this that perpetual-motion machines are a practical impossibility.

Precisely similar ideas are applicable to the molecules which form the air of a room. These also move about independently, and frequently bump into one another. The classical mechanics now predicts that the whole energy of motion will be changed into radiation, so that the molecules will shortly be found lying at rest on the floor—as the steel balls were. In actual

* From *A History of Philosophy* (New York: Henry Holt & Company, 1914), p. 397.

fact they continue to move with undiminished energy, forming a perpetual-motion machine in defiance of the classical mechanics.

—Sir James Jeans*

5.5 PROOF

If a point is controversial or so original that the reader is likely to say "Show me," the author needs to prove it. To do this he almost always must cite examples. **In proof the point to be demonstrated is the author's thesis, and the examples supporting the thesis are his evidence.** The more original or controversial the thesis, the more important the evidence. "Education is useful" is neither original nor controversial. It is a platitude. It could be "proved," but for the average reader the argument would be a waste of time. On the other hand, "high school graduates are adequately prepared for college" happens to be quite controversial, and several books have recently appeared giving evidence *pro* and *con*. Notice that an author arguing this point can choose from several types of evidence. The simplest type of evidence may be *personal experience*. The author can draw on his own observations, remarking, for example, that most of his high school teachers were intelligent and well trained; his classes were limited in size; he scored in the top ten percent on College Board examinations; college courses have not proved excessively difficult and so forth. If the author has studied his subject, he can supplement personal experience with other types of evidence. He can use *source material*—for example, he can refer to surveys published by the Department of Health, Education and Welfare. He can use *testimony* by quoting prominent authorities. Or he can use *direct observation* by making his own survey or interviewing selected teachers and educators. Whatever course he takes, the results will appear in his essay as evidence.

Consider the following three selections. The first, by the critic Hippolyte Taine, is an attempt to prove that Charles Dickens was con-

* From *Physics and Philosophy* (New York: The Macmillan Company, 1943), pp. 124-5.

temptuous of the British aristocracy. The treatment is popular in the sense that it is intended to appeal to the intelligent general reader. The examples are vivid and entertaining. However, because Taine fails to qualify or consider exceptions, a professional scholar would consider the comment superficial. The second example—on the high cost of air—is more formal. It is from a collection of articles in a journal intended for the general reader with a scholarly turn of mind. It consists of two rather specialized examples (purifying normal air, purifying polluted air) described in language that is precise rather than immediate. It also includes two footnotes citing articles on air pollution. The third example—on *Othello*—is highly technical. It is intended for experts only. It assumes knowledge of a previous article, it cites a source—the Elizabethan homilies —that is unknown to most readers and it provides systematic documentation. Its basic method, nevertheless, is the same one used by Taine. The citation from the homilies is **evidence** that Elizabethans believed in "Judas' repentance"; and the citations from *Othello* are **evidence** that Shakespeare's hero practiced "Judas' repentance." Of the three passages given, it is the one that most nearly approximates rigorous proof.

I.

Another fault generated by habitual domineering and conflict is pride. It flourishes in an aristocratic nation, and no one has derided the aristocracy more harshly than Dickens. Every portrait is a sarcasm: James Harthouse, a dandy disgusted with everything, chiefly himself, and rightly so; Lord Frederick Verisopht, a gullible sot, whose wit consists in staring at people and sucking the end of his cane. Lord Feenix, a slot-machine for parliamentary phrases, now out of order and hardly able to conclude the absurd orations into which he launches on the slightest pretext; Mrs. Skewton, a hideous old ruin, coquetting to the last, parading her daughter through the salons of England in order to sell her to some vain husband, and insisting that her own deathbed be draped in rose-colored curtains; Sir John Chester, a rascal in high life, who, lest he be compromised, refuses, with an exquisite grace as he finishes his chocolate, to help his bastard son.

—HIPPOLYTE TAINE*

* From *A History of English Literature*, tr. H. Van Laun (New York: Henry Altemus Co., 1908), III, 231.

II.

Air was once regarded by economists as free goods. More and more we confront the situation of having to spend money to process air before we can use it in such activities as assembling vacuum tubes and building precision gyroscopes. In some places normal meteorological conditions concentrate the pollutants released by our factories and automobiles. A few people have been killed by such concentrations and many more are uncomfortable and perhaps endangered.[1] Processes which stop the release of pollutants from automobiles are being developed and will be required as standard equipment in California within a few years. Larger-scale processes to promote air mixing or to wash out some kinds of impurities appear impractical at present,[2] but they may appear more practical in the future.

—RICHARD C. RAYMOND*

III.

A number of Shakespearean scholars and critics have told me in correspondance and private conversation that, while they accept my reading of *Othello* in general ("The Damnation of Othello," *PMLA*, LXVIII [1953], 1068-78), they think that, in view of Othello's final anguish, he might be regarded as repentant and hence as saved rather than damned. This is a point I should have taken up in my article. I now ask the indulgence of the editor for an additional note.

In the Elizabethan "Homily of Repentance" it is pointed out that the anguished recognition of guilt does not in itself constitute true repentance:

> We read in the gospel, that Judas was so sorrowful and heavy, yea, that he was filled with such anguish and vexation of mind, for that which he had done, that he could not abide to live any longer. Did not he also, afore he hanged himself, make an open confession of his fault, when he said, *I have sinned, betraying the innocent blood?* . . . It is evident and plain then, that although we be never so earnestly sorry for our sins, acknowledge and confess them; yet all these things

[1] "Lung Cancer is Linked to Auto Fumes," *Philadelphia Inquirer*, June 9, 1962.
[2] Robert L. Daugherty, "The Control of Air Pollution," *Engineering and Science*, (April, 1960), p. 16.
* From "Problems of Industrial Conversion," in *Disarmament: Its Politics and Economics*, ed. Seymour Melman (Boston: American Academy of Arts and Sciences, 1962), p. 168.

shall be but means to bring us to utter desperation, except we do steadfastly believe that God our heavenly father will, for his son Jesus Christ's sake, pardon and forgive us our offences and trespasses, and utterly put them out of remembrance in his sight. Therefore . . . they that teach repentance without Christ, and a lively faith in the mercy of God, do only teach Cain's or Judas' repentance.[1]

Christian repentance, then, is sharply distinguished from "Judas' repentance"; the latter is an overwhelming sense of guilt without faith in the mercy of God. This distinction, a restatement of the traditional commonplace of the heinousness of the sin of despair, would have been familiar doctrine for the members of Shakespeare's audience, every one of whom was reached by the homilies.

It is precisely "Judas' repentance" which Othello displays. No glimmer of faith in the mercy of God appears in Othello's assertion that the "demidevil" Iago has "ensnared my soul" (v. ii. 301-302). Further, Othello has no hope of salvation (v.ii. 273-275): "When we shall meet at compt,/ This look of thine will hurl my soul from heaven,/And fiends will snatch at it." When he continues, "Whip me, ye devils,/From the possession of this heavenly sight," he is not only expressing his despair but is already entering upon the punishments of hell in this life.[2] Finally, in committing self-murder he is following Judas' example. His behavior in his last moments, therefore, would have confirmed Elizabethans in the impression that his soul is lost. This impression they would have gained earlier from observing the dramatic irony of his offering Desdemona an opportunity, as

---

[1] *Certain Sermons or Homilies Appointed to be Read in Churches in the Time of the Late Queen Elizabeth* (Oxford Univ. Press, 1832), p. 490. The use of Judas as an instance of repentance without faith is not new with the homilies. As Professor Roy W. Battenhouse has called to my attention, Calvin quotes Biblical commentators who do the same (*Institutes of the Christian Religion*, tr. Henry Beveridge, Edinburgh, 1845, III, iii, 4): "Others . . . have set down two forms of repentance, and, in order to distinguish them, have called the one Legal repentance; or that by which the sinner, stung with a sense of his sin, and overwhelmed with fear of the divine anger, remains in that state of perturbation, unable to escape from it. The other they term Evangelical repentance; or that by which the sinner, though grievously downcast in himself, yet looks up and sees in Christ the cure of his wound, the solace of his terror, the haven of rest from his misery. They give Cain, Saul, and Judas, as examples of legal repentance." Calvin expresses his agreement with this distinction but goes on to insist (III, iii, 5) that although faith and true repentance "cannot be separated, they ought to be distinguished."

[2] *Cf.* Calvin, III, iii, 4: "Their repentance, therefore, was nothing better than a kind of threshold to hell, into which having entered even in the present life, they began to endure the punishment inflicted by presence of the an offended God."

he supposes, for salvation through prayer and then withdrawing it in a rage, not realizing that his own salvation is at issue and forgetting that those who do not forgive will not be forgiven.

—PAUL N. SIEGEL*

5.6 REPRESENTATIVE AND MULTIPLE EXAMPLES

When a single example is used to illustrate, clarify or prove a generalization, it is called a representative example. Two or more examples used for the same generalization are called multiple examples. The examples may be **cited** in a phrase or sentence, or developed at some length. When **developing** examples, the author usually gives details.

The passages already given in this chapter illustrate typical variations. The passage from *Huck Finn* (p. 118) uses **multiple examples** and citation. Several examples are mentioned but no example is developed extensively. The account of medieval student life (pp. 119-20) also uses **multiple examples** and **citation**. Although the quotations are fairly long, they are not discussed by the author. The explanation of Kant's theory of knowledge (pp. 121-2) uses **representative examples.** Although three examples are included in the passage, each example clarifies a *different* generalization. Obviously, the examples are cited, not developed. The selection on the failure of classical mechanics (pp. 122-3) uses a single **representative example.** Within the paragraph describing the motion of billiard balls the author uses **development by detail.** The comments on Dickens and on air pollution (pp. 124-5) use **multiple examples** without development. The article on *Othello* uses a combination of techniques. The second paragraph gives one **representative example** (the quotation from the homilies) developed by means of the subsequent comment. The third paragraph uses **multiple examples.** The first three are **citations** from the text of *Othello.* The fourth ("Finally, in committing self-murder . . .") is **developed** in the two sentences that follow it.

* "The Damnation of Othello: An Addendum," *PMLA*, LXXI (March, 1956), pp. 279-80.

5.7 EXAMPLE IN EXTENDED PASSAGES

Examples are useful in all writing situations. The passages already given in this chapter illustrate the use of examples in narrative, description, exposition and argumentation. Two selections show how examples can be used in extended passages. Although taken from a longer essay, the passage on classical mechanics may be considered a short essay developed by **representative example.** Considered in this way, it has the following outline:

I. Classical mechanics while successful in some areas has failed in others.
II. Classical mechanics can account for simple problems of motion. Ex-example: the motion of billiard balls.
III. Classical mechanics cannot account for molecular motion.

The comment on *Othello* also makes extended use of examples. Notice that the purpose statement is not proved directly. It must be analyzed into two subordinate generalizations. These become the topics of the second and third paragraphs respectively. Proof of the subordinate generalizations constitutes proof of the purpose statement:

I. Othello's repentance is false repentance.
II. Shakespeare's contemporaries believed that repentance was often false "Judas' repentance." Example: Quotation from homily on repentance.
III. Othello's repentance is "Judas' repentance." Examples: Quotations from the play; Othello's suicide.

TERMS TO BE LEARNED

▸ Generalization
▸ Instance
▸ Examples as illustration
▸ Examples as clarification

▸ Examples as proof
▸ Thesis
▸ Evidence
▸ Representative example
▸ Multiple examples
▸ Citation of example
▸ Development of example

Exercises & Theme Topics

I. The following selections use development by example. For each, write out the generalization being supported and the instances given. Then answer the following questions: (1) Are the examples used for illustration, clarification or proof? (2) In terms of the principles governing the use of detail in different writing situations (above, pp. 83-93), how does the author's presentation of his examples reflect his purpose?

A.   **THE LIGHTNESS OF BIRDS**

In addition to conventional lungs, birds possess an accessory system of five or more pairs of air sacs, connected with the lungs, that ramify widely throughout the body. Branches of these sacs extend into the hollow bones, sometimes even into the small toe bones. The air-sac system not only contributes to the birds' lightness of weight but also supplements the lungs as a supercharger (adding to the efficiency of respiration) and serves as a cooling system for the birds' speedy, hot metabolism. It has been estimated that a flying pigeon uses one fourth of its air intake for breathing and three fourths for cooling.

The lungs of man constitute about 5 per cent of his body volume; the respiratory system of a duck, in contrast, makes up 20 per cent of the body volume (2 per cent lungs and 18 per cent air sacs). The anatomical connections of the lungs and air sacs in birds seem to provide a one-way traffic of air through most of the system, bringing in a constant stream of unmixed

129

fresh air, whereas in the lungs of mammals stale air is mixed inefficiently with the fresh. It seems odd that natural selection has never produced a stale air outlet for animals. The air sacs of birds apparently approach this ideal more closely than any other vertebrate adaption.

Even in the foods they select to feed their engines birds conserve weight. They burn "high-octane gasoline." Their foods are rich in caloric energy— seeds, fruits, worms, insects, rodents, fish and so on. They eat no low-calorie foods such as leaves or grass; a wood-burning engine has no place in a flying machine. Furthermore, the food birds eat is burned quickly and efficiently. Fruit fed to a young cedar waxwing passes through its digestive tract in an average time of 27 minutes. A thrush that is fed blackberries will excrete the seeds 45 minutes later. Young bluejays take between 55 and 105 minutes to pass food through their bodies. Moreover, birds utilize a greater portion of the food they eat than do mammals. A three-weeks old stork, eating a pound of food (fish, frogs and other animals), gains about a third of a pound in weight. This 33 per cent utilization of food compares roughly with an average figure of about 10 per cent in a growing animal.

—CARL WELTY*

B.   *MR. DOMBEY AS ARISTOCRAT*

The most complete and the most English portrait of the aristocratic temperament is that of Mr. Dombey, the business man.

This London merchant is as vigorous a type as may be found in our haughtiest chateaux. Like a true nobleman, Dombey identifies his personal interests with those of his house. If he disdains his daughter and yearns for a son, it is that the ancient name of his banking house may be perpetuated. His ancestors were commercial men; he wishes to transmit their traditions and their power. In his opulence and in the scope of his operations, he is a prince, and he has princely sentiments. Such a character could be produced only in a country whose commerce encircles the globe, where merchants are potentates, whence a band of traders has exploited continents, conducted wars, overthrown kingdoms, and established empire over a hundred million men. There is no meanness in the arrogance of such a man as Mr. Dombey, but a terrible tranquillity and aloofness. To find his like, one must reread the *Memoirs* of Saint-Simon. Mr. Dombey has always commanded; that he should yield to anything or anyone never enters

* From "Birds as Flying Machines," in *First Book of Animals*, by the Editors of *Scientific American* (New York: Simon and Schuster, 1955), pp. 132-3.

his mind. He accepts flattery as his due tribute. From his eminence he looks down upon an inferior race created to beseech and to obey. His second wife, the high-spirited Edith Skewton, scorns him; as the arrogance of the merchant is pitted against the arrogance of a daughter of the nobility, their unspoken antipathies rise to an intensity of hatred such as only souls thus born and thus nurtured could contain. Upon her wedding anniversary, Edith, to avenge her pride, leaves Dombey's house, as though she were an adulteress. Then Dombey's cold pride stiffens. Suspecting his daughter of complicity, he drives her away too and prohibits communication with either. He lays an interdict upon the very mention of their names in his presence; even to his guests he manifests the same austerity. Desperate, his heart gnawed by the insult, the chagrin of defeat, the shame of public ridicule, he remains nevertheless firm, haughty, impassive. Ever more audacious business enterprises bring him to ruin and the verge of suicide. Yet the bronze column stands unbroken. Now the exigencies of public morality pervert the theme: Dombey's daughter arrives just in time; she entreats; he softens; she leads him off; he becomes the best of fathers— and spoils a fine novel.

—HIPPOLYTE TAINE*

C. ## *RAPPACCINI'S GARDEN*

Giovanni still found no better occupation than to look down into the garden beneath his window. From its appearance, he judged it to be one of those botanic gardens which were of earlier date in Padua than elsewhere in Italy, or in the world. Or, not improbably it might once have been the pleasure-place of an opulent family for there was the ruin of a marble fountain in the center, sculptured with rare art, but so woefully shattered that it was impossible to trace the original design from the chaos of remaining fragments. The water, however, continued to gush and sparkle into the sunbeams as cheerfully as ever. A little gurgling sound ascended to the young man's window, and made him feel as if the fountain were an immortal spirit that sung its song unceasingly and without heeding the vicissitudes around it, while one century embodied it in marble and another scattered the perishable garniture on the soil. All about the pool into which the water subsided grew various plants, that seemed to require a plentiful supply of moisture for the nourishment of gigantic leaves, and, in some instances, flowers gorgeously magnificent. There was one shrub

* From "English Types in Dickens," in *A History of English Literature*, tr. by H. Van Laun (New York: Henry Altemus Co., 1908), pp. 362-3.

in particular, set in a marble vase in the midst of the pool, that bore a profusion of purple blossoms, each of which had the luster and richness of a gem and the whole together made a show so resplendent that it seemed enough to illuminate the garden, even had there been no sunshine. Every portion of the soil was peopled with plants and herbs, which, if less beautiful, still bore tokens of assiduous care, as if all had their individual virtues, known to the scientific mind that fostered them. Some were placed in urns, rich with old carving, and others in common garden pots; some crept serpent-like along the ground or climbed on high, using whatever means of ascent was offered them. One plant had wreathed itself round a statue of Vertumnus, which was thus quite veiled and shrouded in a drapery of hanging foliage, so happily arranged that it might have served a sculptor for a study.

—NATHANIEL HAWTHORNE*

D.   *THE NEED FOR RULES OF EXPERIENCE*

The common-sense world is one of partial uniformity only. There are areas of experience where we know that uncertainty is the certainty—the weather is an obvious example and to be contrasted with the regularity of day and night. To operate in a world of partial uniformity, we clearly need rules of experience. And the invention of such rules and of abstract ideas related to such rules has been of the utmost importance in the advance of civilization. Long before the idea of number had emerged, primitive people had evolved the conceptual scheme of a three-dimensional world. There were solid objects which could be seen, felt, and kicked; there were shadows that could be seen but neither felt nor kicked. To tie together all the empirical rules about nature, speculative thinking developed such concepts as those involved in animism and mythology.

—JAMES B. CONANT†

E.   *HOBBES AS A SEVENTEENTH-CENTURY THINKER*

The mental history of Hobbes is typical of the mathematical and physical preoccupations of the seventeenth century. His philosophical awakening came at the age of forty, when he accidentally opened a book of Euclid

* From *Rappaccini's Daughter* (1842).

† From *Modern Science and Modern Man* (New York: Columbia University Press, 1952), pp. 108-9.

132

and became enchanted by the certainty of mathematical demonstrations. Along with Euclid he studied Galileo, from whom, it appears, he derived his fundamental mechanical theory, which he proceeded to apply both to the world and to man.[1] Science is the study of causes, but all causes are ultimately reducible to motion. A complete science should begin with a study of simple motions, then proceed to more complex motions in geometry, thence to physics, until we reach the most complex motions in "moral philosophy, in which we are to consider the motions of the mind . . . what causes they have, and of what they be causes."[2] To complete his scheme Hobbes also insisted that the soul is material, a sort of thin, filmy substance, which could thus be assumed to be a part of the mechanical world. The customary theological definition of soul as "incorporeal substance" he ridiculed as meaningless. The soul, he said, has dimension as the body has, though he admitted it has no color. In response to his theological critics, Hobbes declared himself willing to accept on faith such incomprehensible beings as God and the angels, though he suggested with fine irony that "the Scripture favoureth them more, that hold angels and spirits corporeal, than them that hold the contrary."[3]

—LOUIS I. BREDVOLD*

F. *EFFECTS OF THE CIVIL WAR*

The Civil War worked a revolution in American society and economy, North as well as South. Although the roots of modern America go deep into the prewar years, we can date its actual emergency from the war itself. That conflict gave an immense stimulus to industry, speeded up the exploitation of natural resources, the development of large-scale manufacturing, the rise of investment banking, the extension of foreign commerce, and brought to the fore a new generation of "captains of industry" and "masters of capital." It enormously accelerated the construction of the railway and telegraph network and ushered in the railroad age. It put a premium upon inventions and labor-saving devices and witnessed the large-scale application

[1] W. R. Sorley, *History of English Philosophy* (Cambridge, 1920), pp. 49-50. But this early indebtedness to Galileo has been questioned by Frithiof Brandt, *Den mekaniske Naturopfattelse hos Thomas Hobbes* (Copenhagen, 1921), pp. 72-81.

[2] *Elements of Philosophy*, Part I, Chap. VI, especially secs. 5-6 in *English Works*, ed. Sir W. Molesworth, I, 131-132.

[3] *Human Nature*. Chap. XI, secs. 2-5; ed. cited, IV, 59-62.

* From *The Intellectual Milieu of John Dryden* (Ann Arbor: University of Michigan Press, 1956), pp. 53-4.

of these to agriculture as well as to industry. It threw open vast new areas for farming and grazing, developed fresh markets for farm produce, and inaugurated both the agricultural revolution and the farm problem. It created conditions favorable to the growth of cities and offered work to the hundreds of thousands of immigrants who soon crowded into the New World. In the South, defeat largely destroyed the planter class, freed the Negro, revolutionized farm economy, brought a new middle class to the fore, and laid the foundations for that New South which was to emerge during the next generation. In the North it opened up new fields to investment and to speculation, created a host of war millionaires, and hastened the process of the concentration of control of resources, industry, and finance in the great urban centers, the subordination of the South and West to the Northeast, and the creation of new class divisions to take the place of the old.

—ALLEN NEVINS and
HENRY STEEL COMMAGER*

II. Select one of the following generalizations. Write a paragraph using it as the stated or implied topic sentence, and developing it by examples used as illustration.

A. A university president has many responsibilities.
B. You can easily spend a day doing nothing.
C. One outstanding feature of Lincoln's personality was his compassion.
D. Hamlet's "To be or not to be" soliloquy reveals his personality.
E. The car was a beat-up wreck.
F. A walk through the campus at this time of year is a delightful (amusing, depressing, etc.) experience.

III. Using one of the following generalizations as your topic sentence, write a paragraph using examples as evidence *pro* or *con*. At the end of the paragraph, indicate the sort of audience you have in mind—e.g., the general public, a well-educated group of nonspecialists, a scholarly audience.

* From *The Pocket History of the United States* (New York: Pocket Books, Inc., 1943), pp. 257-8.

A. Registration procedures should be simplified.

B. A woman does not need a college education.

C. Freshmen should (or should not) be allowed to have cars.

D. Hamlet's "To be or not to be" soliloquy is a closely reasoned consideration of death.

E. Television commercials are informative (or misleading).

F. A child needs understanding as well as discipline (or discipline as well as understanding).

IV. Suggestions for themes. Using a purpose statement similar to one of the following, write a theme based on examples. Underline each example used, and for each paragraph indicate in the margin whether the paragraph uses representative or multiple examples, and citation or development of individual examples.

A. Even a day when "nothing happens" can be exciting.

B. Travel is a form of education.

C. The government should (or should not) subsidize parochial schools.

D. Half a loaf is better than none.

E. Vote for the man, not for the party (or for the party, not for the man).

F. The college catalogue should be revised.

Argumentation (I): Induction

6

In argumentation, the author's purpose statement becomes a thesis. The thesis may be a stand taken on a burning political issue, or it may be a highly specialized point like "the protein *collagen* provides an objective measure of biological age." In either case, the author faces the problem of convincing his reader of the truth of his thesis.

Argumentative essays can be placed on a rough scale from popular

137

to technical. Usually—though not inevitably—popular argumentation is less rigorous than technical argumentation. The general reader likes to be entertained while he is being convinced. He does not like to unravel complex theoretical arguments and he is easily bored by long paragraphs and footnotes. The specialist, on the other hand, is primarily interested in the subject. He does not like half-truths and easy generalizations, and if an essay adds to his knowledge of the subject, that will be entertainment enough.

6.1   RHETORICAL AND LOGICAL PROOF

Because of the differing attitudes of readers, argumentative essays use two kinds of proof, usually in combination. **Rhetorical proof is persuasion based on appeal to the attitudes and emotions of the reader rather than on evidence and rigorous logic.** It may be extremely effective, but it will not stand critical examination. Its techniques are for the most part appeals to deep-rooted desires, fears and prejudices. A beautiful girl is posed next to a car to increase sales; a political candidate is called a "radical" or a "fascist" in an editorial; an article on "Pest Control for the Home Garden" introduces five closely-packed pages of advice with the statement, "By following a few simples rules, anyone, even a child, can have a flourishing, pest-free garden."

At its worst, rhetorical proof is simply propaganda. There is, however, nothing intrinsically immoral about using it. We do not expect—or want—a newspaper editorial or popular article to read like a page from *The Political Science Quarterly*; and when we buy a box of cereal, few of us have time to read a complete chemical analysis of its contents. Used properly, rhetorical proof is justified and has its place even in writing that relies chiefly on logical methods. Some of its techniques have been examined in chapter 3, and others will be mentioned in the discussion of propaganda devices in chapter 12.

Logical proof is proof that seeks to convince by formal demonstration. The two methods of logical proof are **induction** and **deduction.** Both of these methods are complex, and a rigorous treatment of either would take us far beyond the limits of practical rhetoric. Inductive proof

138

will be considered in the present chapter, but the consideration will be limited to matters that have a direct bearing on writing. Deduction will be considered in chapter 11. The specialized techniques of technical and scholarly argumentation will be treated in chapter 13.

6.2   INDUCTION AS A METHOD OF ARGUMENT

In its simplest form, **induction is the examination of a group of phenomena for the purpose of formulating general rules or hypotheses applying to all phenomena in the group.** A psychologist who examines a great many neurotic patients and forms the hypothesis "All neurotics had disturbing experiences during childhood" is using induction. So is a child who is regularly beaten by his parents and concludes, "People in authority are dangerous."

Induction necessarily proceeds from **instance** to **generalization.** The writer usually reverses the process. He gives the generalization first. It can be the purpose statement of an essay or the topic sentence of a paragraph. Instances are then given as evidence. The rule is not, however, absolute. A paragraph may give instances first and end with a generalization offered as a **conclusion** rather than a **thesis.** In this case the paragraph follows the **order of investigation.** In longer essays it is usual to combine methods. The author begins with the thesis, cites evidence in the body of the essay, and ends with a restatement of the thesis. The technique insures clarity; hence the common advice to public speakers, "Tell them what you are going to say, say it and then tell them you have said it."

6.3   RIGOR

Since inductive argumentation consists essentially of thesis and supporting evidence, its rigor—its logical validity—depends on these two elements. This means that the author must be able to evaluate and criticize them.

6.4 CRITICISM OF GENERALIZATIONS

A useful distinction can be made between **subjective, probable** and **categorical** generalizations.* **A subjective generalization is one that depends so heavily on personal attitudes that it cannot logically be proved or disproved.** "Cigarettes taste good" is a subjective generalization. The speaker may sincerely believe that cigarettes *do* taste good, but he cannot prove this to a friend who dislikes them. At best he can use rhetorical proof: "If you like me you have to like cigarettes; Marlon Brando likes cigarettes; 50 million Americans can't be wrong" and so forth. In formal argumentation, subjective generalizations are a waste of time. Failure to recognize this fact leads to controversies that can never be resolved for the simple reason that there *is* no logical way to resolve them. Subjective generalizations are necessary and proper in writing intended to entertain, evoke a mood or give personal impressions, but they should be eliminated from writing that seeks to offer logical proof.

A probable generalization is one that is true in most cases but not in all. Probable generalizations are the staple of everyday reasoning, popularizations and political debate, both written and spoken. In their worst form they are glittering generalities and half-truths that do more harm than good. Health fads, hero cults and prejudices of all kinds feed on them. Obviously, in this form they have no place in serious writing.

However, most probable generalizations are useful and, in fact, necessary. We need them because we cannot be experts on every subject and because in many disciplines probabilities are all we have. "A stitch in time saves nine" is a probable generalization. It is not always true, but it is true enough to use as a rule-of-thumb. "An alcoholic is unreliable" is also a probable generalization. It may not always be true, but we would probably not vote for a political candidate who was known to be a heavy drinker. On a more serious level, there are many problems for which the best answers available are probable generalizations. "Slum conditions breed crime" is a statement of probability. Sociologists know that there is a high incidence of crime among individuals from slum environments, but they do not at present understand all of the causative

---

* This discussion of generalizations does not take into account the various **forms** that they can take. For a brief analysis of categorical, hypothetical and disjunctive statements, see the discussion of syllogism in chapter 11.

factors. Do *all* slum conditions breed crime or only a few or only a special combination of conditions; or are external conditions secondary to conditions within the family? Since answers are not available, "slum conditions breed crime" is the best generalization we have, and we show our acceptance of it by investing heavily in urban renewal.

Probable generalizations are frequent even in writing that seeks to be rigorous. When the author uses them he can strengthen his case and avoid misunderstanding by subjecting them to careful examination. First, he should recognize that they are probable and admit the fact to the reader. Second, he should **define** and **qualify** their terms. If he intends the statement "most politicians are wealthy" to be rigorous— as he might if he were writing an essay on the American class structure, he must give his **bases** for distinguishing between "politician" and "nonpolitician," and "wealthy" and "not-wealthy"; and he must state what percentage is represented by the word "most." Third, in presenting evidence he should discuss **negative** as well as **positive examples.** What are the exceptions, and what should be said about them?

Categorical generalizations are generalizations that hold true in all cases meeting a stipulated set of conditions. Rigorous thought seeks the ideal of making all of its generalizations categorical. This ideal is approximated in the pure sciences and in situations where the range of subject matter is sufficiently limited so that all cases can be considered by the investigator. The Law of Conservation of Energy is a categorical generalization. So are the statements "In the sample taken all those individuals convicted of felonies had records of juvenile offenses by age fifteen"; and "The first twenty-six lines of *Paradise Lost* include an invocation to the Muse, a statement of the poem's subject matter and Milton's epic proposition." On the other hand, The Law of Supply and Demand is a probable generalization; and "All men are mortal," while categorical to an insurance agent, is simply "ambiguous writing" to a Christian theologian.

6.5 CRITICISM OF EVIDENCE

From the standpoint of practical rhetoric a writer should ask three questions about his evidence: (1) Is it presented honestly and without distortion? (2) Is there sufficient evidence to prove the point convincingly? (3) Have exceptions been taken into account? Other questions that can be asked about evidence concern the way in which evidence is presented; for example, is it immediate, precise and necessary? These have been considered in the chapter on example (chapter 5).

6.6 ARGUMENT BY THESIS AND EVIDENCE

Argument by thesis and evidence is the most common method for term papers, examination essays and short technical papers. It is simple, convenient and persuasive. To appreciate its usefulness consider the steps involved in writing, say, a short critical essay on F. Scott Fitzgerald's novel *The Great Gatsby*.

The author's first problem is finding a **thesis.** A "book report" or plot summary will be unsatisfactory. The author wants to learn something while he writes the essay and, if possible, offer his reader fresh insights. Also, his probable readers (certainly his instructor) will not need to be convinced that the novel is "good" and will already be familiar with the story line. Perception and creativity are extremely important at this point. The author needs them if he is to produce something of genuine interest, and the more they enter into the formulation of the thesis, the more rewarding the essay will be to all concerned.

Let us assume that during his first reading of the novel the author has noticed that color is mentioned frequently. Perhaps the references to color are systematic; it may be that they are intended to contribute positively to the novel's theme or character portrayal. With these possibilities in mind the author reexamines the novel. At this point he is making an **empirical** study. Let us assume that after he has considered several references to color individually, he decides that they are—as he suspected—used for a definite purpose. He can now formulate a tentative thesis: "Fitzgerald makes extensive use of color to make his writing graphic."

The next step is to **analyze** (that is, to divide) the thesis into manageable subtopics. If the author has underlined or listed the color references, he can examine them to decide what subtopics are most appropriate.

142

Consideration of possible ways to subdivide the thesis itself will suggest others. Two solutions appear promising. If only a few colors—say, red, blue and white—are significant, the essay can be divided into three subtopics treating each color individually. On the other hand, if a great many colors have to be considered, this approach might result in a large number of choppy paragraphs. The **alternative** is to subdivide the essay in terms of the *uses* of color. An examination of Fitzgerald's color references shows that this is the best approach. The author now writes the following outline:

I. Fitzgerald uses color to make his writing graphic.
   a. Analysis [*i.e.,* Method]: Atmosphere and symbolism.
II. Colors are used to suggest atmosphere.
III. Colors are used symbolically.

At this point the author should examine his generalizations critically. Is the thesis subjective, probable or categorical? Can it be proved at all, and if so, how rigorous can the proof be made? Even without training in formal logic, the author should be able to see that the word "graphic" is vague. What is graphic to one person may be tedious to another. As stated, therefore, the thesis is rather subjective. To improve the rigor of his essay, the author needs to define his terms. The definition of "graphic" will be in the nature of an axiom. If the reader accepts it, the thesis can be proved with considerable rigor. If not, the reader will know that he is quarreling with the author's definitions, not his evidence. Although the author can draw his definition from an authoritative source like a dictionary or handbook of literary terms, he also has the right to give his own definition. Since "graphic" is a fairly simple word, we may assume that the author will decide to define it for himself—recognizing, of course, that his or anyone else's definition may be questioned. Having reached this decision, he writes: "Graphic writing is writing that is vivid and has a clear purpose. Creation of atmosphere through detail, and definition of theme through imagery and symbolism are among the important elements of graphic writing."

With this definition, the thesis is capable of genuine proof. Note that whether the thesis is probable or categorical depends on the novel. If *all* color references are used as symbols or to create atmosphere, and if the author can show this by listing or statistical summary, the thesis will be categorical. If there are exceptions, or if the author treats typical

143

examples without trying to be comprehensive, the thesis will remain probable.

The same process of criticism used for the thesis may be used for the subtopics. Within the subtopics, the development will take the form of examples given as evidence. We can assume that the essay does not need to be comprehensive. Multiple examples will be used, but there is no need to cite every color reference in the novel. The outline now looks like this:

I. Fitzgerald uses color to make his writing graphic.
   a. Method: Atmosphere and symbolism.
   b. Background: Definition of "graphic."
II. Colors are used to suggest atmosphere.
   a. Examples of rose and white.
   b. Examples of yellow.
   c. Example (one only) of gray.
III. Colors are used for symbolism.
   a. Brief definition of symbol.
   b. Example of white used for Daisy Buchanan
   c. Examples of green for America, Daisy, money.
   d. Examples of blue for aristocracy.

The last step before actual writing is criticism of evidence. If the author has read carefully, he can be sure that his examples are—to the best of his ability—chosen fairly and presented without distortion. Since he does not intend to be comprehensive, several typical examples in each section will be sufficient. From the outline, it appears that the author has not found any examples that are exceptions to his thesis, but he might check his list of color references again to make sure. Finally, in regard to presentation of examples, citations should be specific and direct quotation should be used freely. Footnotes giving page references may or may not be needed, depending on the circumstances.

▶ 6.7 ARGUMENT BY "GIVING REASONS"; CAUSE AND EFFECT

When the writer's thesis has the form "This is true because . . ." or "This should be done because . . .," his essay becomes argumentation by **"giving reasons."** This type of essay is related in method and structure to argumentation based on **cause and effect.** Just as inductive argumentation usually reverses the process of induction itself by giving the hypothesis at the beginning of the essay as the thesis to be proved, so in argumentation by giving reasons and cause and effect, the conclusion justified by the reasons or the effect produced by the causes usually becomes the thesis of the essay. The thesis is introduced and explained in the introduction, and the reasons (or causes) are presented and supported in the major subdivisions of the essay. The form is illustrated by the following outline:

I. America's international position is strengthened by its overseas force in Germany because this force deters Russian aggression, strengthens German morale and gives hope to the people of Eastern Europe.

II. The American overseas force deters Russian aggression. (Discussion and evidence.)

III. It strengthens German morale. (Discussion and evidence.)

IV. It gives hope to the peoples of Eastern Europe. (Discussion and evidence.)

V. Conclusion: Restate thesis and comment on the danger of gradual reductions in size of the American force.

Clearly both the form and the problems in this type of argument are similar to those of argument by thesis and evidence. In addition to the problems already discussed in connection with the essay on *The Great Gatsby,* however, the writer of an essay based on "giving reasons" or cause and effect must deal with problems of relationship. To test the adequacy of his argument he should ask the following questions:

1. Is the cause sufficient to produce the desired effect? In section II of the essay outlined above, for example, the writer should ask whether the American overseas force is powerful enough seriously to deter the Russian army in the event that the Russians decided on a policy of war. If the answer is yes, the writer should say so and explain why in the course of developing section II.

2. Would another (more desirable) cause produce the same effect? For example, would a program of technical and economic assistance do more to strengthen German morale and cost less than maintaining a division of American troops in Germany?

145

3. Will the cause produce undesirable effects? For example, does the presence of American troops in Germany produce anti-American sentiment; does the program contribute to the drain on American gold reserves and therefore weaken (rather than strengthen) the American international position? Again, these questions should be discussed in the appropriate sections of the essay.

6.8 STEPS IN DEVELOPING AN ARGUMENTATIVE ESSAY

The preceding examples deal with essays on literary and political topics, but the procedures outlined are useful no matter what the subject matter. They can be summarized as five steps in developing an argumentative essay:

1. Investigation of subject.
2. Formulation of thesis.
3. Analysis of thesis.
4. Criticism of generalizations.
5. Criticism of evidence (or causes).

To describe these steps takes several pages. In practice, they become habits and are performed automatically as routine parts of the writer's task.

TERMS TO BE LEARNED

- ▸ Rhetorical proof
- ▸ Logical proof
- ▸ Induction
- ▸ Three types of generalization
- ▸ Three questions for criticism of evidence
- ▸ Three questions for criticism of argument by cause and effect
- ▸ Five steps in developing an argumentative essay

Exercises & Theme Topics

I. The following student essay on the use of color in *The Great Gatsby* follows generally the outline given on p. 144. It is deficient, however, in several respects. List four ways in which it fails to be adequate argumentation. Consider the author's generalizations, his analyses, his selection and presentation of evidence.

THE USE OF COLOR IN THE GREAT GATSBY

In *The Great Gatsby*, Fitzgerald makes extensive use of particular colors in a general or a physical sense. However, certain of these colors through their repeated use assume either a definite symbolism or a definite pattern. This employment of color is for two purposes: to make the scenes and characters more graphic, and to give expressions which have a concrete meaning an abstract or deeper meaning.

In a general sense, Fitzgerald uses colors, such as rose, white, yellow and gray, to help produce the atmosphere of a particular scene.

Rose and white, rather subtle tones, are employed to depict the Buchanan's home. These colors perhaps suggest a sense of warmth and welcome; yet, at the same time, suggest a certain sense of coolness and detachment. The "white color theme" is further illustrated by the dresses which Daisy and Jordan are wearing. These, too, add to the atmosphere of aloofness and impersonality.

Yellow, a vibrant hue, is often used to produce the setting for Gatsby's parties. In these instances, the yellow lends an air of vivaciousness, of heightened excitement. It produces an electric atmosphere in which the guests seem to have all of their senses sharpened to their greatest sensitivity. The guests are so alive to all of the exciting possibilities of the evening that they make the air itself hum with vitality. The characters and the physical setting, which outline the scene, are filled in and animated by this wild display of vivid, glowing color, which seems to have been thrown into the air so that it might fall and lend something of its life to the people and events.

Gray, a drabber tone, is employed to create the mood of the valley of ashes. It imparts a feeling of dreariness, and almost a feeling of deadness, as if all that was bright and full of life is now dull and dead. Further, the color leaves a strong feeling of disgust and a taste of bitter ashes.

In a symbolic sense, Fitzgerald uses colors, namely, white, green, and blue, to lend an abstract meaning to the context of passages with concrete meanings.

The recurrent use of white and rose (or roses) in connection with Daisy leaves an impression of Daisy herself. In her youth, Daisy lived in a white house, drove a white car, and often wore white. This recurrence perhaps suggests an aloof, pristine person, interested only in those things in life which have little deep meaning—in short an oversophisticated person.

Green may be thought to have three symbolic meanings. Although different in what they signify, all three relate to one another and depend on each other, so that they act as a whole to produce one unified symbol.

The first, and perhaps the most involved of the three, relates green to the American dream. In this connection, green denotes America itself, the land of opportunity. It symbolizes the lush promises that become reality, the awakening of the sense of wonder, and the awakening of the physical senses to these promises and realities.

In the second sense, green may be related to Daisy. She, too, is a promise of new exciting things, the best of life, and the hope for a fresh start. The green light on her boat dock is, in a sense, a manifestation of Daisy. Like the light, Daisy is something which is unattainable to Gatsby. He strives to reach her, but can never do so because she is beyond him and her promise is in the past, buried by the present.

In the final connotation, green may represent money. Since paper money is often referred to as "greenbacks," this, then would only seem a natural assumption.

These three symbolisms have materialism as their unifying factor. In each of these symbols, the American dream, Daisy, and money, materialism is the key that provides insight into the symbol's meaning, as it relates to the work.

The color blue appears at intervals throughout *The Great Gatsby*. "This blue lawn,"[1] and "the blue leaves"[2] are the most notable examples of the use of blue in connection with Gatsby. It seems to leave an impression of the thoroughbreds, the bluebloods of society, with which Gatsby wants to be associated, but is not actually a part of. Blue implies a richness, a luxuriance in Gatsby's surroundings. Furthermore, it may symbolize what Gatsby wants to be. He wants to appear to be aristocratic, to be the best,

---

[1] F. Scott Fitzgerald, *The Great Gatsby* (New York: Charles Scribner's Sons, 1953), p. 152.

[2] *Ibid.*, p. 182.

to have the best, but only to impress Daisy. He want to have her with him as before. He seems to think that presenting a wealthy front which would match the wealth and luxury that Daisy had always had, would be the best way to lure her to him.

All of these colors, rose, white, yellow, gray, green, and blue appear in recurrent patterns in connection with one person or concept. The patterns do not always have a symbolic meaning, but rather, are associated with a person or concept. For instance, every use of white with Daisy is not symbolic, but associative. The same is true with Gatsby and yellow. In other words, the yellow is associated with Gatsby in a vibrant, splashy sense. In order to continue this impression, the particular color appears with Gatsby, as a part of Gatsby himself. The use of rose with Daisy, and the other colors with their respective persons or concepts, follows the same pattern of color to person, or color to concept.

In summary, because of the nature of *The Great Gatsby*, all of these colors are an important, integral part of the novel. The employment of color in description, in setting the atmosphere of scenes, and in symbolism agrees with the poetic diction of the work, because the application of color is a poetic method of description and characterization. Furthermore, inasmuch as the narrator has poetic tendencies, he is inclined to ascribe particular colors to the various characters and scenes in *The Great Gatsby*.

II. Outline and write a short essay (500-700 words) supporting a thesis that you consider important. As preparation review the evidence available to you. Will you depend on personal experience or will you use source material and/or testimony? Do you have *enough* evidence, or will you need to do additional preparation to make an effective case? Is your thesis capable of rigorous proof? Have you taken this fact into account in your development and presentation? If your essay is based on "giving reasons" or cause and effect, have you taken into account the requirements for valid argument using this method?

Comparison and Contrast

7

Comparison and contrast are among the basic tools of the writer. They can be used in individual images, as in metaphor or simile; in sentences or paragraphs or as organizing principles for an entire essay. Because of failure to understand the structure of comparison, many writers fail to use it effectively. Therefore we will begin with an analysis of the structure of comparison as revealed in its simplest form, the simile, and continue with a discussion of its more general uses.

7.1 STRUCTURE OF COMPARISON

The simile "my love is like a red, red rose" is familiar to almost everyone. It is an image in which two different elements, a girl ("my love") and a flower are compared. Since all comparisons have at least two elements, it is useful to have labels for them. Literary critics use a variety of terms. For clarity we will simply call the two elements of comparison **subject** and **object**. The **subject** is what the writer is immediately concerned with. In the simile given, it is "my love." The **object** is that to which the subject is compared; in this case, "rose." All similes and metaphors have both a subject and an object, although in metaphor the subject is often implied, as in the metaphor "the wind howled," where the subject is the sound of the wind, but is not stated explicitly.

When comparison is used on a larger scale than in metaphor and simile, the two elements are often both **subjects.** For example, a writer may compare communism and democracy. In this case, both forms of government are his subjects and neither is an object in the sense that "rose" is an object for "my love."

The comparison of a girl to a rose is so commonplace we tend to take it for granted. Actually, it is a rather complex image. At first glance there seems to be little in common between subject and object. However, careful consideration reveals several common factors—for example, beauty, fragility, sweetness, perhaps even the slight suggestion of peril arising from the fact that the rose has thorns. The most important common factor is *beauty,* and the image is a means of emphasizing the beauty of a girl, whom we have not seen, by comparing it to something beautiful which is a part of everyone's experience. All comparisons must have such a common factor. It is called the **basis** of the comparison. Without it the comparison is pointless, as, for example, the comparison of an automobile to the sea, or a flower to a refrigerator.

Finally, the comparison must have an **effect.** The rose image does more than call our attention to the girl's beauty. It has the **effect** of praise and is an appropriate part of the poem in which it appears since the poet's larger purpose is to praise his beloved.

To summarize, every comparison must have the following parts to be effective:

1. **subject** and **object;** or two **subjects**
2. **basis**
3. **effect**

Three common comparisons, arranged in order of increasing complexity, will illustrate these parts. The first is an analogy: "Currency during an inflation is much like a medicine that is continually diluted by a druggist so he will have more to sell." Here the **subject** is *currency,* and the **object** is *medicine.* The **basis** is *decreasing strength,* because of inflation in the one and dilution in the other. The **effect** is *clarification* or *explanation* of a difficult point. Most analogies, and almost all visual ones, work in this way.

The colloquial metaphor "crazy music" is more difficult. In fact, many colloquial images are hard to explain. Why, for example, should "blue" suggest sadness, "square" suggest awkwardness or lack of tact or a cucumber suggest coolness? "Crazy music" is somewhat simpler than the preceding examples. It is an implied comparison of the impression made by a musical composition (subject) with the impression made by an insane person (object). Clearly, the **basis** is either disorganization or extreme excitement or both. The **effect** is partly to inform, and the image is thus related to analogy. But the image also emphasizes the quality of the music. Since this is probably the most important reason for using it, we could say its effect is *emphasis.*

It was remarked in chapter 3 that deliberate imagery is the most important kind of imagery from the writer's point of view, since it is controlled and often invented to serve a specific purpose. It is also the most subtle form of imagery. In the psalms, for example, David is described as suffering "like a woman in travail." The **subject** of this image is David's suffering, which is caused by his feeling of guilt. The **object** is the suffering of a woman in travail (that is, childbirth). Clearly, the **basis** is pain. The **effect** seems at first merely emphasis. However, the matter is not so simple. Emphasis could be achieved by any number of objects. David's suffering could be compared to that of a man with a severe wound, with a broken arm or with cancer. What makes the

153

original object superior to these alternatives? The answer lies in the implications of the object. Cancer, for example, is a degenerative disease that usually results in death. A man with advanced cancer suffers without hope. On the other hand, childbirth is a creative form of suffering. It soon passes, and when it does, it is replaced by the joy of a new child. In the same way, suffering caused by conscience is creative. It is a sign the guilty person recognizes his faults and wishes to atone for them. When such suffering has passed, it is replaced by peace and joy—by what is often called a spiritual rebirth. Thus the effect of the image from the psalms is *hope* as well as *emphasis*. The image is a means of commenting on the situation being described. It is especially effective because it compresses many interrelated ideas into a few vivid and specific words.

7.2 COMPARISON AND CONTRAST IN SENTENCES AND PARAGRAPHS

When the writer compares two things in separate clauses of a sentence or in separate sentences, he is usually talking about both of them. The sentence, "Renaissance man, like modern man, was primarily concerned with getting ahead in the world," is a case in point. It is from an essay comparing modern and Renaissance man, and both topics interest the author. They are therefore both **subjects.** The **basis** is "interest in getting ahead," and the comparison is emphatic because in most respects modern man differs from his Renaissance counterpart. The **effect** is particularly important. The author's overall purpose in his essay was to prove Renaissance and modern cultures have much in common. Therefore the effect of the sample comparison is to *illustrate* or *prove* the author's purpose. Note that the elements of the comparison would remain unchanged if it were presented in two sentences instead of one; for example: "Renaissance man was primarily interested in getting ahead in the world. In this respect he was no different from the practical businessman of the twentieth century." In fact, the structure of the comparison would be the same no matter how far it was extended.

Contrast is an important variation of comparison. It also must have at least two elements, and these are almost always **subjects.** Its **basis** is the reverse of comparison. In a good comparison, two dissimilar elements are compared in order to bring out a basis they have in common. In contrast, two similar elements are placed together in order to show some essential **difference** between them. The more the two subjects are like one another, the more emphatically their differences will emerge. In a contrast of communism and democracy, for example, the author might write, "The communist state has elections, but these are manipulated so the people have no real choice. In a democracy the elections are all-important, for they represent a real choice by the voters." Here the subjects are communism and democracy. They are similar in that they are both forms of government, both constitutional and both (theoretically) subject to the will of the people. The **basis** is the **difference,** namely the fact that communist elections are "manipulated" whereas democratic elections are genuine. The **effect** of the contrast is to point out the falseness of the communist system, and since this is the author's overall purpose, the effect is to *illustrate* or *prove* the purpose.

7.3 CONTINUOUS AND DISCONTINUOUS FORMS

When comparison or contrast is used as a method of paragraph development the subjects are usually analyzed and compared point-by-point. For example, one could compare a Ford and Chevrolet automobile in a single sentence: "The Ford is better than [or worse than] the Chevrolet." However, one could also consider several aspects of the cars, such as appearance, economy, maneuverability, cost and ease of repair. In this case there would be ample material for a paragraph and perhaps for an entire essay.

The following paragraphs illustrate two different forms of point-by-point development. The first—a paragraph of contrast—employs **continuous** development. The two subjects are treated continuously throughout the paragraph so that the writing tends to fall into an a-b, a-b, a-b pattern. Of course, the pattern is varied somewhat to avoid monotony. The two subjects are (a) spoken and (b) written English. They are contrasted in

155

terms of several specific points. Note that the individual points of contrast have been carefully selected so they all illustrate the same essential difference, the *lack of expressiveness* of written English. *Lack of expressiveness* is thus the **basis** of each contrast and also the unifying idea of the paragraph as a whole. The **effect** is to prove the author's main point.

> Even a moment's reflection will show that the spoken American language is backed by expressive features lacking in the written language. . . . Written English, lacking clear indication of such features, must be so managed that it compensates for what it lacks. It must be more carefully organized than speech in order to overcome its communicative deficiencies as compared with speech. In speech we safeguard meaning by the use of intonation, stress, gesture, and voice qualities. In writing, we must deal with our medium in such a way that the meaning cannot possibly be misunderstood. In the absence of an actual external hearer capable of interrupting and demanding further explanation, a clear writer is always conscious of "a reader over his shoulder." All this despite the fact that writing, being permanent, as compared with speech, which is evanescent, allows not only reading but also rereading.
>
> —HAROLD WHITEHALL*

The second illustration is a comparison. It is in two distinct sections that are emphasized in this case by the paragraph division, and its development is **discontinuous** rather than continuous. The points of comparison of the first subject are grouped together in the first paragraph; and these are followed by a paragraph containing the points of comparison of the second subject. The form is thus not a-b, a-b, a-b; but a-a-a, b-b-b.

> The scientist is a man who applies pure thought, that is, logic, and if possible, mathematics, to the heterogeneous facts of nature. He is not a pure thinker, for he lives in a mixed world. For him there remains always the world of things which have appreciable qualities. When the agricultural college at Berkeley was being projected, a dirt farmer who offered his advice did not see the need for such a school. He said, "When I want to know about a soil I smell it, and taste it, and roll it between my fingers, and

* From *Structural Essentials of English* (New York: Harcourt, Brace & Co., Inc., 1956), p. 2.

then I know all about it." Professor Hilgard, who was to be the director of the "Cow College," assured him that the pupils would be taught to do all this, and to analyze the soil as well. There are sciences, like physics, where this kind of thing counts for little and others, like medicine, where it still counts for a great deal.

For the artist there is something analogous. His pure contemplation of values, his pure appreciation, is disturbed by the multiplicity of the world before him. People often think of the poet as simply having something organically growing in his soul. There is that beautiful word "inspiration." They do not realize the heterogeneity of his material, and the large amount of critical discrimination needed to put it in order. When we look at a landscape, with its harmony of mood, the blending of all the elements that compose it, we do not stop to think that those elements have for the most part nothing to do with each other, that they belong together only in the vision of the artist, and that to a closer observer the heterogeneity is overwhelming.

—LEO STEIN*

The two preceding examples are merely selections from an almost infinite variety of ways in which comparison and contrast can be used. If they are useful, they are so because they help to define extremes between which most writing falls. The writer should not restrict himself to the patterns illustrated; rather, he should use them as starting points for his own experiments in the form.

7.4 COMPARISON AND CONTRAST AS METHODS OF DEVELOPMENT

Often comparison and contrast are carried on throughout an entire essay. Essays based on these techniques are often given double titles, as, for example, "Jefferson and Washington," "The Ford versus the Chevrolet," "Physics and Philosophy."

Whatever its title, the essay based on comparison and contrast will

* From *Appreciation: Painting, Poetry and Prose* (New York: The Modern Library, 1947), pp. 17-8.

have as its purpose statement an assertion about the **basis** of the comparison which forms the body of the essay; and the **effect** of each individual comparison or contrast will be to illustrate or prove the purpose statement. The **subjects** of the comparison or contrast will be treated either **continuously** throughout the developing section, or **discontinuously,** with one section devoted to each subject. Only those aspects of the subjects which tend to demonstrate the purpose statement will be strictly relevant, although others may occasionally be included for the purpose of variety or qualification. The two outlines below are from student essays comparing Renaissance and modern man. They illustrate both the emphasis on a common **basis** for individual comparisons and the alternative ways of organizing an essay of comparison. The same principles would, of course, apply to an essay of contrast.

A. (Continuous comparison)

I. Renaissance man was just as worldly as modern man. (The **basis** of later comparisons will thus be *worldliness*, which should be defined in the introduction.)
II. Renaissance interest in wealth and modern interest in wealth.
III. Renaissance interest in power and modern interest in power.
IV. Renaissance deviation from Christian morality and modern deviation from Christian morality.
V. Conclusion: reemphasize similarity of two outlooks.

B. (Discontinuous comparison)

I. Renaissance man was just as worldly as modern man.
II. Renaissance man:
    a. Interest in wealth.
    b. Interest in power.
    c. Deviation from Christian morality.
III. Modern man:
    a. Interest in wealth.
    b. Interest in power.
    c. Deviation from Christian morality.
IV. Conclusion: reemphasize similarity of two outlooks.

For the most part, simplicity is a virtue in outlining, and these outlines, which are intentionally simple, would serve as the bases of quite satisfactory essays. They should not, however, be considered fixed forms, and the author should always attempt to modify his outline to suit his specific purpose. If the preceding outlines were developed, the most natural method would be to illustrate each of the points by means of *examples* drawn from Renaissance history, biography and literature; and from the observation of modern society. The more apt the examples, the more convincing the essay would be; and the more numerous, the closer the essay would come to being an adequate *proof* of the author's purpose statement.

The essay below will serve as a final example of the use of comparison and contrast. In this case, the method is contrast. The organization is simple, and can be expressed in the following outline:

I.   British, French and American films have strikingly different moral attitudes.
II. British films: emphasize conscience.
III. French films: emphasize opposition between nature and human wishes.
IV. American films: emphasize optimism.

Clearly, the contrast has three (rather than the usual two) **subjects.** The **basis** is "moral attitudes," as the purpose statement makes clear. Since the essay is one of contrast, it places like things (popular films) together in order to show an essential difference, this being the contrast in moral attitudes illustrated in II, III, and IV respectively. The **effect** of the contrast is to prove or illustrate the purpose statement. Despite the simplicity of its plan (perhaps because of it), the essay resulting from the outline is clear and stimulating.

BRITISH, FRENCH AND AMERICAN FILMS

The dramatic productions of a particular culture at a particular time, or even over a considerable period, tend to exhibit a distinctive plot configuration. This configuration gives the various individual dramas the distinctive atmosphere which we can recognize as pervading them all. Obviously a group of plots or even a single plot is exceedingly complex. Nevertheless a certain basic plan may be discerned: we can see that one pattern from among the range of dramatic alternatives has been chosen for major emphasis.

Looking back over the films which we have been discussing, we shall now indicate briefly the essential plot configuration which distinguishes each of the three groups of films with which we have been concerned, the British, the French, and the American.

The essential plot in British films is that of the conflict of forbidden impulses with conscience. Either one of contending forces may win out and we may follow the guilt-ridden course of the wrong-doer or experience the regrets of the lost opportunity virtuously renounced. In the happy instance, wishes may coincide with the demands of virtue and a fatherly fate will reward the good children. The world is presided over by authorities who are wise and good and against whom the wilful and unlucky may contend. But the counterpart of these authorities is also implanted in the individual soul; the evil-doer will be self-condemned as well as pursued by the authorities.

British films evoke the feeling that danger lies in ourselves, especially in our impulses of destructiveness. In a cautionary way they show what happens if these impulses break through, particularly where the weak become the victims. Thus they afford a catharsis at the same time that they demonstrate the value of defenses by showing the consequences of their giving way. The character who embodies dangerous impulses is apt to be a superior person, one who should be able to control his own destructiveness, and in whom it is all the more terrible to see it get out of hand. Violence is not simply a destructive force but a breaking both of the pattern within the individual personality and of the order which prevails in his world. The complete murderer is one who disputes the rule of just authorities, in his pride setting himself up as an arbiter of life and death, and doomed by his own struggle. While violence is on one side related to a whole social framework, it has also another side of intimacy and isolation. The act of violence is slowly prepared and may be preceded by special closeness between murderer and victim. Violence is thus often pervaded by the tenderness which in ordinary circumstances serves to ward it off.

Self-accusation is prominent in British films and may be evoked by wishes no less than by acts. Characters feel guilty when circumstances beyond their control produce fatalities coinciding with unconscious wishes. Lovers tempted to overstep lawful bounds draw back alarmed by guilty apprehensions. However, the pure in heart find that the authorities of this world and the next are their allies. The hero, temporarily distressed by a false charge, discovers that the police know all along that he is innocent and are quietly working side by side with him. The fine young couple who for the moment fear that fate has brought them together only to separate them learn that even death can be set aside so that they can be joined.

British films preserve, in a modern idiom (the peculiarities of which we shall not analyze here), many of the themes of Shakespearean drama. There are heroes who like Macbeth are carried away by criminal impulses and then punished; heroes who like Hamlet suffer pangs of conscience for crimes they did not commit. And there are young couples briefly and playfully threatened by the same fate which intended all along to wed them as Prospero did with his daughter and Ferdinand. The image of a perfect father, like Hamlet Sr., still presides over the scene, and constitutes the model for an exacting conscience.

In the major plot configuration of French films, human wishes are opposed by the nature of life itself. The main issue is not one of inner or outer conflicts in which we may win or lose, be virtuous or get penalized. It is a contest in which we all lose in the end and the problem is to learn to accept it. There are inevitable love disappointments, the world is not arranged to collaborate with our wishes, people grow older, lovers become fathers, the old must give way to the young, and eventually everyone dies. The desire for justice is ranged alongside other human wishes which are more likely than not to be frustrated. French films repeatedly present these aspects of life so that we may inure ourselves to them and master the pain they cause us. It is the Mithridates principle of taking a little poison every day so that by and by one becomes less vulnerable to it.

It is in keeping with this tendency that French films so often take as their central character an aging man. He is not the triumphant hero whom we wish to become nor the criminal hero whom we fear to become, but simply what we must become: old. In him we see concentrated disappointment, lost hopes, change, decline of physical powers, and imminent death. We can observe his sadly comic struggle against his fate as he refuses to realize that he is no longer eligible to be the lover of a young girl, or learn from him the compensations of later life as he renounces the role of lover for that of father. He helps to reconcile us both to our past and to our future. We see in him our own father no longer dominant and powerful but a sharer of our common human fate. He who was in possession of things which we as children were denied is now seen suffering disappointments more grievous than we suffered then. In making peace with him we also make peace with our own future.

The young hero no less than the aging one in French films is likely to be disappointed. We see him in his pursuit of a beloved woman about whom he gradually learns much that is contrary to his wishes. He is not spared the discovery that this woman is involved with another man, and we in following his fate may work through our own similar disillusion-

161

ments. Knowledge which at first glance increases sorrow in the end mitigates the pain which, we see, could not be avoided.

We must learn that the world is not arranged to fulfill our demands for justice any more than to satisfy our longings for happiness. Human agencies of justice are obtuse and inefficient, and there are no divine ones. We are shown how the innocent are convicted, how the guilty are exonerated; they may even confess without being believed. Where justice is done, it is made clear that this is a happy accident. A clue uncovered by chance a moment earlier or later makes the difference between life and death of an innocent man. No one is watching over him, nor is he able to be the master of his own fate. Things may turn out happily. The suicidal bullet misses, the brain tumor may be operable, the hostages facing execution may be rescued at the last moment, the aging couple may find an unexpected revival of pleasure in life. The pleasure, no less sweet for that, is tinged with sadness; we know it is only a reprieve.

The major plot configuration in American films contrasts with both the British and the French. Winning is terrifically important and always possible though it may be a tough fight. The conflict is not an internal one; it is not our own impulses which endanger us nor our own scruples that stand in our way. The hazards are all external, but they are not rooted in the nature of life itself. They are the hazards of a particular situation with which we find ourselves confronted. The hero is typically in a strange town where there are apt to be dangerous men and women of ambiguous character and where the forces of law and order are not to be relied on. If he sizes up the situation correctly, if he does not go off half-cocked but is still able to beat the other fellow to the punch once he is sure who the enemy is, if he relies on no one but himself, if he demands sufficient evidence of virtue from the girl, he will emerge triumphant. He will defeat the dangerous men, get the right girl, and show the authorities what's what.

When he is a child, he is the comic hero, showing off, blundering, cocky, scared, called on to perform beyond his capacities, and pulling through by surprising spurts of activity and with the help of favorable circumstances. He is completely harmless, free from sexual or aggressive impulses, and the world around him reflects his own innocuous character. Its threats are playful and its reproaches ridiculous. When he is a man he is the melodrama hero and the world changes to reflect his changed potentialities; it becomes dangerous and seriously accusing, and launches him on his fighting career. The majority of the melodramas show him coming through successfully. A minority reveal various perils which lie off the main track; they are cautionary tales. The hero may succumb to his attacker; this is his bad dream. The men around him may be less dangerous than he suspects.

Under the delusion that he attacks in self-defense, he may initiate hostilities; then he will lose. In this case he is crazy. Without being deluded to this extent, out of greed and overconfidence, he may try to get away with murder; he commits the crime of which he is usually only suspected and he has to pay for it. The girl may turn out to be worse than he believed. He will have to go off without her; then he is lonely. He may not be able to produce anyone on whom to pin the blame for the crimes of which he is falsely accused; then he is a victim of circumstances. If circumstances fail to collaborate with his need to blame someone else, he may even end by blaming himself. These are the various hazards which the usual melodrama hero safely passes on the way.

The fantasy which provides for defeating dangerous men, winning the right girl, and coming out in the clear, is produced under the auspices of two major mechanisms: projection and denial. Self-accusations are embodied in the blundering police and destructive impulses in the unprovoked attacker. The beloved woman seems to be involved with another man but investigation ends in the gratifying demonstration that she never loved anyone but the hero. The love disappointment to which the French movie hero is repeatedly exposed is here denied.

The external world may be dangerous but manageable, or at other times, uncontrollable but gratifying. Where things seem to get out of control the results turn out to be wish-fulfilling. The overturning automobile throws the girl into the hero's arms, the rocking boat tosses the heroine's rival into the waves. The world that is uncontrollable but gratifying expresses an omnipotence fantasy while at the same time eliminating guilt. As soon as an internal problem is replaced by an external one, we can see the promise of success. The hero suffering from kleptomania becomes involved in investigating the activities of a gang of thieves; the amnesiac hero pursues his memories only long enough to unearth blues of someone else's crime before he rises impatiently from the psychiatrist's couch to embark on a successful detective job.

The world, which is not effectively policed, does not need to be policed at all. The hero, the self-appointed investigator and agent of justice, is able to set things right independently. The world thus appears as a kind of workable anarchic arrangement where, although hostilities are far from eliminated, life need not be nasty, brutish, and short, at any rate not for anyone we care about. The unofficial supervisors of private morals, the comic onlookers, are just as superfluous as the police. No one has any intention of doing anything naughty; only the mistakenly suspicious onlooker fails to recognize the natural goodness of the clean-cut young people.

American film plots are pervaded by false appearances. In this shadowy

163

but temporarily vivid guise, the content of what is projected and denied tends to reappear. It is in false appearances that the forbidden wishes are realized which the hero and heroine so rarely carry into action. In a false appearance the heroine is promiscuous, the hero is a murderer, the young couple carry on an illicit affair, two men friends share the favors of a woman. This device makes it possible to eat our cake and have it, since we can enjoy the suggested wish-fulfillments without emphatic guilt we know that the characters with whom we identify have not done anything. The contention of American films is that we should not feel guilty for mere wishes. The hero and heroine are threatened with penalties for the incriminating appearance but in the end are absolved. The misguided police or the foolish onlooker in comedies convey a self-accusation from which the hero and heroine struggle to dissociate themselves, a vestige of archaic conscience which is to be dispensed with.

What the plot unfolds is a process of proof. Something is undone rather than done: the false appearance is negated. The hero and heroine do not become committed to any irretrievable act whose consequences they must bear. Nor do they usually undergo any character transformation, ennoblement or degradation, gain or loss of hope, acceptance of a new role or the diminution and regrets of age. They succeed in proving what they were all along. They emerge from the shadow of the false appearance. What has changed is other people's impressions of them. In so far as the hero and heroine may be unsure of who or what they are except as they see themselves mirrored in the eyes of others, they have succeeded in establishing for themselves a desirable identity. In so far as they struggle against a projected archaic conscience that persecutes the wish as if it were the act, they win a victory for a more tolerant and discriminating morality.

—Martha Wolfenstein
and Nathan Leites*

TERMS TO BE LEARNED

▸ Comparison
▸ Subject
▸ Object

* Reprinted with permission of The Free Press from *Movies: A Psychological Study* by Martha Wolfenstein and Nathan Leites. Copyright 1950 by The Free Press, a corporation.

▶ Basis
▶ Effect
▶ Contrast
▶ Continuous comparison
▶ Discontinuous comparison

Exercises & Theme Topics

I. List subject, object, basis and effect for the following images:

Lincoln stood during the crisis like an oak tree in a high wind.
I-beam
golden hair
Italy is shaped like a boot.
His eyes glittered like silver coins.
I felt all broken up after hearing the news.
Her hair hung down her pallid cheeks like wet seaweed on a clam.

II. Comment on the following student essay as an example of development by comparison. What techniques of comparison does it use? In what ways is the use of comparison adequate? How could it be improved?

"SIMILARITIES IN THE PHILOSOPHIES OF DARWIN AND MARX AND ENGELS"

Along with the scientific advances of the nineteenth century, came many new developments in philosophical thought. Two of these nineteenth-century philosophies which had tremendous effect on the thinking of succeeding decades were Darwin's *Origin of Species* and Marx and Engels' *Communist Manifesto*. Although these widely known and highly controversial philosophies are unrelated in many ways, they are quite similar in others and show several basic parallels in philosophical thinking.

165

One of the most obvious similarities is the concern for over-production. Although Darwin is concerned with biological over-production and Marx and Engels direct their attention toward over-production in industry and agriculture, the idea that over-production must be balanced by a system of checks is paralleled by both philosophies. Darwin asserts that population increases by a geometric ratio, and that population would expand far beyond the earth's ability to accommodate it if unchecked for only a short time. Population expansion, however, is checked by competition for available food and shelter and changes in climate which may favor one species over another. As one example, Darwin points out that the very severe winter of 1854-55 greatly reduced the bird population around his home, thus checking a population expansion which had begun the previous spring.

Marx and Engels are concerned with quite another kind of over-production. This is economic over-production. According to them, under a bourgeois controlled, capitalist society, production is forced higher and higher until industrial output exceeds the needs of the consumer. This over-production is then checked by inflation and sometimes depression.

Even more basic than over-production, checks, and balances is the evolutionary theory advanced by the two philosophies. Darwin's evolution is biological and is brought about by natural selection. In this selection process only the strongest and most adaptable creatures are able to survive. Nature carries out her selection, says Darwin, through such things as changes in climate or food supply. Thus, any one of these changes might turn the survival odds greatly in favor of one creature and greatly against another. The creature who is not favored must then adapt or face extinction. From these facts, it might be assumed that Darwin believes that dinosaurs, for example, were unable to survive because they were unable to adapt to changes in environment, and that the species that has become man was able to survive because man has been able to adapt himself to these changes.

The evolutionary theory of Marx and Engels involves man in a political instead of a biological sense. They carefully point out that the modern bourgeoisie was begun about the end of the Middle Ages. In the beginning this class was composed merely of freed serfs who began working independent of overlords. From this evolved what is known as the "middle class." According to Marx and Engels, because this class was adaptable, it now controls governments of the West and exploits the working man or proletariat. However, they believe that the bourgeoisie has now ceased to be adaptable and that its destruction is inevitable. They hold that the bourgeoisie is creating the environment of its own destruction by suppressing the proletariat and making them more aware of themselves as a class.

Thus, eventually a revolt will take place and society will evolve into a community controlled by the proletariat.

Marx and Engels are certain that political evolution will come about through revolution. A great appeal to the working class is made at the end of their manifesto. "Let the ruling classes tremble at a Communist revolution. The proletarians have nothing to lose but their chains. They have a world to win. Workingmen of all countries, unite!"

III. The following selections illustrate the use of comparison and contrast by professional writers to develop paragraphs and larger units in the essay. State in each case whether the author is using comparison or contrast or both, and whether his organization is continuous or discontinuous. Then identify subject, basis and effect for each selection. Note: the last example, Milton's "L'Allegro" and "Il Penseroso," is optional. If your instructor assigns it, work out an outline for each poem. Comment on the similarities and differences of structure. Then make a detailed list of the points of comparison and contrast treated by Milton.

A.   ***GOOD GUYS AND BAD GUYS***

One afternoon, hearing gunfire from the room where our television set is installed, I went in with that losing intention of fraternizing with my son for a little while. There sat Catbird with the cretinous expression I have learned to recognize. A Western was in progress.

"What's going on?" I asked.

He looked at me in wonder. "What do you mean, what's going on? Don't you know?"

"Well, no. Tell me!"

He was kind to me. Explained as though I were the child.

"Well, the Bad Guy is trying to steal Her father's ranch. But the Good Guy won't let him. Bullet figured out the plot."

"Who is Bullet?"

"Why, the Good Guy's horse." He didn't add "You dope," but his tone implied it.

"Now wait," I said, "which one is the Good Guy?"

"The one with the white hat."

"Then the one with the black hat is the Bad Guy?"

"Anybody knows that," said Catbird.

For a time I watched the picture, and I realized that I had been ignoring a part of our life that everybody knows. I was interested in the characterizations. The girl, known as Her or She, was a blonde, very pretty but completely unvoluptuous because these are Family Pictures. Sometimes she wore a simple gingham dress and sometimes a leather skirt and boots, but always she had a bit of a bow in her hair and her face was untroubled with emotion or, one might almost say, intelligence. This also is part of the convention. She is a symbol, and any acting would get her thrown out of the picture by popular acclaim.

The Good Guy not only wore a white hat but light-colored clothes, shining boots, tight riding pants, and a shirt embroidered with scrolls and flowers. In my young days I used to work with cattle, and our costume was blue jeans, a leather jacket, and boots with run-over heels. The cleaning bill alone of the gorgeous screen cowboy would have been four times what our pay was in a year.

The Good Guy had very little change of facial expression. He went through his fantastic set of adventures with no show of emotion. This is another convention and proves that he is very brave and very pure. He is also scrubbed and has an immaculate shave.

I turned my attention to the Bad Guy. He wore a black hat and dark clothing, but his clothing was definitely not only unclean but unpressed. He had a stubble of beard but the greatest contrast was in his face. His was not an immobile face. He leered, he sneered, he had a nasty laugh. He bullied and shouted. He looked evil. While he did not swear, because this is a Family Picture, he said things like "Wall dog it" and "You rat" and "I'll cut off your ears and eat 'em" which would indicate that his language was not only coarse but might, off screen, be vulgar. He was, in a word a Bad Guy. I found a certain interest in the Bad Guy which was lacking in the Good Guy.

"Which one do you like best?" I asked.

Catbird removed his anaesthetized eyes from the screen. "What do you mean?"

"Do you like the Good Guy or the Bad Guy?"

He sighed at my ignorance and looked back at the screen. "Are you kidding?" he asked. "The Good Guy, of course."

—JOHN STEINBECK*

* From "How to Tell Good Guys from Bad Guys," in *The Reporter*, XII (March 10, 1955), 42-4. Copyright © 1955 by John Steinbeck. Appeared originally in *The Reporter*. Reprinted by permission of McIntosh and Otis, Inc.

B.   *CALFORNIA LAND*

   The stubborn and enduring land of California has changed less than its
people. From an aeroplane the "coloured counties" are seen spread out like
a giant relief map. Mount Shasta looms to the north, Mount Whitney to
the south; the Sierra Nevada forms a wall to the east; and beyond Whitney,
where the Sierra appears to go underground, the desert takes over. There
are the long interior valleys; and there are the tumbled, rough, and wooded
Coast Ranges through which rivers and creeks break to the sea. Below,
incredible, lies the vast and varied land, its mountains and deserts empty
and mute today, while over the accessible valleys and coastal plains a
congested and diverse population clusters close to a few centers like wasps
around heavy-hanging nests. A constant stream of automobiles, looking
from the air like lines of black ants on the march, fills the passes over
the Sierra barrier, moving westward to the favored spots. The hills are
empty except for lumbering operations wherever there is a good stand of
trees; the mining towns of the Mother Lode and the old rancherias are
shabby and deserted, or have been taken over by "summer people." The
banks of rivers and creeks are empty save for sporadic invasions of fishermen;
and the desert is without human occupants except for a citified overflow
which follows in the wake of air-cooling installations, swimming pools, and
motels.
   What would an air view have revealed in the days of the gold rush? The
same lines of black ants moving in the same westerly direction over the
same passes, on horseback, and in covered wagons drawn by oxen, traveling
more slowly than today's immigrants but with the same doggedness as these
later ones, heading in part for the same centers, in part stopping in the
hill country where ranches, mining camps, and saw and grist mills were
scattered along streams and in the forests.
   Hovering over the same land, but continuing our flight back in time, we
view another trek, this one on foot or on mule and horseback, coming up
from the south, northward along the rim of the sea. The time is the
'seventies of the eighteenth century, and the travelers, Spaniards pushing
out of Mexico, keeping a sharp eye for a sheltered and sunny and likely
spot for mission, rancheria, or presidio as they move slowly on.
   If we take a last backward flight in time, the Spaniard is no longer seen.
This is the time before his coming; the golden land belongs wholly and
undisputedly to its native sons and daughters. No lines of black ants move
over the high passes or come up from the south in this view. Indeed, we

169

must fly low to see the narrow trails meandering beside a stream, or across country to an oak flat, or up into the hills. At first there seem to be neither houses nor people, but presently a frame with surf fish strung on it to dry on a sunny beach, a clearing in the trees, a thin blue wisp of smoke from a wood fire, serve to guide the eyes to the weathered roof of a low redwood house, to an earth-covered circular house, to a thatched house, to a brush shelter. We see an old woman tending the fire outside a house, a man spearing fish beside a stream, a half-grown boy paddling downstream in a dugout canoe. A young woman, her baby in a basket carrier on her back, gathers wild iris on a hillside; a hunter brings down a deer with bow and arrow. These people step noiselessly over the ground, barefoot or in soft deerskin moccasins, and their naked or near-naked copper-colored bodies blend in semicamouflage against the colors of the earth. Such clothes as they wear, a skirt of shredded bark, a buckskin breechclout, an occasional fur or feather cape, also blend into the natural background. Their voices, whether in ordinary conversation, or in song or prayer or mourning cry, are light-toned, neither harsh nor loud.

The high mountains are empty. But people are living in the hills as far up as oak trees grow and wherever manzanita and other berries abundant, and wherever there are deer; along fish-filled streams; and where a river flows into the sea; and on the desert. Even so unlikely a place as Death Valley has men who call it home.

—Theodora Kroeber*

C.   THE LITERATURE OF KNOWLEDGE AND THE LITERATURE OF POWER

Books . . . do not suggest an idea coextensive and interchangeable with the idea of Literature; since much literature . . . may never come into books, and much that *does* come into books may connect itself with no literary interest. But a far more important correction, applicable to the common vague idea of literature, is to be sought not so much in a better definition of literature as in a sharper distinction of the two functions which it fulfils. In that great social organ which, collectively we call literature, there may be distinguished two separate offices that may blend and often *do* so, but capable, severally, of a severe insulation, and naturally fitted for reciprocal repulsion. There is, first, the literature of *knowledge*;

* From *Ishi in Two Worlds* (Berkeley: University of California Press, 1961), pp. 11-3. Reprinted by permission.

and secondly, the literature of *power*. The function of the first is—to *teach*; the function of the second is—to *move*: the first is a rudder; the second, an oar or a sail. The first speaks to the *mere* discursive understanding; the second speaks ultimately, it may happen, to the higher understanding or reason, but always *through* affections of pleasure and sympathy. Remotely, it may travel towards an object seat in what Lord Bacon calls dry light; but proximately, it does and must operate,—else it ceases to be a literature of *power*,—on and through that *humid* light which clothes itself in the mists and glittering *iris* of human passions, desires, and genial emotions.

Men have so little reflected on the higher functions of literature as to find it a paradox if one should describe it as a mean or subordinate purpose of books to give information. But this is a paradox only in the sense which makes it honourable to be paradoxical. Whenever we talk in ordinary language of seeking information or gaining knowledge, we understand the words as connected with something of absolute novelty. But it is the grandeur of all truth which *can* occupy a very high place in human interests that it is never absolutely novel to the meanest of minds: it exists eternally by way of germ or latent principle in the lowest as in the highest, needing to be developed, but never to be planted. To be capable of transplantation is the immediate criterion of a truth that ranges on a lower scale. Besides which, there is a rarer thing than truth,—namely, *power* or deep sympathy with truth. What is the effect, for instance, upon society, of children? By the pity, by the tenderness, and by the peculiar modes of admiration, which connect themselves with the helplessness, with the innocence, and with the simplicity of children, not only are the primal affections strengthened and continually renewed, but the qualities which are dearest in the sight of heaven,—the frailty, for instance, which' appeals to forbearance, the innocence which symbolizes the heavenly, and the simplicity which is most alien from the worldly,—are kept up in perpetual remembrance, and their ideals are continually refreshed. A purpose of the same nature is answered by the higher literature, viz. the literature of power. What do you learn from "Paradise Lost?" Nothing at all. What do you learn from a cookery-book? Something new, something that you did not know before, in every paragraph. But would you therefore put the wretched cookery-book on a higher level of estimation than the divine poem? What you owe to Milton is not any knowledge, of which a million separate items are still but a million of advancing steps on the same earthly level; what you owe is *power*,—that is, exercise and expansion to your own latent capacity of sympathy with the infinite, where every pulse and each separate influx is a step upwards, a step ascending as upon a Jacob's ladder from earth to mysterious altitudes above the earth. *All* the steps of knowledge, from first

171

to last, carry you further on the same plane, but could never raise you one foot above your ancient level of earth; whereas the very *first* step in power is a flight—is an ascending movement into another element where earth is forgotten.

—THOMAS DE QUINCEY*

D. *"THE TOWN MOUSE AND THE COUNTRY MOUSE"*

A Country Mouse, a plain, sensible sort of fellow, was once visited by a former companion of his, who lived in a neighboring city. The Country Mouse put before his friend some fine peas, some choice bacon, and a bit of rare, old Stilton, and called upon him to eat heartily of the good cheer. The City Mouse nibbled a little here and there in a dainty manner, wondering at the pleasure his host took in such coarse and ordinary fare. In the after-dinner chat the Town Mouse said to the Country Mouse, "Really, my good friend, that you can keep in such spirits in this dismal, dead-and-alive kind of place surprises me altogether. You see here no life, no gayety, no society in short, but go on and on, in a dull, humdrum sort of way, from one year's end to another. Come now with me, this very night, and see with your own eyes what a life I lead." The Country Mouse consented, and as soon as it fell dark, off they started for the city, where they arrived just as a splendid supper, given by the master of the house where our town friend lived, was over and the guests had departed. The City Mouse soon got together a heap of dainties on a corner of the handsome Turkey carpet. The Country Mouse, who had never even heard the names of half the meats set before him, was hesitating where he should begin when the room-door creaked, opened, and in entered a servant with a light. The companions ran off, but everything soon being quiet again, they returned to their repast, when once more the door opened, and the son of the master of the house came in with a great bounce, followed by his little Terrier, who ran sniffing to the very spot where our friends had just been. The City Mouse was by that time safe in his hole—which, by the way, he had not been thoughtful enough to show to his friend, who could find no better shelter than that afforded by a sofa, behind which he waited in fear and trembling till quietness was again restored. The City Mouse then called upon him to resume his supper, but the Country Mouse said, "No, No; I shall be off as fast as I can. I would rather have a crust with peace

* From "Letters to a Young Man Whose Education Has Been Neglected" (1823).

172

and quietness than all your fine things in the midst of such alarm and frights as these."

—AESOP*

E.

"L'ALLEGRO" AND "IL PENSEROSO"

"L'Allegro"

Hence loathed Melancholy
  Of Cerberus and blackest Midnight born,
In Stygian cave forlorn
  'Mongst horrid shapes, and shrieks, and sights unholy,
Find out some uncouth cell,   5
  Where brooding Darkness spreads his jealous wings,
And the night-raven sings;
  There under ebon shades and low-browed rocks,
As ragged as thy locks,
  In dark Cimmerian desert ever dwell.   10
But come thou Goddess fair and free,
In Heaven yclept Euphrosyne,
And by men, heart-easing Mirth,
Whom lovely Venus at a birth
With two sister Graces more   15
To ivy-crowned Bacchus bore;
Or whether (as some sager sing)
The frolic wind that breathes the spring,
Zephyr with Aurora playing,
As he met her once a-Maying,   20
There on beds of violets blue,
And fresh-blown roses washed in dew,
Filled her with thee, a daughter fair,
So buxom, blithe, and debonair.
    Haste thee Nymph, and bring with thee   25
Jest and youthful Jollity,
Quips and Cranks, and wanton Wiles,
Nods, and Becks, and wreathed Smiles,
Such as hang on Hebe's cheek,
And love to live in dimple sleek;   30
Sport that wrinkled Care derides,
And Laughter holding both his sides.

* From *Fables*.

Come, and trip it as ye go
On the light fantastic toe,
35 And in thy right hand lead with thee,
The mountain nymph, sweet Liberty;
And if I give thee honor due,
Mirth, admit me of thy crew,
To live with her, and live with thee,
40 In unreproved pleasures free;
To hear the lark begin his flight,
And singing startle the dull night,
From his watch-tower in the skies,
Till the dappled dawn doth rise;
45 Then to come in spite of sorrow,
And at my window bid good-morrow,
Through the sweet-briar, or the vine,
Or the twisted eglantine.
While the cock with lively din,
50 Scatters the rear of darkness thin,
And to the stack or the barn door,
Stoutly struts his dames before;
Oft listening how the hounds and horn
Cheerly rouse the slumbering Morn,
55 From the side of some hoar hill,
Through the high wood echoing shrill.
Sometime walking not unseen
By hedgerow elms, on hillocks green,
Right against the eastern gate,
60 Where the great sun begins his state,
Robed in flames and amber light,
The clouds in thousand liveries dight;
While the ploughman near at hand,
Whistles o'er the furrowed land,
65 And the milkmaid singeth blithe,
And the mower whets his scythe,
And every shepherd tells his tale
Under the hawthorn in the dale.
    Straight mine eye hath caught new pleasures
70 Whist the landscape round it measures:
Russet lawns and fallows gray,
Where the nibbling flocks do stray,

Mountains on whose barren breast
The laboring clouds do often rest,
Meadows trim with daisies pied,   75
Shallow brooks and rivers wide.
Towers and battlements it sees
Bosomed high in tufted trees,
Where perhaps some beauty lies,
The cynosure of neighboring eyes.   80
Hard by, a cottage chimney smokes,
From betwixt two aged oaks,
Where Corydon and Thyrsis met,
Are at their savory dinner set
Of herbs and other country messes,   85
Which the neat-handed Phillis dresses;
And then in haste her bower she leaves,
With Thestylis to bind the sheaves;
Or if the earlier season lead,
To the tanned haycock in the mead.   90
    Sometimes with secure delight
The upland hamlets will invite,
When the merry bells ring round,
And the jocund rebecks sound
To many a youth and many a maid,   95
Dancing in the chequered shade;
And young and old come forth to play
On a sunshine holiday,
Till the livelong daylight fail;
Then to the spicy nut-brown ale,   100
With stories told of many a feat,
How fairy Mab the junkets eat;
She was pinched and pulled she said,
And he by friar's lantern led
Tells how the drudging goblin sweat,   105
To earn his cream-bowl duly set,
When in one night, ere glimpse of morn,
His shadowy flail hath threshed the corn
That ten day-laborers could not end;
Then lies him down the lubber fiend,   110
And stretched out all the chimney's length,
Basks at the fire his hairy strength;

175

And crop-full out of doors he flings,
Ere the first cock his matin rings.
115 Thus done the tales, to bed they creep,
By whispering winds soon lulled asleep.
    Towered cities please us then,
And the busy hum of men,
Where throngs of knights and barons bold
120 In weeds of peace high triumphs hold,
With store of ladies, whose bright eyes
Rain influence, and judge the prize
Of wit or arms, while both contend
To win her grace whom all commend.
125 There let Hymen oft appear
In saffron robe, with taper clear,
And pomp, and feast, and revelry,
With masque and antique pageantry;
Such sights as youthful poets dream
130 On summer eves by haunted stream.
Then to the well-trod stage anon,
If Jonson's learned sock be on,
Or sweetest Shakespeare, Fancy's child,
Warble his native wood-notes wild;
135 And ever against eating cares,
Lap me in soft Lydian airs,
Married to immortal verse,
Such as the meeting soul may pierce
In notes with many a winding bout
140 Of linked sweetness long drawn out,
With wanton heed and giddy cunning,
The melting voice through mazes running,
Untwisting all the chains that tie
The hidden soul of harmony;
145 That Orpheus' self may heave his head
From golden slumber on a bed
Of heaped Elysian flowers, and hear
Such strains as would have won the ear
Of Pluto, to have quite set free
150 His half-regained Eurydice.
    These delights if thou canst give,
Mirth with thee I mean to live.

176

"*Il Penseroso*"

Hence vain deluding Joys,
  The brood of Folly without father bred,
How little you bested,
  Or fill the fixed mind with all your toys;
Dwell in some idle brain,   5
  And fancies fond with gaudy shapes possess,
As thick and numberless
  As the gay motes that people the sunbeams,
Or likest hovering dreams,
  The fickle pensioners of Morpheus' train.   10
But hail thou Goddess, sage and holy,
Hail divinest Melancholy,
Whose saintly visage is too bright
To hit the sense of human sight,
And therefore to our weaker view   15
O'erlaid with black, staid Wisdom's hue;
Black, but such as in esteem
Prince Memnon's sister might beseem,
Or that starred Ethiop queen that strove
To set her beauty's praise above   20
The sea nymphs, and their powers offended;
Yet thou art higher far descended:
Thee bright-haired Vesta long of yore
To solitary Saturn bore;
His daughter she (in Saturn's reign   25
Such mixture was not held a stain).
Oft in glimmering bowers and glades
He met her, and in secret shades
Of woody Ida's inmost grove,
Whilst yet there was no fear of Jove.   30
      Come pensive Nun, devout and pure,
Sober, steadfast, and demure,
All in a robe of darkest grain,
Flowing with majestic train,
And sable stole of cypress lawn,   35
Over thy decent shoulders drawn.
Come, but keep thy wonted state,
With even step and musing gait,

177

And looks commercing with the skies,
40 Thy rapt soul sitting in thine eyes;
There held in holy passion still,
Forget thyself to marble, till
With a sad leaden downward cast,
Thou fix them on the earth as fast.
45 And join with thee calm Peace and Quiet,
Spare Fast, that oft with gods doth diet,
And hears the Muses in a ring
Aye round about Jove's altar sing.
And add to these retired Leisure,
50 That in trim gardens takes his pleasure;
But first and chiefest, with thee bring
Him that yon soars on golden wing,
Guiding the fiery-wheeled throne,
The Cherub Contemplation;
55 And the mute Silence hist along,
'Less Philomel will deign a song,
In her sweetest saddest plight,
Smoothing the rugged brow of Night,
While Cynthia checks her dragon yoke,
60 Gently o'er the accustomed oak;
Sweet bird that shunn'st the noise of folly,
Most musical, most melancholy!
Thee chauntress oft the woods among,
I woo to hear thy even-song;
65 And missing thee, I walk unseen
On the dry smooth-shaven green,
To behold the wandering moon,
Riding near her highest noon,
Like one that had been led astray
70 Through the Heaven's wide pathless way;
And oft, as if her head she bowed,
Stooping through a fleecy cloud.
Oft on a plat of rising ground
I hear the far-off curfew sound,
75 Over some wide-watered shore,
Swinging slow with sullen roar;
Or if the air will not permit,
Some still removed place will fit,

Where glowing embers through the room
Teach light to counterfeit a gloom,   80
Far from all resort of mirth,
Save the cricket on the hearth,
Or the bellman's drowsy charm,
To bless the doors from nightly harm.
Or let my lamp at midnight hour   85
Be seen in some high lonely tower,
Where I may oft outwatch the Bear,
With thrice great Hermes, or unsphere
The spirit of Plato to unfold
What worlds or what vast regions hold   90
The immortal mind that hath forsook
Her mansion in this fleshly nook;
And of those daemons that are found
In fire, air, flood, or under ground,
Whose power hath a true consent   95
With planet or with element.
Sometime let gorgeous Tragedy
In sceptred pall come sweeping by,
Presenting Thebes, or Pelops' line,
Or the tale of Troy divine,   100
Or what (though rare) of later age
Ennobled hath the buskined stage.
     But, O sad Virgin, that thy power
Might raise Musaeus from his bower,
Or bid the soul of Orpheus sing   105
Such notes as, warbled to the string,
Drew iron tears down Pluto's cheek,
And made Hell grant what Love did seek;
Or call up him that left half told
The story of Cambuscan bold   110
Of Camball, and of Algarsife,
And who had Canace to wife,
That owned the virtuous ring and glass,
And of the wondrous horse of brass,
On which the Tartar king did ride;   115
And if aught else great bards beside
In sage and solemn tunes have sung,
Of tourneys and of trophies hung,

Of forests and enchantments drear,
120 Where more is meant than meets the ear.
    Thus Night oft see me in thy pale career,
Til civil-suited Morn appear,
Not tricked and frounced as she was wont
With the Attic boy to hunt,
125 But kerchieft in a comely cloud,
While rocking winds are piping loud,
Or ushered with a shower still,
When the gust hath blown his fill,
Ending on the rustling leaves,
130 With minute-drops from off the eaves.
And when the sun begins to fling
His flaring beams, me Goddess bring
To arched walks of twilight groves,
And shadows brown that Silvan loves,
135 Of pine or monumental oak,
Where the rude axe with heaved stroke
Was never heard the nymphs to daunt,
Or fright them from their hallowed haunt.
There in close covert by some brook,
140 Where no profaner eye may look,
Hide me from Day's garish eye,
While the bee with honied thigh,
That at her flowery work doth sing,
And the waters murmuring,
145 With such consort as they keep,
Entice the dewy-feathered Sleep;
And let some strange mysterious dream
Wave at his wings in airy stream
Of lively portraiture displayed,
150 Softly on my eyelids laid.
And as I wake, sweet music breathe
Above, about, or underneath,
Sent by some spirit to mortals good,
Or the unseen Genius of the wood.
155   But let my due feet never fail
To walk the studious cloister's pale,
And love the high embowed roof,
With antic pillars massy proof,

180

And storied windows richly dight,
Casting a dim religious light.   160
There let the pealing organ blow
To the full-voiced choir below,
In service high and anthems clear,
As may with sweetness, through mine ear,
Dissolve me into ecstasies,   165
And bring all Heaven before mine eyes.
    And may at last my weary age
Find out the peaceful hermitage,
The hairy gown and mossy cell,
Where I may sit and rightly spell   170
Of every star that Heaven doth shew,
And every herb that sips the dew;
Till old experience do attain
To something like prophetic strain.
    These pleasures Melancholy give,   175
And I with thee will choose to live.

—JOHN MILTON*

IV. Select one or more of the following topics. For each topic selected, write a paragraph of comparison or contrast. At the end of the paragraph state the basis and effect of the comparison or contrast.

Town and country
Train travel and automobile travel
Poetry and prose
The engineering student and the liberal arts student
College and high school
Study and recreation
The Middle Ages and the Renaissance

V. Select one of the above topics or a similar topic suggested by your instructor. Use it as the basis of an essay developed by comparison and contrast (minimum length, 500 words). Your essay should be accompanied by an outline that clearly indicates the techniques you have used.

* "L'Allegro" and "Il Penseroso" (1632?).

Definition

8

One of the chief causes of vague writing is failure to define terms. Words like "love," "democracy," "good" or "beauty" are notorious for meaning different things to different people. Unless they are defined, it is impossible for reader and writer to have a genuine meeting of minds. The "big words" are not the only ones that need definition. Words that everybody "knows he knows"—words like "fact," "symbol" or "order"—

turn out on inspection to have several possible meanings. If they are key words in an essay, the writer needs to state which of the possible meanings he will use. Otherwise he may use the words inconsistently or the reader may assume a meaning different from the appropriate one.

It is impossible to stress the importance of definition too strongly. Definition is essential to all levels of expository and argumentative writing from the simplest to the most formal, and failure to define leads endlessly to confusion, empty debate and misinterpretation. A set of contest rules states "Late entries will not be accepted." If the writer stops here the reader will be as ignorant as before, but considerably more anxious. The writer must give an exact definition of "late" so he adds, "An entry will be judged late if it is postmarked after 12:00 midnight, March 11, 1966." The pamphlet accompanying United States Income Tax forms is an example of writing in which exact definitions are vitally important. Exemptions can be claimed for "dependents," but what is a "dependent?" The form therefore includes a three-column definition of the term. Deductions are allowed for "charitable contributions." This necessitates a two-column definition ending with a list of contributions that are *not* included in the term "charitable." The adequacy of these and similar definitions directly affects government revenues, the income of the taxpayer and legal cases of tax evasion, not to mention the taxpayer's somewhat frayed emotions. The fact that some definitions on the form are ambiguous and that filling out one's income tax is still a frustrating experience illustrates the difficulty of formulating definitions that are exact but at the same time simple enough for easy comprehension. The art of writing contracts is to a large extent the art of writing exact definitions. Legal interpretation also depends heavily on definition. The question of whether "separate but equal" schools for children of different races was constitutional, for example, hinged on the definition of the "equal rights" provision of the Constitution.

8.1 FORMAL DEFINITION

Definition depends on relating the term to be defined to a larger **class** or **genus**. To define the term "John P. Williams, III," for example, one must place it in one of several possible larger categories, for example, the class of students, the class of American citizens or the class of basketball players. By the same token "students" is a member of the class of "human beings," "human beings" is a member of the class of "vertebrates" and so forth.

The object of formal definition is to state the class in which a term belongs and then to give the basis for distinguishing the term from other terms in the class referred to. The basis for distinguishing the term is called the **differentia,** and in a given definition one or more **differentiae** may be necessary. "John Williams is the basketball player with dark hair" is a sufficient definition if all other players have blond hair. If several players have dark hair, a second **differentia** is needed: "John Williams is the basketball player with dark hair and a scar on his left wrist."

Formal definition consists of giving the term to be defined, the class or genus in which it belongs and one or more differentiae. "Man is a thinking animal" is a formal definition. "Man" is the term, "animal" is the class, and "thinking" is the differentia.

8.2 PRECISION AND RELEVANCE

The two most important attributes of formal definition are **precision** and **relevance. A precise definition is one that is unambiguous.** It can be interpreted in only one way. In a contest, "Entries will not be accepted after Friday, March 11" might be ambiguous. To make it precise, the writer revises it to read "Entries will not be accepted if postmarked after midnight, Friday, March 11, 1966." **A relevant definition is one that applies to the situation in which it is used.** Because terms can usually be assigned to more than one class the writer often has a choice as to what definition he will use, and his choice will depend on purpose and context. "John Williams is the basketball player with dark hair and a scar on his left wrist" would be **relevant** in a conversation during a basketball game, but **irrelevant** in most other contexts. For the student directory John Williams is "Senior; res.: Middletown, Ohio; campus: 215 Rush Dorm." And for the infirmary, John is "Caucasian male, 21, admitted 2/19/65 with severe cold." Each of these definitions uses a different **class** and set of **differentiae,** but each is valid. In complex situations, formulation of a relevant definition may require careful thought, but it is of central importance. In cases where the author states his preference for one of several possible definitions—either his own or one derived from a dictionary or other authoritative source—the definition may be called **stipulative.**

▶ 8.3   AIDS TO DEFINITION

Even in a dictionary, formal definition is supplemented by techniques that explain and clarify. The more extended the definition, the more helpful these techniques become. The simplest aid to definition is the use of a **synonym** or **equivalent term.** More complex aids include historical definition, definition by example, definition by enumeration of attributes and definition by contrast: (1) **Historical definition clarifies the meaning of a term by explaining how it was used in the past. Etymology is a type of historical definition.** (2) **In definition by example the term is defined by one or more typical instances.** It is a way of showing, rather than asserting, what the term means. (3) **Definition by enumeration clarifies the meaning of a term by listing its characteristics (or attributes).** (4) **Definition by contrast gives examples or attributes showing what the term does *not* include.** Consider the following examples:

1. **Formal definition:**

    TERM   CLASS   DIFFERENTIA (1)   DIFFERENTIA (2)
    A ⌐chair¬ is a ⌐seat,¬ ⌐usually movable,¬ ⌐for one person.¬

2. **Synonym:**

    A chair is a seat.

3. Historical definitions

    a. By etymology:
       Chair is derived through French and Latin from Greek *kathedra,* a compound of *kata,* meaning *down,* and the root of *hezesthai, to sit.*

b. By usage:
Chair: a seat for one person. *Cursor Mundi* (1300) : "Was never yeitt king ne kaiser, pat ever sait in slic *chaier*." Wyclif (1382) : "He turnyde vpsadoun the bordis of chaungeris, and the *chaiers* of men sellynge culveris." Merlin (1450) : "He sholde do sette ther a *cheyer*." Howard (1564) : "In a *chaire* fast besides him." Shakespeare (1601) : "Like a Barbers *chaire* that fits all buttokes." Steele (1704) : "Get *chairs* . . . and leave us." Johnson (1751) : "mistaking a lady's lap for my own *chair*."

4. Definition by **example** and by **contrast**:
The Japanese student asked me what "chair" meant. I pointed to the object he was sitting on. "That," I said, "is a chair." Pointing to where I was sitting, I added, "This is not a chair. It is a sofa."

5. Definition by **enumeration** and **contrast**:
A chair usually has four legs and a back, and may have arms. A seat with three legs and no back is usually called a stool.

Notice how several techniques are combined in the composite definition given in the sixth edition of *Webster's Collegiate Dictionary*:
chair (char), *n.* OF. *chaiere,* fr. L. *cathedra,* fr. Gr., *kathedra,* fr. *kata* down—root of *hezesthai* to sit. 1. A seat, usually movable, for one person. It usually has four legs and a back, and may have arms.

8.4 CLASSIFICATION AND ANALYSIS OF MEANINGS

When a term is used in more than one sense, its meanings can be **classified** and discussed individually. In a dictionary different meanings are numbered, and a separate definition is given for each. *Chair,* for example, is used as a noun in four different senses. After giving the most common definition of *chair* (quoted above), Webster's adds:

2. An official seat of authority, state, or dignity; hence, the office or place of authority, dignity, etc., or the dignity itself; specif., the office of a

187

professor, judge, etc. **3.** A sedan chair. **4.** The presiding officer of an assembly; a chairman.

In simple cases, the writer need only give the definition appropriate to the subject. The definition can be derived from an authoritative source like the dictionary or it can be formulated by the author to meet the immediate situation. In the latter case the author accepts responsibility for the definition. The method insures **relevance,** but if the definition is superficial or eccentric the whole essay will suffer. In **extended definition** it is often necessary to discuss several possible meanings, to explain them and to justify the preferred meaning. Whether the definition is brief or extended, recognition that the term can be used in several ways is a safeguard against inconsistency.

Analysis is related to enumeration. The author lists the components of the term—its subclasses, parts, different functions, etc.—and discusses each. The discussion thus becomes a cumulative definition of the term. An entry on "United States Government" in a one-volume encyclopedia begins, "The Federal Government of the United States is divided into three branches: the executive, the judicial and the legislative." After commenting on the historical causes of this division, the entry continues with an extended discussion of the history and function of each branch. When the reader finishes, he has a concise, if somewhat sketchy, definition of "United States Government."

Since **classification** and **analysis** are techniques of organization as well as definition, they are often used as a method of development in essays of extended definition. The entry on "United States Government," for example, may be considered a short essay of definition with the following outline:

I. The American Government is divided into three branches: the executive, the judicial and the legislative.
II. The executive branch offers leadership, controls the administration of laws and has veto power, subject to review, over laws passed by the legislative branch.
III. The judicial branch reviews laws.
IV. The legislative branch passes laws.

8.5 ANNOTATED EXAMPLES OF DEFINITION

Everyone "knows he knows" what the word *myth* means. Consider, however, the following definitions. Note especially the way they reflect **relevance** to the author's purpose.

1. Brief formal definition:

TERM   CLASS   DIFFERENTIA

A myth—that is a story about gods and legendary heroes—is always a

delight to read.

2. Dictionary definition (*The American College Dictionary**):

TERM   DIFFERENTIAE   CLASS

myth (mĭth), *n.* 1. a traditional or legendary story, usually concerning

ATTRIBUTES

some superhuman being or some alleged person or event, whether without

or with a determinable basis of fact or a natural explanation; esp., a tra-

EQUIVALENT

ditional or legendary story usually concerning deities or demigods and

CLASS

the creation of the world and its inhabitants. 2. stories or matter of

EXAMPLE OF USAGE   DIFFERENTIA   CLASS   DIFFERENTIAE

this kind: *in the realm of myth.* 3. any invented story. 4. an imaginary or

CLASS   DIFFERENTIA (1)   CLASS   DIFFERENTIA (2)

fictitious thing or person. 5. *Sociol.* a collective belief that is built up

CONTRAST

in response to the wishes of the group rather than an analysis of the basis

* (New York: Random House, Inc., 1958), p. 805.

189

HISTORY (ETYMOLOGY)

of the wishes. [t. NL: s. *mȳthus*, mod. var. of LL *mȳthos*, t. Gk.: word,

SYNONYM

speech, tale, legend, myth]—**Syn.** 1. See **legend.**

3. Handbook definition (*Reader's Companion to World Literature*†):

TERM DIFFERENTIA (1) CLASS   DIFFERENTIAE

myth: a traditional tale common to the members of a tribe, race, or nation,

ATTRIBUTES

usually involving the supernatural and serving to explain some natural

EXAMPLE

phenomenon. The story of Persephone is a clear example: it was common

to the peoples of classical antiquity, and its account of how Persephone

(daughter of Demeter, goddess of grain) was carried off to the Under-

world by Hades but was allowed to return and visit her mother for half

of each year, supplied an explanation of the alternation of the seasons.

COMMENT

The explanatory purpose of many myths is now obscure, for a myth often

continues to live as a tale in its own right after its explanation has been

supplanted.

CONTRAST

It must be emphasized that a myth is not a specific literary work, but

a floating tale. Myths are often given literary treatment (as in Aeschylus'

Prometheus Bound and *Oresteia*), but the myth is the raw material for

these plays, not the plays themselves.

† Lillian H. Hornstein and G. D. Percy (New York: The Dryden Press, 1956), pp. 309-10.

4. Extended definition using classification of meanings ("Foreword," *The Quest for Myth,** a book on the literary aspects of myth):

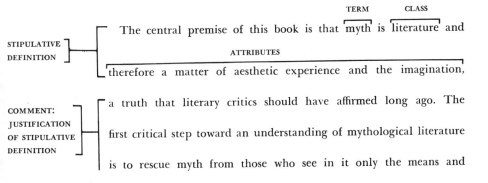

... misleading ideas about myth are abroad. The *psychoanalysts* tell

us that a myth is a collocation of sex symbols and is little different

TERM · CLASS · DIFFERENTIA

from a dream. The *semanticists* take myth to be a kind of curious

EQUIVALENT TERM · TERM

intellectual puzzle involving the shuffling about of signs and symbols

DIFFERENTIAE · CLASS · DIFFERENTIA

—an activity alleged to occupy both the waking and sleeping hours

ATTRIBUTES

of "primitive men." The *apologists of religion* reduce myth to dogma

TERM · CLASS

or a system of rationalized belief which they tell us must be es-

SYNONYM · DIFFERENTIA

tablished before we can hope to create a new poetry and a new

culture.

CLASSIFICATION OF MEANINGS

The central premise of this book is that myth is literature and

TERM · CLASS

therefore a matter of aesthetic experience and the imagination,

ATTRIBUTES

STIPULATIVE DEFINITION

a truth that literary critics should have affirmed long ago. The first critical step toward an understanding of mythological literature is to rescue myth from those who see in it only the means and

COMMENT: JUSTIFICATION OF STIPULATIVE DEFINITION

* Richard Chase (Baton Rouge: Louisiana State University Press, 1949), p. vi.

ends of philosophy, religious dogma, psychoanalysis, or semantics. It is my hope that the present study takes this step.

5. Extended definition using analysis ("The Possible Nature of a 'Mythology' to Come" in *Myth and Mythmaking*,* an essay on the psychology of myth; numbers and italics are as given in the original):

The following definitions are arranged according to aspects, under each of which one or more kinds, or classes, of myths may be distinguished.

DEFINITION

TERM

1. *Formal, descriptive definition. A* myth *manifestly consists of*

DIFFERENTIA (1)   DIFFERENTIA (2)

the essential features of an important, *more or less natural/preter-*

DIFFERENTIA (3)

natural situation or event *(that has a basic thema)* *in which at*

DIFFERENTIA (4)

least one extraordinary, more or less natural/preternatural psychic

DIFFERENTIA (5)

entity is involved—all this as sensibly represented in one channel

or another. Let us consider this definition part by part.

COMMENT BY ASPECTS OR PARTS OF THE DEFINITION

SYNONYM   SUPPLEMENTARY SYNONYMS

1.1 *an* event *(series of actions or interactions)* *sensibly represented*

DIFFERENTIA

in one channel or another, that is, a myth is *not* an actual occurrence,

CONTRAST

but an occurrence (more or less actual/imaginary) represented in

HISTORY

sensory terms, not in conceptual, theoretical terms. The early Greek

* Henry A. Murray (New York: George Braziller, Inc., 1960), p. 319.

(TO END OF PARAGRAPH)   AUTHORITY

mythos meant "the thing spoken" or uttered by the mouth (Spence),

including "the thing spoken during a religious ceremony." Since these

were magical words identical with their meanings, one could say that

mythos referred to *both* the actual *words* which represented the

SYNONYM

preternatural (imagined) event enacted by the mute performers of

SYNONYM

the rite, *and* the preternatural (imagined) *event* represented by the

words. The preternatural event consisted chiefly of the imagined

SYNONYM

actions of one or more gods, the audible imitation (description) of

SYNONYM

which by means of words and the visible imitation (enaction) of

which by means of muscles was felt to be unquestionably efficacious.

From these sacred tales and rituals, in imitation of the imagined

actions of *superhuman* beings, evolved the written and then audibly

spoken and visibly enacted secular tragedies of the Greek theater

in imitation of the imagined actions of *human* beings. The term

Aristotle gave to the events or series of actions represented by the

SYNONYM

masked actors of the drama was *mythos* (translated "plot").

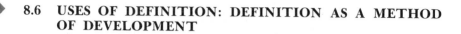

8.6 USES OF DEFINITION: DEFINITION AS A METHOD OF DEVELOPMENT

A definition can be given in a single phrase or extended to the length of an entire essay or book. In general, the writer includes definition for "key terms"—that is, terms that are important to the success of a paragraph, subdivision or essay. Since "key terms" are often introduced at the beginning of an essay, definition is a common feature of the "background material" presented in the introduction. For the same reason, paragraphs acting as introductions to subdivisions of an essay often include definitions.

Essays of extended definition are quite common. Any encyclopedia or "handbook of terms" will provide examples. Cardinal Newman's *The Idea of a University* is a book-length definition of what a university ought to be; and Charles Lamb's essay "Poor Relations" uses extended definition as the basis for an informal, humorous essay.* As a brief example of extended definition, consider the following passage from a lecture by William James on pragmatism.

"WHAT PRAGMATISM MEANS"

Some years ago, being with a camping party in the mountains, I returned from a solitary ramble to find every one engaged in a ferocious metaphysical dispute. The *corpus* of the dispute was a squirrel—a live squirrel supposed to be clinging to one side of a tree-trunk; while over against the tree's opposite side a human being was imagined to stand. This human witness tries to get sight of the squirrel by moving rapidly around the tree, but no matter how fast he goes, the squirrel moves as fast in the opposite direction, and always keeps the tree between himself and the man, so that never a glimpse of him is caught. The resultant metaphysical problem now is this: *Does the man go round the squirrel or not?* He goes round the tree, sure enough, and the squirrel is on the tree; but does he go round the squirrel? In the unlimited leisure of the wilderness, discussion had been

---

* See Exercises, III A and III B of this chapter.

194

worn threadbare. Every one had taken sides, and was obstinate; and the numbers on both sides were even. Each side, when I appeared therefore appealed to me to make it a majority. Mindful of the scholastic adage that whenever you meet a contradiction you must make a distinction, I immediately sought and found one, as follows: "Which party is right," I said, "depends on what you *practically mean* by 'going round' the squirrel. If you mean passing from the north of him to the east, then to the south, then to the west, and then to the north of him again, obviously the man does go round him, for he occupies these successive positions. But if on the contrary you mean being first in front of him, then on the right of him, then behind him, then on his left, and finally in front again, it is quite as obvious that the man fails to go round him, for by the compensating movements the squirrel makes, he keeps his belly turned towards the man all the time, and his back turned away. Make the distinction, and there is no occasion for any farther dispute. You are both right and both wrong according as you conceive the verb 'to go round' in one practical fashion or the other."

Although one or two of the hotter disputants called my speech a shuffling evasion, saying they wanted no quibbling or scholastic hair-splitting, but meant just plain honest English 'round,' the majority seemed to think that the distinction had assuaged the dispute.

I tell this trivial anecdote because it is a peculiarly simple example of what I wish now to speak of as *the pragmatic method*. The pragmatic method is primarily a method of settling metaphysical disputes that otherwise might be interminable. Is the world one or many?—fated or free?—material or spiritual?—here are notions either of which may or may not hold good of the world; and disputes over such notions are unending. The pragmatic method in such cases is to try to interpret each notion by tracing its respective practical consequences. What difference would it practically make to any one if this notion rather than that notion were true? If no practical difference whatever can be traced, then the alternatives mean practically the same thing, and all dispute is idle. Whenever a dispute is serious, we ought to be able to show some practical difference that must follow from one side or the other's being right.

—WILLIAM JAMES*

* From *Pragmatism, A New Name for Some Old Ways of Thinking* . . . (New York: Longmans, Green and Co., 1943), pp. 43-6. "The lectures that follow were delivered at the Lowell Institute in Boston in November and December, 1906, and in January, 1907, at Columbia University, in New York. They are printed as delivered. . . ." Author's Preface.

8.7 DICTIONARIES

Dictionaries are useful sources for basic definitions. They are authoritative but they are not final authorities, and this fact should always be kept in mind by the writer. Dictionary definitions are necessarily brief. They may be superficial or they may be irrelevant to the matter at hand. The situation is further complicated by the fact that many popularly sold dictionaries are sloppy and inaccurate or are unrevised (or lightly revised) reprints of nineteenth-century dictionaries.

The better dictionaries are either **unabridged** or **abridged**. Unabridged dictionaries are more comprehensive but both bulky and prohibitively expensive. When he needs to refer to an unabridged dictionary, the writer usually visits the library. Abridged dictionaries are convenient and inexpensive. Every writer should have a good abridged dictionary of his own, should study it so that he knows its special features, and should make a habit of using it. The following dictionaries are recommended.

Unabridged:

The Oxford English Dictionary. 12 volumes and Supplement. Oxford: The Clarendon Press, 1933.

Webster's New International Dictionary. Third Edition. Springfield, Mass.: G. & C. Merriam Co., 1961. [Note: Some authorities still prefer the second edition.]

New Standard Dictionary. New York: Funk & Wagnalls Company, 1952.

Abridged:

The American College Dictionary. New York: Random House, Inc., 1958.

The New College Standard Dictionary. New York: Funk & Wagnalls Company, 1950.

Thorndike-Barnhart Comprehensive Desk Dictionary. New York: Doubleday & Company, Inc., 1957.

Webster's New Collegiate Dictionary. Seventh Edition. Springfield, Mass.: G. & C. Merriam Co., 1961.

Webster's New World Dictionary. Cleveland: The World Publishing Company, 1964.

The Winston Dictionary. College Edition. New York: Holt, Rinehart and Winston, Inc., 1963.

TERMS TO BE LEARNED

▶ Formal definition
▶ Term
▶ Class (or genus)
▶ *Differentia*
▶ Precision
▶ Relevance
▶ Five aids to definition
▶ Classification of meaning
▶ Analysis of meaning

Exercises & Theme Topics

I. Select one of the following words. Write out the definitions given in four standard abridged dictionaries. For the *first meaning* listed in each dictionary, identify term, class, *differentiae* and any "aids to definition" used. Then comment on the differences between the definitions. Are all equally precise? Are all equally relevant? Is there any reason for preferring one dictionary to another?

order, class, category, word, idea, symbol, need, prestige, current, epoch, foundation, political, distinction, dependent, charity

II. Select two words that you did not look up from the list in exercise I and write your own definition. After writing the definition, compare it with the definition given in a good abridged dictionary and comment.

III. Comment on the techniques of definition used in the following selections.

A.

A poor relation—is the most irrelevant thing in nature,—a piece of impertinent correspondency,—an odious approximation,—a haunting conscience,—a preposterous shadow, lengthening in the noontide of your prosperity,—an unwelcome remembrancer,—a perpetually recurring mortification,—a drain on your purse,—a more intolerable dun upon your pride,— a drawback upon success,—a rebuke to your rising,—a stain in your blood, —a blot on your scutcheon,—a rent in your garment,—a death's head at your banquet,—Agathocles' pot,—a Mordecai in your gate,—a Lazarus at your door,—a lion in your path,—a frog in your chamber,—a fly in your ointment, —a mote in your eye,—a triumph to your enemy, an apology to your friends, —the one thing not needful,—the hail in harvest,—the ounce of sour in a pound of sweet.

—CHARLES LAMB*

B.

A University is a place of concourse, whither students come from every quarter for every kind of knowledge. You cannot have the best of every kind everywhere; you must go to some great city or emporium for it. There you have all the choicest productions of nature and art all together, which you find each in its own separate place elsewhere. All the riches of the land, and of the earth, are carried up thither; there are the best markets, and there the best workmen. It is the center of trade, the supreme court of fashion, the umpire of rival talents, and the standard of things rare and precious. It is the place for seeing galleries of first-rate pictures, and for hearing wonderful voices and performers of transcendent skill. It is the place for great preachers, great orators, great nobles, great statesmen. In the nature of things, greatness and unity go together; excellence implies a center. And such, for the third or fourth time, is a University; I hope I do not weary out the reader by repeating it. It is the place to which a thousand schools make contributions; in which the intellect may safely range and speculate, sure to find its equal in some antagonist activity, and

* From *Poor Relations* (1833).

its judge in the tribunal of truth. It is a place where inquiry is pushed forward, and discoveries verified and perfected, and rashness rendered innocuous, and error exposed, by the collision of mind with mind, and knowledge with knowledge. It is the place where the professor becomes eloquent, and is a missionary and a preacher, displaying his science in its most complete and most winning form, pouring it forth with the zeal of enthusiasm, and lighting up his own love of it in the breasts of his hearers. It is the place where the catechist makes good his ground as he goes, treading in the truth day by day into the ready memory, and wedging and tightening it into the expanding reason. It is a place which wins the admiration of the young by its celebrity, kindles the affections of the middle-aged by its beauty, and rivets the fidelity of the old by its associations. It is a seat of wisdom, a light of the world, a minister of the faith, an Alma Mater of the rising generation . . .

—JOHN HENRY NEWMAN*

C.   *"MEDICAL AND DENTAL EXPENSES"*

If you itemize deductions, you can deduct, within the limits described below, the amount you paid during the year (not compensated by hospital, health or accident insurance) for medical or dental expenses for yourself, your wife, or any dependent who received over half of his support from you whether or not the dependent had $600 or more income. List on the attachment the name and amount paid to each person or institution.

You can deduct amounts paid for the prevention, cure, correction, or treatment of a physical or mental defect or illness. If you pay someone for both nursing and domestic duties, you can deduct only the nursing cost.

You can deduct amounts paid for transportation primarily for and essential to medical care, but not for any other travel expense even if it benefits your health. Meals and lodging while you are away from home receiving medical treatment may not be treated as medical expense unless they are part of a hospital bill or are included in the cost of care in a similar institution.

Subject to the Limitations Set Forth Below, You CAN Deduct as Medical Expenses Payments To or For:

Physicians, dentists, nurses, and hospitals
Drugs or medicines

* From *The Idea of a University* (1852).

199

Transportation necessary to get medical care
Eyeglasses, artificial teeth, medical or surgical appliances, braces, etc.
X-ray examinations or treatment
Premiums on hospital or medical insurance

You CANNOT Deduct Payments For:

Funeral expenses and cemetery plot
Illegal operations or drugs
Travel ordered or suggested by your doctor for rest or change
Premiums on life insurance
Cosmetics

—INTERNAL REVENUE SERVICE*

D. "*BAROQUE MUSIC*"

The music of the period c. 1600-1750, following upon that of the Renaissance. It is also frequently referred to as the "thorough-bass period." The
term *baroque* (probably from Port. *barrocco*, a pearl of irregular form)
was used formerly, and still is today, in a decidedly depreciatory sense, as
meaning "grotesque," "in corrupt taste" [cf. Webster], "overladen with
scroll-work," etc. Its application to the Fine Arts was based on the opinon
(Jacob Burckhardt) that 17th-century style in architecture and paintings
was a debased Renaissance style. This opinion, however, was thoroughly
revised about 1900 by Heinrich Wolfflin, who was the first to point out the
positive contributions and the great artistic qualities of Baroque art, and
to vindicate the term Baroque from any implication of inferiority. More
recently, musical historians have followed suit and have adopted the term
alongside others such as Renaissance, Gothic, Rococo. In view of this situation, the resistance which the term "Baroque music" is still encountering in
some circles is hardly justified. If understood properly, this term has the
advantage of placing an important and well-defined period of music history
within the general frame of cultural development, and of avoiding the
emphasis on a special feature of somewhat secondary importance which is
implied in the term "thorough-bass period"—a term which, by the way, does
not properly include one of the most important branches of 17th-century
music, namely, that for organ and harpsichord.
Both the beginning and the end of the Baroque period in music are

* From *Federal Income Tax Forms for 1963, General Instructions* (U.S. Treasury
Department), p. 7.

rather clearly defined, much more so than those of most other periods, particularly the Renaissance. Baroque music starts about 1600 with the rise of monody, opera, oratorio, cantata, recitative, and closes 150 years later, with the death of Bach and Handel. Preparatory phenomena are, on the one hand, the ballettos and villanellas with their reaction against the Flemish polyphony, and on the other hand, the style of the Venetian School (G. Gabrieli), the pomp and splendor of which exceed the limitations of true Renaissance art and foreshadow the aesthetic basis of Baroque style. It may be noticed that throughout the 17th century, the tradition of Renaissance music persisted to some extent in the Roman School, and that on the other hand, a new period, the Rococo, had already begun when Bach and Handel were writing their greatest masterpieces, the true culmination points of Baroque music.

Generally speaking the Baroque period is an era of ecstasy and exuberance, of dynamic tensions and of sweeping gestures, an era of longing and of self-denial, much in contrast to the assuredness and self-reliance of the Renaissance. It is the period in which men liked to consider this life as the "vale of tears," in which the statues of the Saints look rapturously toward heaven, in which the clouds and the infinite landscape were discovered. Much of this attitude is reflected in the expressive melodies of the 17th century, in its long coloraturas, in its pathetic recitative, its frequent use of chromaticism, its capricious rhythms. Particularly the early Baroque music (prior to 1650) shows, in its canzonas and toccatas, striking traits of capriciousness, exuberance, and irregularity, while later composers such as Carissimi and Corelli brought about a trend towards greater restraint and regularity of style. On the other hand, the structural, or, as one might call it, the architectural element in Baroque music must not be overlooked. More than any other period, the 17th century has contributed toward the development and establishment of clearly defined types and forms, such as the ostinato-forms, the variations, the suite, the sonata, the da-capo aria, the rondo, the concerto, the opera, the oratorio, the cantata.

From the point of view of style, Baroque music is characterized chiefly by the thorough-bass technique, leading to a texture of two principal contours, melody and bass, with the intervening space being filled in by improvised harmony. In Germany, however, the contrasting style of true polyphony not only persisted but reached, in Bach, its very acme of perfection and greatness. A third principle of Baroque style is the stile concertante, that is, contrasting effects, a principle which expressed itself in the abrupt changes of the early canzona as well as in the col-tutti alternation of the concerto grosso and in the echo-effects of vocal and of organ music. Other basic conceptions of Baroque music are improvisation and ornamentation. Lastly, mention must be made of the final establishment of tonic and dominant as the principal chords of harmony and, about 1650 (Carissimi), of four-measure phrases.

At the beginning of the 17th century we find three great figures still rooted in the tradition of the Renaissance but inaugurating the novel trends of Baroque music, namely, Monteverdi, G. Gabrieli, and Sweelinck. They may be considered as the sources of three main streams running through Baroque music, that is, vocal, instrumental, and organ music, to which, in turn, the three styles mentioned above can be roughly coordinated, namely, accompanied melody, concerto style, and contrapuntal style.

The first of these streams, starting in Florence (Caccini, Peri, later Monteverdi), produces the monodic style with the recitative and aria, and with the composite forms of the cantata, opera, and oratorio (passion). The second, "Venetian," stream finds its realization in the instrumental canzona, the violin sonata, the trio-sonata in its two varieties, sonata da chiesa and sonata da camera, and in the orchestral forms of the concerto grosso, the French overture, and the sinfonia. The last stream, starting with Sweelinck and Frescobaldi, but continuing chiefly in Germany (Scheidt, Froberger, Buxtehude, Pachelbel, Kuhnau, Muffat, Fischer, Bach), leads to the fugue, organ chorale (choral prelude), toccata, and suite (the latter also in France).

—WILLI APEL*

E.   *"OF TRUTH"*

"What is truth?" said jesting Pilate, and would not stay for an answer. Certainly there be those that delight in giddiness and count it a bondage to fix a belief, affecting free will in thinking as well as in acting. And though the sects of philosophers of that kind be gone, yet there remain certain discoursing wits which are of the same veins, though there be not so much blood in them as was in those of the ancients. But it is not only the difficulty and labor which men take in finding out of truth, nor again that when it is found imposeth upon men's thoughts, that doth bring lies in favor; but a natural, though corrupt, love of the lie itself. One of the later school of the Grecians examineth the matter and is at a stand to think what should be in it, that men should love lies, where neither they make for pleasure as with poets, nor for advantage as with the merchant, but

---

* From *Harvard Dictionary of Music* (Cambridge: Harvard University Press, 1947), pp. 76-7. Reprinted by permission.

for the lie's sake. But I cannot tell: this same truth is a naked and open daylight, that doth not show the masks and mummeries and triumphs of the world, half so stately and daintily as candlelights. Truth may perhaps come to the price of a pearl, that showeth best by day; but it will not rise to the price of a diamond or carbuncle, that showeth best in varied lights.

A mixture of a lie doth ever add pleasure. Doth any man doubt that if there were taken out of men's minds vain opinions, flattering hopes, false valuations, imaginations as one would, and the like, but it would leave the minds of a number of men poor shrunken things, full of melancholy and indisposition, and unpleasing to themselves? One of the Fathers, in great severity, called poesy *vinum daebonum*, because it filleth the imagination and yet it is but with the shadow of a lie. But it is not the lie that passeth through the mind, but the lie that sinketh in and settleth in it, that doth the hurt, such as we spake of before.

But howsoever these things are thus in men's depraved judgments and affections, yet truth, which only doth judge itself, teacheth that the inquiry of truth, which is the love-making or wooing of it, the knowledge of truth, which is the presence of it, and the belief of truth, which is the enjoying of it, is the sovereign good of human nature. The first creature of God, in the works of the days, was the light of the sense; the last was the light of reason; and his sabbath work ever since is the illumination of his Spirit. First he breathed light upon the face of the matter of chaos; then he breathed light into the face of his chosen. The poet that beautified the sect that was otherwise inferior to the rest, saith yet excellently well: "It is a pleasure to stand upon the shore and to see ships tossed upon the sea; a pleasure to stand in the window of a castle and to see a battle and the adventures thereof below; but no pleasure is comparable to the standing upon the vantage ground of truth (a hill not to be commanded, and where the air is always clear and serene), and to see the errors and wanderings and mists and tempests in the vale below": so always that this prospect be with pity, and not with swelling or pride. Certainly, it is heaven upon earth to have a man's mind move in charity, rest in Providence, and turn upon the poles of truth.

To pass from theological and philosophical truth to the truth of civil business, it will be acknowledged even by those that practice it not that clear and round dealing is the honor of man's nature, and that mixture of falsehood is like alloy in coin of gold and silver, which may make the metal work the better, but it embaseth it. For these winding and crooked courses are the goings of the serpent, which goeth basely upon the belly and not upon the feet. There is no vice that doth so cover a man with shame as to be found false and perfidious. And therefore Montaigne saith prettily, when he inquired the reason why the word of the lie should be such a disgrace and such an odious charge. Saith he, "If it be well weighed to say that a man lieth is as much to say as that he is brave towards God and a coward towards men." For a lie faces God, and shrinks from man. Surely the wickedness or falsehood and breach of faith cannot possibly be so highly expressed as in that it shall be the last peal to call the judgments of God upon the generations of men: it being foretold that, when Christ cometh, "he shall not find faith upon the earth."

—SIR FRANCIS BACON*

IV. Write an extended definition (500-700 words) of one of the following or a similar term of your own choice.

beauty, thought, newspaper, nonsense, tragedy, comedy, The Law of Supply and Demand, bread, anxiety, order, fact, space

* From *Essays, or Counsels Civil and Moral* (1625).

Style (II)

9

In chapter 3 style was examined in terms of **tone, word choice** and certain basic types of **imagery.** The present chapter extends the discussion of style to **sentence structure.** Although the reader is not always conscious of the fact, sentence structure makes a significant contribution to the tone of the essay. It is a means of avoiding monotony, and it helps orient the reader toward the type of writing being employed—formal, informal, emotional, expository, etc. It is also a means of gaining coherence, creating emphasis and indicating shades of difference. Because beginners are not used to considering sentence structure as an aspect of writing that can be controlled easily, they usually disregard it. In practice this means that most student essays are written in the informal style of the popular magazine articles. Yet ability to control sentence structure is a shortcut to increasing the author's range of style and improving his use of any one style.

9.1 SENTENCE TYPES

To talk about sentence structure objectively, it is necessary to distinguish between types of structure. This is done on the basis of four grammatical components of the sentence: subject, verb, object and modifier, abbreviated S, V, O and M. A clause is indicated by the subscript "c," as M_c, and a phrase by subscript "p," as M_p.

Traditional grammar recognizes three basic sentence types: simple, compound and complex.

1. **A simple sentence** consists of one main clause. "John runs" and "John and Fred went to the store" are both simple sentences. The first has the structure SV; the second, the structure $S_1S_2VM_p$.

2. **A compound sentence** consists of two or more main clauses joined by a coordinating conjunction, a semicolon or a comma. "John runs, and Mary dances" is a compound sentence, as is "There are three factors influencing the efficiency of a jet engine, and each of these influences the other two." The first has the structure SV, SV; the second, $VMSM_p$, SM_pVMO.

3. **A complex sentence** consists of one main clause and one or more subordinate clauses. "John runs when he is late for school" is a complex sentence with the structure SVM_c. "The man who took the money ought to know where it is hidden" has the structure SM_cVO_c.

4. A **compound-complex sentence** is, as the label indicates, a sentence with two or more main clauses and one or more subordinate clauses. "The man who took the money ought to know where it is, and he should return it immediately" has the structure SM_cVO_c, SVOM.

Control of sentence types is important for emphasis and tone. When used following a series of complex sentences, for example, a simple sentence "stands out." It *emphasizes* the point it makes. In the same way, a short sentence followed by several long sentences is emphatic.

Coordination is a way of indicating that two or more ideas are of equal value. In relation to sentence structure it refers to two or more main clauses joined by a coordinating conjunction, semicolon or equivalent punctuation. **Subordination** indicates that one idea is less important than, or contingent upon, another. In relation to sentence structure it refers to use of a main clause together with one or more subordinate clauses in which the less important or contingent ideas are expressed. Use of coordination for two ideas, one of which is logically subordinate to the other, is **faulty coordination.** Likewise a sentence in which the main clause is less important than the subordinate clause exhibits **faulty subordination.**

A. *Faulty*: It is a well-known fact that landing is the most dangerous part of flying.

 Better: Landing is the most dangerous part of flying.

B. *Faulty*: I finished work at five o'clock, and I went to the movies.

 Better: When I finished work at five o'clock, I went to the movies.

 Best: At five o'clock, when I finished work, I went to the movies.

C. *Faulty*: It was the Indian trader who pioneered the way for civilization. He was opposed by the storekeeper and the farmer, but still he was successful.

 Better: In spite of opposition from the storekeeper and the farmer, the Indian trader pioneered the way for civilization.

Sentence structure also contributes to the **tone** of the essay. A great many brief, simple sentences make the essay seem naïve—it begins to sound like writing produced by (or for) young children. In a child's textbook or a fairy tale, constant use of simple sentences can be very effective, but in most situations they lead the reader to question the maturity of the writer.

Consistent use of compound sentences is often a feature of impressionistic writing and description, suggesting the relaxed, somewhat undisciplined flow of thoughts and images in the mind. It is less frequent in exposition and argumentation, types of writing in which logical relations, qualification and subordination are usually necessary for clarity. In these situations, complex sentences are frequent, and the more formal the writing, the more frequent they are likely to be. Writing that deals with theoretical matters has perhaps the largest proportion of complex sentences. On the other hand, complexity is not desirable for its own sake, and complex sentences can become a bad habit. When they are too frequent or too involved, they make the writing opaque, a form of jargon.

Writing tends to fall into three categories parallel to the categories of **usage.** Colloquial and informal writing—fiction, narration, newspaper reporting and popular articles—is generally simpler than formal writing. Sentences are short, and simple and compound sentences predominate. In formal and technical writing, sentences are longer and the proportion of compound and complex sentences is much larger.

The following passage is informal and intended to entertain as well as to convey information. Note the alternation of short, simple sentences with longer compound and complex sentences. Identify each sentence by type. Which type predominates? What is the function of the extremely short sentences? What is the function of the complex sentences? Comment on the contribution of sentence structure to the effectiveness of the passage.

Italians are pleased and perplexed. Every year since the end of the war they have seen the number of foreign visitors to their country increase at an incredibly rapid rate. The phenomenon has now reached unprecedented, practically inexplicable, and almost alarming proportions. In the 1950's the tourists numbered eight, ten, twelve million yearly. A little later, only yesterday, they were fifteen, seventeen, nineteen million. They have now passed the twenty million mark, a proportion of more than one tourist to every two and a half Italians, and the total is still growing. It appears that, if circumstances remain favorable, the travelers will reach thirty million within a decade, and will eventually match and even surpass the number of native inhabitants in the peninsula. Nothing daunts foreigners. Nothing frightens them. Nothing stops them. They arrive in a steady stream, by all forms of transport and even on foot, by day and night, from the sea or via the Alps. What is but a small trickle in the winter months grows in the spring to the size of a stream, and, in April, May, and June, turns into a monsoon flood, breaking all dikes, covering everything in sight. It begins to recede in September. It never completely dries up.

—Luigi Barzini*

9.2 SENTENCE ORDER

Sentences can be classified according to the order of their components. In general, the writer uses the order that gives his ideas the proper emphasis. Since the points of emphasis in a sentence are the beginning and the end, these positions are particularly important in a consideration of possible arrangements.

1. **Standard** sentence order in English is Subject-Verb-Object (SVO); or, if the verb is intransitive, Subject-Verb (SV). In **standard** order modifiers are usually placed before the word modified: MSV; SMV; SVMO. Phrases and clauses usually *follow* the word modified: SM_cV; SVM_c; $SVOM_c$.

2. **Inversion** occurs when standard order is modified for emphasis. Typical inversions include SOV, OVS, VSO.

    Standard: He ran fast. (SVM)
    Inverted: Why did he run fast? (V_1SV_2M)

    Standard: He went to bed after he finished dinner. ($SVMM_c$)
    Inverted: After he finished dinner, he went to bed. (M_cSVM)

    Standard: Nothing is in the box. (SVM)
    Inverted: There is nothing in the box. (VSM)

    Standard: He always gets what he wants. ($SMVO_c$)
    Inverted: What he wants he always gets. (O_cSMV)

* From *The Italians* (New York: Atheneum, 1964), p. 1.

209

3. **Interruption** (abbreviated I) occurs when the normal progression of the sentence is interrupted by a parenthetical expression or a long modifier. Typical interruptions are SIVO and SVIO.

    Standard: John called a taxi when he learned the plane was on time. (SVOM$_c$)

    Interrupted: John—when he knew the plane was on time—called a taxi. (SIVO)

    Standard: Poison is kept in a locked cabinet according to hospital regulations. (SVM$_1$M$_2$)

    Interrupted: Poison is kept (according to hospital regulations) in a locked cabinet. (SVIM)

4. **A loose sentence** is a sentence that ends with one or more elements—usually modifiers—not essential to completion of the meaning of the main clause. The longer the end elements, the **looser** the structure. Most English sentences show some degree of looseness.

5. **A periodic sentence** is one in which the meaning of the main clause is not completed until the end of the sentence. To have marked periodicity, a sentence must be fairly long. Inversion and interruption are commonly used to delay completion of the sense of the main clause.

    Standard: Movies are enjoyable.
                   Movies are enjoyable most of the time.

    Loose: Movies are enjoyable most of the time, though seldom very tragic or very funny.

                   The movie is the diversion of slaves, the pastime of illiterate wretches harried by wants and worries, the astutely poisoned pablum of a multitude condemned by the forces of Moloch to this vile degradation.

                                                           —GEORGES DUHAMEL

    Periodic: Next—admittedly superficial but still a pleasant form of relaxation—come Westerns. If asked to name the greatest movie cowboy of them all, the man who epitomizes both the toughness and the curious gentleness of the men who tamed the West, the

man who could always outdraw and outfight the meanest gunslinger but would never shoot him in the back or take advantage
of the most tarnished dancehall queen, the average moviegoer
will unhesitatingly name Gary Cooper.

When in the Course of human events it becomes necessary for
one people to dissolve the political bands which have connected
them with another, and to assume among the powers of the
earth, the separate and equal station to which the Laws of
Nature and of Nature's God entitle them, a decent respect to
the opinions of mankind requires that they should declare the
causes which impel them to the separation.

—Declaration of Independence

9.3   VARIETY; SUSTAINED USES

Knowledge of sentence structure helps the writer to achieve a lively
and pleasing **variety**. Variation of sentence types and sentence order
can do much to sustain reader interest and avoid the impression of
monotony.

More specific effects are possible when sentence structure is used
functionally in sustained passages. A markedly **loose** style suggests
informality and immediacy. Aside from idiomatic uses as in questions,
inversion and **interruption** are more formal. They call attention to
themselves and therefore suggest a greater degree of conscious control—
of artifice—than loose structure. They can be used occasionally for special
effects, particularly emphasis; or they can be used regularly. In the latter
case they are usually used in conjunction with *periodic* style. Sustained
periodic style, although the exception rather than the rule in English,
allows for ornate elaboration and powerful emphasis. For this reason
it is used most frequently in ceremonial and consciously artistic writing.

Consider the following examples.

1.   Generally **loose** structure:

All week long, red-eyed citizens wandered through their streets, looking
for friends or loved ones, comparing experiences, recounting tales of tragedy

211

and heroism. Soldiers with bayonets patrolled streets, or baby-sat with be-grimed children who had to be wheedled out of tears with jokes and C rations. Families fortunate enough to have heat, water or electricity opened their doors to the homeless. In the streets of the towns, volunteer workers joined military personnel in the unending job of picking up the pieces. In Seward a 30-ton fishing boat lay incongruously in a patch of woods several hundred yards from the shore. In the dockside railroad yard, a big switching engine rested on its side 200 ft. from the tracks.

*—Time**

2. More **formal; interruption** especially prominent:

The starfish (does anyone among us remember this?) wraps its arms around the oyster, clamping on with its suckerlike feet, and proceeds, not to kill it quickly which it can't do, but to exhaust it, hour after hour. In that horrible embrace, more silent than that of locked couples drowned in the moment of love, a foredoomed struggle between two muscular structures goes on to the limit of strength, without pause and with hardly a motion visible. But then there is no referee, no other creature of the sea is watching, nobody cares but the oysterman and he isn't there; he could know about it only at low tide anyway. The oyster is alone with its agony and the long hopeless fight that it must engage in, for that is its nature, exactly as if it had a chance; in some circles this is called a moral preroga-tive. It can't even know what the incubus is but only that it doesn't shift, all it does is pull, with a single unrelenting force on the two halves of the shell. For a long time, resisting hunger and dehydration and the lack of oxygen, the captive keeps its valves shut, but at last weakness sets in. Al-ready dying, it still resists, until suddenly the muscles are limp. The shell gapes a little. The starfish has placed itself in the right position for this moment, with its mouth, which is on the inside of its central disk, against one end of the oyster. It sticks its stomach out through its mouth into the opening; suction and digestion do the rest.

—Eleanor Clark†

3. Generally **periodic** structure:

Everything which another man would have hidden, everything the publi-cation of which would have made another man hang himself, was matter

* April 10, 1964, p. 23.
† From *The Oysters of Locmariaquer* (New York: Pantheon, 1964), pp. 98-100.

of gay and clamorous exultation to his James Boswell's weak and diseased mind. What silly things he said, what bitter retorts he provoked, how at one place he was troubled with evil presentments which came to nothing, how at another place, on waking from a drunken doze, he read the prayer-book and took a hair of the dog that had bitten him, how he went to see men hanged and came away maudlin, how he added five hundred pounds to the fortune of one of his babies because she was not scared at Johnson's ugly face, how he was frightened out of his wits at sea, and how the sailors quieted him as they would have quieted a child, how tipsy he was at Lady Cork's one evening and how much his merriment annoyed the ladies, how impertinent he was to the Duchess of Argyll and with what stately contempt she put down his impertinence, how Colonel Macleod sneered to his face at his impudent obtrusiveness, how his father and the very wife of his bosom laughed and fretted at his fooleries; all these things he proclaimed to all the world, as if they had been subjects for pride and ostentatious rejoicing. All the caprices of his temper, all the illusions of his vanity, all his hypochondriac whimsies, all his castles in the air, he displayed with a cool self-complacency, a perfect unconsciousness that he was making a fool of himself, to which it is impossible to find a parallel in the whole history of mankind. He has used many people ill; but assuredly he has used nobody so ill as himself.

—THOMAS BABINGTON MACAULAY*

9.4 PARALLELISM

Parallelism is the repetition of like grammatical structures for the sake of coherence or emphasis. It can be used within the sentence, between sentences and in larger units of the essay. Parallelism is often reinforced by **repetition** of key words or phrases. When the parallel elements are similar in rhythm as well as structure, the result is **balance**. When the parallel elements contrast with one another, the result is **antithesis**. When several parallel elements are coordinate and arranged in order of descending or ascending importance (**climax**) the result is **gradation**.

* From "Samuel Johnson" (1831).

PRACTICAL RHETORIC

1. **Parallelism** of phrase and clause:

   I went to the store, found the salesman, and returned the radio. (SV_1M_1, V_2O_1, V_3O_2)

   The speaker told who he was and what he would discuss. (SVO_{c1}, O_{c2})

2. **Parallelism** between sentences:

   There are several reasons why Communist China should not be considered a great power. Her agriculture is insufficient to support her population. Her industrial production is still extremely low compared to countries like the United States, Germany, Russia and Japan. Her army, although large, lacks transport, and much of its heavy armor is obsolescent. Finally, her navy, which would be a key factor in an attack on Formosa, is almost nonexistent.

3. **Balance**:

   Honor and glory; aid and comfort; pride and prejudice; by hook or by crook; like father, like son

   Einstein pondered his equations, and Hitler pondered the philosophy of *Mein Kampf*.

   What other generals considered reckless, Lee considered sound strategy. What Northern soldiers considered beyond the limit of endurance, Lee's soldiers accepted as normal duty.

4. **Antithesis**:

   Only the brave deserve the fair.

   It is not what you do but how you do it that counts.

   Thus the Puritan was made up of two different men, the one all self-abasement, penitence, gratitude, passion; the other proud, calm, inflexible, sagacious. He prostrated himself in the dust before his Maker; but he set his foot on the neck of his king.

   —THOMAS BABINGTON MACAULAY

Democracy gives freedom to act with responsibility. It does not license irresponsible action.

5. **Gradation:**

Some are born great, some achieve greatness, and some have greatness thrust upon them.

—WILLIAM SHAKESPEARE

He willed his money to his children, his home to his wife, his manuscripts to his university, and his genius to the American people.

We hold these truths to be self-evident, that all men are created equal, that they are endowed by their Creator with certain unalienable Rights, that among these are Life, Liberty and the pursuit of Happiness.

—*Declaration of Independence*

9.5 USES OF PARALLELISM

Parallelism and its special forms are devices of **coherence** and **emphasis.** They show **connection** between coordinate ideas, and **contrast** between opposing ones. In expository writing they clarify the author's meaning, and in other types of writing they can be used as devices to intensify the reader's emotional response. As has been noted, parallelism is often reinforced by **repetition** of key words and phrases.

The passages quoted above (9.3) illustrate sustained uses of controlled sentence structure and contain significant instances of parallelism and repetition. Note, for example, that the first selection (pp. 211-2) falls neatly into two units of three parallel sentences each. In the second unit the parallelism is reinforced by **repetition** of prepositional phrases at the beginning of each sentence: "In the streets. . . . In Seward. . . . In the dockside railroad yard. . . ." The selection by Macaulay is particularly rich in examples of parallelism, balance, antithesis and gradation. Underline two or three and be prepared to comment on them.

215

9.6 PARALLELISM AS A DEVICE OF ORGANIZATION

Parallelism can be used between paragraphs as well as sentences. When two paragraphs of comparison have a parallel structure, the similarity of their content is emphasized. In paragraphs of contrast, parallelism is a way of bringing out differences.

Parallelism can also be used in larger units of the essay. Making subtopics parallel in structure is a way of insuring **unity**. In this connection, it is helpful to make sentences that introduce subtopics of an outline parallel in structure, and, where appropriate, to use similar methods of development. Even when it will be concealed in the written essay, parallelism in the outline helps the writer focus his thoughts and avoid digression. Notice the extensive use of parallelism in the following outline:

I. Darwin and Marx are both concerned with overproduction and evolution.
II. Both are concerned with overproduction.
    a. Darwin and overproduction.
       Examples.
    b. Marx and overproduction.
       Examples.
III. Both are concerned with evolution.
    a. Darwin and evolution.
       Examples.
    b. Marx and evolution.
       Examples.

TERMS TO BE LEARNED

▸ Simple, compound and complex sentences
▸ Standard order
▸ Inversion
▸ Interruption
▸ Loose sentence

▸ Periodic sentence
▸ Parallelism
▸ Balance
▸ Antithesis
▸ Gradation

Exercises & Theme Topics

I. Comment on the sentence structure of one or more of the following selections using the terms given above. How does the sentence structure affect the author's tone? How does it reflect his purpose?

A.

An avalanche of questions followed these discoveries. Are the properties of the gene explained by the properties of the DNA? How does DNA carry genetic information when no *chemical* difference can be detected between the DNA nucleotides of different species? When a cell makes new DNA, what preserves the genetic information? What could not be questioned was the dramatic fact that, at last, a fateful meeting had occurred between biology, chemistry and physics. All lines of demarcation were now erased. For DNA is a *chemical* compound carrying *biological* information somewhere within its *physical* structure.

—WILLIAM S. BECK*

B.

Thus the Puritan was made up of two different men, the one all self-abasement, penitence, gratitude, passion; the other proud, calm, inflexible, sagacious. He prostrated himself in the dust before his Maker; but he set his foot on the neck of his king. In his devotional retirement, he prayed with convulsions, and groans, and tears. He was half-maddened by glorious

* From "The Riddle of Life," in *Adventures of the Mind* (New York: Vintage Books, 1960), pp. 47-8.

217

or terrible illusions. He heard the lyres of angels or the tempting whispers of friends. He caught a gleam of the Beatific Vision, or woke screaming from dreams of everlasting fire. Like Vane, he thought himself intrusted with the sceptre of the millennial year. Like Fleetwood, he cried in the bitterness of his soul that God had hid his face from him. But when he took his seat in the council, or girt on his sword for war, these tempestuous workings of the soul had left no perceptible trace behind them. People who saw nothing of the godly but their uncouth visages, and heard nothing from them but their groans and their whining hymns, might laugh at them. But those had little reason to laugh who encountered them in the hall of debate or in the field of battle. These fanatics brought to civil and military affairs a coolness of judgment and an immutability of purpose which some writers have thought inconsistent with their religious zeal, but which were in fact the necessary effects of it. The intensity of their feelings on one subject made them tranquil on every other. One overpowering sentiment had subjected to itself pity and hatred, ambition and fear. Death had lost its terrors and pleasure its charms. They had their smiles and their tears, their raptures and their sorrows, but not for the things of this world. Enthusiasm had made them Stoics, had cleared their minds from every vulgar passion and prejudice, and raised them above the influence of danger and of corruption. It sometimes might lead them to pursue unwise ends, but never to choose unwise means. They went through the world, like Sir Artegal's iron man Talus with his flail, crushing and trampling down oppressors, mingling with human beings, but having neither part nor lot in human infirmities, insensible to fatigue, to pleasure, and to pain, not to be pierced by any weapon, not to be withstood by any barrier.

—Thomas Babington Macaulay*

C.

Why are you going to college? Not to enhance your parents' social position; not to get high marks; not to get the ultimate answers, which not even *we* can furnish. To use our own professional jargon, you come to college to get a liberal education. We must admit that we do not altogether know what a liberal education is, but we have some fairly good ideas on the subject. We do not entirely follow these ideas. None of us, for example, believes that there is a magic in piling up a certain number of hour-credits. Yet, sixty credits and you get your diploma. And that diploma is supposed to admit you to the company of educated men and women. Why not

* From "Milton" (1825).

fifty-five or sixty-five? We do not know. Indeed if you pressed us we should have to admit that some students are liberally educated with thirty credits while others will not belong to the educated company if they take sixty times sixty hours of credit. Do not measure your education by simple arithmetic.

Elect your courses with care. If you go to a college which requires that you juggle five courses at once, you will do well to find one easy berth and sleep in it; otherwise you cannot do justice to the other four. This is a secret practice acceptable and accepted by all. But in general easy courses should be avoided simply because they are easy and do not give you your father's money's worth.

Do not select your courses with an eye to a specific job or type of occupation. More of you will make this mistake than not, and it is one of the most serious you can make. In the first place, we know at least that a liberal education involves a balance and harmony of interests. Secondly, your interests and talents are by no means fully appreciated or explored when you come to us. You do not want to wake up in your senior year and wish that you had not missed many important and interesting things. Thousands of seniors do.

When you come to college you are intellectually very young and have not yet learned to proceed safely or efficiently under your own intellectual power. You are what your environment and your elders have made you. Your ideas are not your own. The first thing you must learn is to stand on your own ideas. This is why you should not take us and our ideas too seriously. Broaden your horizon so that as you become more and more able to take care of yourself you will move intelligently. Do considerable mental visiting in your first years in college. Try to encounter the major points of view represented on the faculty and among the students. Entertain them the more seriously the more they differ from your own. You may return to your own, but if you do it will be with greater tolerance and broader understanding.

—ROGER W. HOLMES*

D. "THE OLD CHARNEL TRAIL"

Spawn of Evil, by Paul I. Wellman, 350 pages, Doubleday, $5.95

Legend, song and the movies have portrayed the desperadoes of the U.S. frontier as Robin Hoods. This may have had some validity in the case

* From "What Every Freshman Should Know," *The American Mercury*, LI (November, 1940), 273-80.

of folk heroes like Jesse James and Billy the Kid, on whom the wide open plains imposed a certain gallantry. But in earlier days, when the West was still east of the Mississippi, the frontier spawned a group of brutal outlaws lauded in no song or story. They gouged out eyes, bit off noses, scalped, never robbed without murdering, casually shot women and children. They disposed of bodies by splitting them open, filling them with stones and dumping them in the river.

Exploring this neglected part of the U.S. frontier with the help of diaries and a somewhat pervervid dramatic style, Paul Wellman, a novelist and historian of the West, has produced a lively account of a criminal empire which "exerted an influence of bale and woe for a full generation and held all of interior America in a web of terror."

After the turbulence of the Revolutionary War, people swarmed into the Ohio and Mississippi River valleys. They found no land of their dreams but a forbidding forest. The favorite rendezvous of almost every crook in the region was a cave on the banks of the Ohio on the Kentucky-Illinois border. More than 50 feet wide and 140 feet deep, the cave provided all that a hardened criminal could ask for: prostitutes in one cranny, gambling in another; heaps of counterfeit coin; and an escape hatch in the rear. The cave, Wellman writes, was the "lair of the worst cutthroats, freebooters and gallows-birds this continent ever witnessed."

Micajah and Wiley Harpe killed for the fun of it; they rarely made a profit. Followed by a retinue of three prostitutes and some offspring of indeterminate parentage, they roamed Tennessee and Kentucky murdering anybody who seemed defenseless: old peddlers, itinerant fiddlers, children, slaves. Hospitality especially infuriated them. When a woman gave them lodging for a night, they tomahawked a fellow lodger because he was snoring too loudly. They slit the throat of the woman's baby while pretending to rock it; finally they knifed the woman.

Lumbering frontier justice eventually caught up with the Harpes. Wiley was hanged and Micajah was shot. While Micajah was dying, a man whose family had been wiped out by the Harpes slowly cut off his head with a knife. "You're a God-damned rough butcher," gurgled Micajah, "but cut on and be damned!"

Billy Potts owned a tavern in Ford's Ferry, Ky. Its floor was covered with bloodstains; outside, the grounds were filled with shallow graves. Travelers who stayed overnight could not depend on getting up again next morning. Billy's son, a chip off the old block, was caught robbing by two farmers, was forced to leave the state. Years later he returned with a hefty bankroll and a beard. He decided to surprise the folks by not letting on who he was. Not recognizing him, Daddy cheerfully sank a knife into his back, fleeced him, and went to bed boasting to his wife. Next morning he learned his victim's identity from other outlaws. At least, Potts had the grace to shut down the tavern.

John Murrell was educated, and thought big. The son of a prostitute, he was taught by Mama to rob her clients while she had them in bed. One day, Murrell robbed his mother and set out on his own. He became a slave snatcher. Pretending to be an Abolitionist, he talked slaves into running away with him, then sold them to another slaver. If the slave balked, Murrell killed him. At one point, Murrell spent a year in jail for horse stealing, where he was branded, whipped, and pilloried. He came out determined to take his revenge on the whole South by fomenting a slave revolt—and getting some loot for himself during the fracas. He boasted: "I'll have the pleasure and honor of knowing that by my management I have glutted the earth with more human gore, and destroyed more property, than any other robber who has ever lived in America or in the known world." The uprising was scheduled for July 4, 1835. But the slaves, as well as Murrell, talked too much. The plot was discovered, and Murrell went to prison for ten years. When he came out, he was so broken he became a harmless blacksmith.

*—Time**

E.

Tir'd with all these, for restful death I cry:
As, to behold desert a beggar born,
And needy nothing trimm'd in jollity,
And purest faith unhappily forsworn,
And gilded honour shamefully misplac'd,　　5
And maiden virtue rudely strumpeted,
And right perfection wrongfully disgrac'd,
And strength by limping sway disabled,
And art made tongue-tied by authority,
And folly, doctor-like, controlling skill,　　10
And simple truth miscall'd simplicity,
And captive good attending captain ill:
　　Tir'd with all these, from these would I be gone,
　　Save that, to die, I leave my love alone.

—WILLIAM SHAKESPEARE†

* April 10, 1964, pp. 108-9. Courtesy TIME; copyright Time Inc. 1964.
† From *Sonnets*, Sonnet 66 (1609).

221

F.   *SEBASTIAN*

I remember Sebastian as a boy, six years my senior, gloriously messing about with water-colours in the homely aura of a stately kerosene lamp whose pink silk shade seems painted by his own very wet brush, now that it glows in my memory. I see myself, a child of four or five, on tiptoe, straining and fidgeting, trying to get a better glimpse of the paintbox beyond my half-brother's moving elbow; sticky reds and blues, so well-licked and worn that the enamel gleams in their cavities. There is a slight clatter every time Sebastian mixes his colours on the inside of the tin lid, and the water in the glass before him is clouded with magic hues. His dark hair, closely cropped, renders a small birthmark visible above his rose-red diaphaneous ear,—I have clambered onto a chair by now—but he continues to pay no attention to me, until with a precarious lunge, I try to dab the bluest cake in the box, and then, with a shove of his shoulder he pushes me away, still not turning, still as silent and distant, as always in regard to me. I remember peering over the banisters and seeing him come up the stairs, after school, dressed in the black regulation uniform with that leather belt I secretly coveted, mounting slowly, slouchingly, lugging his piebald satchel behind him, patting the banisters and now and then pulling himself up over two or three steps at a time. My lips pursed, I squeeze out a white spittal which falls down and down, always missing Sebastian; and this I do not because I want to annoy him, but merely as a wistful and vain attempt to make him notice my existence. I have a vivid recollection, too, of his riding a bicycle with very low handle-bars along a sun-dappled path in the park of our countryplace, spinning on slowly, the pedals motionless, and I trotting behind, trotting a little faster as his sandled foot presses down the pedal; I am doing my best to keep pace with his tick-tick-sizzling back-wheel, but he heeds me not and soon leaves me hopelessly behind, very out of breath and still trotting.

Then later on, when he was sixteen and I ten, he would sometimes help me with my lessons, explaining things in such a rapid impatient way, that nothing ever came of his assistance and after a while he would pocket his pencil and stalk out of the room. At that period he was tall and sallow-complexioned with a dark shadow above his upper lip. His hair was now glossily parted, and he wrote verse in a black copybook which he kept locked up in his drawer.

I once discovered where he kept the key (in a chink of the wall near the white Dutch stove in his room) and I opened that drawer. There was the copybook; also the photograph of a sister of one of his schoolmates;

some gold coins; and a small muslin bag of violet sweets. The poems were written in English. We had had English lessons at home not long before my father's death, and although I never could learn to speak the language fluently, I read and wrote it with comparative ease. I dimly recollect the verse was very romantic, full of dark roses and stars and the call of the sea; but one detail stands out perfectly plain in my memory: the signature under each poem was a little black chess-knight drawn in ink.

—VLADIMIR NABOKOV*

II. Using the selections in exercise I find two examples each of standard order, inversion, interruption, loose sentence, periodic sentence, parallelism, balance and antithesis. After each, indicate the structure using S, V, O, M, I, and subscript c (clause).

III. Comment on the variety and effectiveness of sentence structure in the following student essay. Show by means of an outline the author's use of parallelism between sections as an organizational device. How could the essay be improved?

"CAMPUS LOYALTIES"

We all know someone so loyal that his only desire at every moment is to be punctual at his next appointment. This person represents only one example of a life filled with loyalties. Indeed a person's every action is controlled by loyalties—not only the ultimate loyalties to the state or to God, but also such everyday loyalties as to an accident victim or to punctuality. These loyalties come into conflict a hundred times a day, as when the punctual man has five minutes to drive across town but does not wish to violate traffic laws. In such cases the conflict is usually resolved easily. The more important loyalty wins.

College students, being in a transition stage between dependence and independence, between irresponsibility and responsibility, have more than their share of conflicting loyalties, and these conflicts affect their behavior.

* From THE REAL LIFE OF SEBASTIAN KNIGHT by Vladimir Nabokov. Copyright 1941, © 1959 by New Directions. Reprinted by permission of the publisher, New Directions.

On the outcome of the battle for ascendency among their loyalties may depend their success in college. Students can, in fact, be classified into two groups on the basis of their primary loyalty. For some students the primary loyalty is schoolwork; for others, schoolwork is second to extra-curricular loyalties.

Students in the first category have no gods but academic success. Whether their main objective is knowledge or a diploma, praise from teachers or the envy of their classmates, a reward from their parents or an attractive job offer after graduation, schoolwork comes first.

But book-loyal students are not all alike. They can be distinguished according to the power of this loyalty. Students who are at their desks almost constantly obviously place a high priority on schoolwork—the power of their loyalty to studying overcomes all obstacles. Whether their study habits are good or bad, they stick to their work despite all temptations. Movies are out, dates are out, bull sessions are out. These students have few friends, their mothers worry, their education for life will of course be incomplete. Their world is bounded by their dormitory room, the library, and the cafeteria (where they invariably eat and run). This group is small, but its importance cannot be overlooked, despite an apparent paradox: the poorest as well as the best students are in this group. The best chemists may come from it, and the Freshman washed out by Thanksgiving may come from it. If the strength of one's loyalty to an objective were the only requirement for achievement, there would be many more poorly-adjusted chemists today, but such is not the case.

Many students, on the other hand, are primarily loyal to their work but not in the same way as those previously discussed. School for them, in other words, has top priority at quiz time and at term paper time; but in between, other loyalties take precedence. The student is able to relax and enjoy himself every now and then. He may join a fraternity. He may read novels. He may play golf in the afternoon. Whatever he does for relaxation, he is in the majority. Although such students differ from students in the first group in that they allow many loyalties to enter their lives from time to time, they differ among themselves in the importance that they assign to these other loyalties. They range from the student who takes off an hour or two a week for TV to the one who spends just enough time on his work to make a "Gentleman's C." Many of the most intelligent students are also among the laziest, and they fall into this group.

In the second major category are the students whose other loyalties are always more powerful than loyalty to schoolwork. For them work is an inconvenience, and assignments are unreasonable impositions to be done only when they do not interfere with other, more important activities.

There are four non-academic loyalties, plus a fifth which is a sort of non-loyalty. All are found on the typical college campus, although fortunately they are not too numerous. The pure types, of course, exist only in theory. Some students have more than one non-academic loyalty, and those pursuing each loyalty do so to different degrees.

The Extra-curricker's main loyalties are best pursued at a large university where students have a good deal of autonomy. Given a sizeable student body and an indifferent or overburdened faculty advisor, a student can simultaneously join the band, run for campus office, chair a committee, and write for the campus newspaper. The Debate Club, student theatricals, the "Y," the Young Democrats, Young Republicans, and Youth Labor League, the Chess Club, the Choral Society, the yearbook, and the Campus Quarterly all claim their members (or victims), and the list could easily be made twice as long. In most cases the Extra-curricker's are not wasting their college days, and to a certain extent they serve their university. Their loyalties, however, will not lead to a diploma. Many is the student who has flunked out after a year or two of brilliant extracurricular successes.

Although most athletes compete for other reasons, the Athlete with a capital *A* gives sports his entire, undivided attention. For him, courses are what you do between games. The Athlete is likely to have a short half-life at most colleges and universities. If he somehow manages to survive, he will stick around for his diploma only so long as he keeps making the team. Usually, his goal after graduation is to enter professional athletics.

The Crusader is quite a different type but equally in demand on the college campus. There are countless causes which, in the minds of many students, deserve a greater loyalty than course work. Some Crusaders drop out; others flunk out: school can seem quite unimportant beside the Call of the Oppressed. And on the typical campus the Crusader has ideal material to work with. He is close to young, permeable minds; and he sees much work to be done.

Less glorious are the Good-time Charlies. Most colleges have a full supply of co-eds, countless bridge games, and a cluster of drive-ins, beer joints, and dance halls within easy walking (or driving) distance. Charlie makes good use of them. He spends his evenings with the boys, his week-ends beside a hot combo or at the beach, and his vacations—he leaves two days early—in New York or Nassau. He lives from week-end to week-end until the week-ends run out.

The final group of students with non-academic loyalties actually have no loyalties at all. School for them is secondary, but they do not know what is primary. They came to college merely because they graduated from high school and did not want to work, or because their parents and friends

225

expected them to go to college. College keeps them out of the army or the employment office but offers them no positive goal. Many a co-ed drops out when she finds a husband; many a shirker drops out when the going gets tough. School cannot be a substitute loyalty for something else or merely a way of passing time. Students who think it can are, in essence, Time-biders. When they find their real loyalty, they leave school.

These, then, are American college students and their various loyalties. Pure stereotypes are few and seldom found, but mixtures in various and varying proportions of Studiers, Extra-currickers, Athletes, Crusaders, Good-time Charlies, and Time-biders are numerous. A student's college life is necessarily a reflection of his loyalties.

IV. Write an informal paragraph on "movies," "cars," "books" or a similar topic. How many types of sentence structure have you used? Have you used any markedly loose or periodic sentences? After answering this question, rewrite your paragraph in a more formal style, emphasizing either looseness or periodicity.

V. Select a topic from the theme suggestions for chapters 7 or 8. Write an outline using parallelism between subtopics. When writing the essay from the outline, experiment with sentence structure. Try to use several types of structure functionally; that is, for variety, emphasis and (if appropriate) emotional appeal. You may, if you wish, use marked looseness or periodicity, but this is not necessary.

Introductions and Conclusions

In an introduction, the writer puts his best foot forward. He needs to make a favorable impression and to arouse interest. He must also explain his purpose and give enough background to allow the reader to follow the subsequent discussion. Although a narrative or an essay of description may not need a formal introduction, an expository or argumentative essay almost always does. The rule for conclusions is less strict. For a

227

short essay, a sentence or two is usually enough; a longer essay may require more, perhaps a paragraph or a separate section with several paragraphs.

10.1 INTRODUCTIONS

There are four parts of the standard introduction. Only one is essential; the others are optional. Moreover, with the exception of the **approach step** they can be given in any order that is clear and emphatic. The parts are: (1) **statement of purpose,** (2) **statement of method,** (3) **background,** (4) **approach step.** The **statement of purpose** is a version of the statement that begins the outline. The outline purpose statement may be used *verbatim,* but is usually revised to fit naturally into the context of the introduction. Frequently the revision is so extensive that, although the idea remains the same, the language of the two statements is completely different. The statement of purpose should be in a position of emphasis. In formal writing it is acceptable to call attention to purpose by introducing the statement with a phrase like "I will seek to show that . . ." or "The object of the present study is to. . . ." In less formal writing, this kind of directness usually seems stilted.

The **statement of method** (also called *division* or *partition*) tells the reader what the major subdivisions of the essay will be. It is included where clarity is particularly important, either because the subject is difficult or because the essay is so long that without it the reader may lose his way. The statement of method can be combined with the statement of purpose, but it is usually given separately. It can be informal, or it can be given in such a way that it calls attention to itself; as, for example, when the author writes, "To understand why federal aid to the arts is dangerous, we must consider how it would affect the creative process, the relation between the artist and his public and the economics of the art market." Formal statements of method, like formal statements of purpose, are likely to seem stilted in brief, relatively straightforward essays. Also they are usually unnecessary when the author uses chronological arrangement, or where the method is obvious without them.

Background includes all material that the author considers necessary to an understanding of his purpose and method. What he includes will

228

vary with his audience and subject. In general, the more specialized the essay, the more important the background material becomes. Among common types of background material are **definitions** of important terms, **history** of the subject or the author's experience with it, **explanation** of the significance of the subject or method, **qualification** and **limitation**. Background material is easy to supply, but it should be chosen with care. Most introductions need some background material. Too much, however, is just as bad as too little.

The **approach step** is nonessential but highly desirable in writing intended for the general public. It is a device to catch the reader's attention or arouse his interest. When used, it comes first in the introduction. It is usually only a sentence or two, but can be extended to the length of a paragraph. **Anecdotes** and **quotations** are favorite kinds of approach step. Striking facts, maxims, intriguing questions and paradoxes are also common. The chief problem in using an approach step is finding one that works. A striking fact that is not really striking, a joke that fails to amuse, an anecdote that bores or a quotation that is a platitude will do more harm than good.

10.2 ANNOTATED EXAMPLES

1. A student essay illustrating all four parts of the standard introduction:

APPROACH STEP

PURPOSE

BACKGROUND
(QUALIFICATION)

METHOD

Half a century ago the entire graduating class of Midstate University consisted of eighteen young men. This year, the graduating class will be over fifteen hundred, and one third will be women. Yet the University has gained more over the years than size and the presence of the female sex, no matter how impressive both of these gains may be. In the year 1964 there is a spirit of vitality and dedication abroad that is felt by almost every student. This does not mean that every student is absorbed in his work, that every class is an exciting discovery, or that every professor is inspiring. Far from it. There are students who are confused and poorly prepared, boring classes, and mediocre teachers. In spite of these facts, however, the spirit is there. It can be felt in class discussions and "bull sessions," in student attitudes toward assigned work, and in the plans that students have for their careers.

2. An expository article; semi-formal:

PURPOSE

METHOD

BACKGROUND
(QUALIFICATION)

BACKGROUND
(EXPLANATION)

The effects of modern knowledge upon our mental life have been many and various, and seem likely, in the future, to become even greater than they have been hitherto. The life of the mind is traditionally divided into three aspects: thinking, willing and feeling. There is no great scientific validity in this division, but it is convenient for purposes of discussion, and I shall, therefore, follow it. It is obvious that the primary effect of modern knowledge is on our thinking, but it has already had important effects in the sphere of will, and should have equally important effects in the sphere of feeling, though as yet these are very imperfectly developed. I will begin with the purely intellectual effects.

—BERTRAND RUSSELL*

3. Popular reporting:

BACKGROUND
(HISTORY)

PURPOSE

BACKGROUND
(EXPLANATION BY
BRIEF EXAMPLES
OF CHANGE)

It is almost 25 years since I decided that the snowy enchantment of northern winters was more agreeable to read about on a Florida beach than to take part in. Since then, except for the war years, I have made the annual journey back to my winter home in Key West with a regularity that some of my friends consider monotonous.

It has never seemed monotonous to me, for there is nothing static about the scenes to which I am returning. No state can grow from twenty-seventh to ninth in population in this brief time without such growth showing.

I have seen small towns like Orlando and St. Petersburg turning into big cities. Familiar pinewoods have given way to mile upon mile of tilled and planted fields. In the sky the flight of planes and missiles has become as commonplace as the slow soaring of buzzards and man-of-war birds used to be.

The Navy and Air Force, which swarmed into Florida during World War II, have remained and grown to such proportions that each year the Governor gives them a Military Appreciation Dinner. For them Florida is a year-round state. For more and more people the simple fact of air conditioning is making it so.

Florida ranks fifth in the Nation—after Texas, New York, Cali-

* From "The Expanding Mental Universe," in *Adventures of the Mind* (New York: Vintage Books, 1960), pp. 295-6.

fornia, and Illinois—in total number of dwellings with air conditioning. Indoor weather control has not only made homes livable through the hottest summer months, but has induced northern industries to move plants and even their headquarters here.

—BENEDICT THIELEN*

10.3 CONCLUSIONS

For brief essays and informal essays in general, an informal conclusion consisting of a few final remarks rounded off with an appropriate concluding sentence is usually adequate. If a formal introduction is necessary, it is set off from the developing section by paragraphing or more emphatic devices like spacing or subheadings. It can include one or all of the following parts: (1) **summary,** (2) **author's comment,** (3) **restatement.**

Summary is a form of listing. The conclusions reached, the steps examined or the points demonstrated are briefly recapitulated. In technical writing, the listing is often explicit: the items are introduced by a heading such as "Summary" or "Conclusions" and the items are numbered. This method is useful in writing that demands the utmost clarity. It is undesirable in most other cases.

Author's comment includes discussion of the conclusions reached, comment on their implications and deductions that follow from them. It is the least mechanical part of the conclusion and affords real opportunity for creative additions. After completing the development of the essay, the author can test the need for additional comment by placing himself in the position of his reader. Assuming that the reader is properly moved or informed by the development, are there any implications that he should know about? If, for example, the author has proved that "The Tory Party is losing strength in its former strongholds," he might conclude with discussion of the effect of this loss of strength on the next general election. Is it likely to put the Labour Party in power, and if so, what policy changes can be expected? Or he might discuss the effect

* From "Florida Rides a Space-age Boom," *The National Geographic*, Vol. 124 (December, 1963), 858.

of the loss of strength on leadership within the Tory Party. Will there be changes? Who will be affected and how? Will new leaders mean new policies? Used creatively, **author's comment** can be a stimulating and exciting part of the essay.

Restatement is a form of repetition. By restating his purpose directly or in different words the author reminds the reader of the original point and emphasizes it.

The **concluding sentence** is the last sentence of the essay. It is usually **author's comment,** but it can be a **restatement** or the last sentence of a **summary.** Concluding sentences should not leave the reader hanging in mid-air. They should round out the essay and should have the quality—often achieved by sentence rhythm—of finality.

10.4 ANNOTATED EXAMPLES

Understanding the why's and wherefore's of a good conclusion depends so much on familiarity with the essay being concluded that excerpts are of limited value as examples. For the sake of illustration, however, four examples are given below. The first is the conclusion of the student essay, the introduction of which was given on page 229. The second is the formal conclusion to a textbook chapter on evolution. The word *summary* is part of the original. The third and fourth examples are less formal and in them major emphasis is placed on **author's comment.** They are the conclusions to the essays by Russell and Thielen, the introductions of which are printed on pp. 230-1.

1. A student essay (cf. p. 229):

RESTATEMENT

SUMMARY

FINAL SENTENCE
AND AUTHOR'S
COMMENT

The new spirit at Midstate plays a vital and growing role in student life. Its influence can be felt all the way from the questions asked by a freshman during an orientation lecture on the honor code to the decision by a senior engineering students to enter the Peace Corps rather than taking a high-paying job in industry after graduation. Whether the new spirit is a passing fashion or something more permanent depends partly on the students and partly on the faculty and administration. If faculty members rise to the challenge by giving their best at all times, and if the administration

232

recognizes the need for increased emphasis on independent work, flexible course programs, and fewer arbitrary regulations, the new spirit will not only grow, it will help to make Midstate one of the great educational centers of the country.

2. A chapter from a textbook:

RESTATEMENT

    Summary.—The plants and animals which are on earth today have reached their present forms through a process of change, and many of them are very different from their ancestors which lived long ago. The general direction of these changes can be traced in the geologic record, and the picture which it presents is supported by other evidences.

SUMMARY

    The distinct peculiarities of the plants or animals of a region are proportional to the degree of isolation of the region, and this can be explained by the operation of a process of evolution in a population more or less separated from other populations. A single pattern of structure in some part of an organism is frequently found performing widely different functions under widely different conditions, and the plants or animals showing such a pattern are regarded as having descended from a common ancestral type. The improvements which have been produced by practical plant and animal breeding and the scientific analysis of observed hereditary changes prove that evolution is possible.

SUMMARY

    The principle of evolution has been recognized for many centuries and numerous explanations of its mechanism have been proposed. Most influential in shaping modern thought have been the theories of Lamarck, Darwin, and De Vries, which may be stated briefly as follows:

    Lamarck (1809) — The continuous use of any part of an organism gradually strengthens that part, and disuse weakens it. The changes thus produced in an individual are passed on to later generations, and the ultimate result is the evolution of a new kind of organism.

    Darwin (1859) — In any one generation of a species there are many more individuals than can live on the available resources. These individuals are not all exactly alike, and some are better fitted than others to live in any specific environment. This selective influence, operating for many generations, brings about evolution.

    De Vries (1901) — A clear distinction is to be made between inherited and non-inherited variations. Experiments indicate that new species may appear by abrupt mutations rather than by the gradual accumulation of small differences.

The modern view is a composite of the best of the earlier theories and the results of more recent studies. Changes produced in the body of an individual by environmental influences do not affect the reproductive tissues and are not inherited. Heritable changes occur in the reproductive cells, but their causes are unknown; they may be large or imperceptibly small, advantageous or detrimental. In CONCLUDING SEN- general, the organism having the best combination of characteristics TENCE (DERIVED for the environment in which it happens to be is most likely to FROM SUMMARY) survive and transmit its characteristics to following generations.

—PAUL WEATHERWAX*

3. An expository article; semi-formal (cf. p. 230):

AUTHOR'S COMMENT   The state of mind which I have been trying to describe is what I mean by wisdom, and it is undoubtedly more precious than rubies. The world needs this kind of wisdom as it has never needed it before. If mankind can acquire it, our new powers over nature offer a prospect of happiness and well-being such as men have never experienced and could scarcely even imagine. If mankind cannot, every increase in cleverness will bring us only nearer to irretrievable disaster. Men have done many good things and many bad ones. CONCLUDING SEN- Some of the good things have been very good. All those who care TENCE (DERIVED for these good things must hope, with what confidence they can FROM AUTHOR'S command, that in this moment of decision the wise choice will be COMMENT) made.

—BERTRAND RUSSELL†

4. Popular reporting (cf. pp. 230-1):

AUTHOR'S COM- When I finally started back down the Keys, six weeks of traveling MENT IN THE had made me forget how intensely blue and pale lime-green their FORM OF A FINAL waters can be. Nowhere else in Florida are they like this. Nowhere DESCRIPTION OF A else in the state can you take a boat, as I did from Key Largo, and FLORIDA SCENE

* From *Plant Biology* (Philadelphia: W. B. Saunders Co., 1942), pp. 371-2. Reprinted by permission.
† From "The Expanding Mental Universe," in *Adventures of the Mind* (New York: Vintage Books, 1960), pp. 305-6.

look down at a living coral reef, now protected as a state park. Like the cypresses of Corkscrew, its 75 square miles of waving sea fans and forests of coral have been saved. Until 1912, when Henry Flagler completed the extension of his Florida East Coast Railroad from the mainland to Key West, the Keys were isolated from the world. Twenty-three years later the Labor Day hurricane of 1935 destroyed Flagler's railroad. But its 40 bridges—one spanning seven miles of open water—remained. Now the Overseas Highway runs over them, and a few hours' drive will take you from the mainland to Key West.

A day after I returned, I climbed to the top of one of Key West's handsome old houses with a friend who was remodeling it. We stood on the white-railed *mirador*, from which the first owner of the house watched for the wrecked ships whose cargoes made him rich.

"Every time I come back I realize Key West really is different," my friend said.

It is. It is the only truly tropical city in the continental United States. It is the only one that rides like a ship a hundred miles out at sea.

I looked down on the town's chimneyless, silver-painted metal roofs. Beyond was the harbor, filled with the shrimp boats that, along with tourists and the Navy, are Key West's principal source of wealth. It was dusk and other vessels were returning: submarines and destroyers, and charter boats laden with some of the hundreds of species of fish that make Florida, especially the Keys, a fisherman's dream.

Long before there was a Miami there was a Key West. The residents prospered on salvaged cargo, fishing, sponging, and cigar making. In the 1830's it was judged the richest city per capita in the South. It no longer is, but its slender-columned old houses wear the dignity of age.

Somewhere below me, hidden in a dark-green sapodilla tree, a mockingbird was singing. As I listened to the extraordinary variety of his song, I remembered that this was the state bird of Florida. FINAL SENTENCE It seemed a good choice.

—BENEDICT THIELEN*

---

* From "Florida Rides a Space-age Boom," *The National Geographic*, Vol. 124 (December, 1963), 903.

TERMS TO BE LEARNED

▶ Four parts of the introduction: statement of purpose; statement of method; background; approach step

▶ Three parts of the conclusion: summary; author's comment; restatement

Exercises & Theme Topics

I. Comment on the following introductions and conclusions taken from student essays. Then select one introduction and one conclusion that you feel need improvement. Rewrite each.

A. *"CONFORMITY"*

Man today lives in a world of anxiety and fear. War has gone beyond the point of human comprehension as newer and deadlier weapons have been developed, and man has become frightened to live. In a state of anxiety such as exists in modern society, man feels helpless. And because man in the West thinks of himself as the master of all situations, he must escape this anxiety and uselessness.

In order to obtain peace of mind he has attempted to abolish the discussion and thought of such things. Man's method is conformity and his strict adherence to its principles has enabled the problems of the world to go unnoticed and unsolved.

This cult of conformity that man has developed has four principles which help man escape his anxiety: rationalization, denial, narcotism, and avoidance.

. . . .

But the cult does not recognize the truth of these critics, and regards them as embittered souls. The cult turns from criticism, their one hope of salvation, and in doing so they insure themselves of a future, but it is a future of denial of life and present realities in the hope that these realities will vanish if they are ignored. But the problems of society and civilization can not dissolve on their own. It will take active interest and creative thinking to vanquish them, and as long as man relies on the cult of conformity for security, these problems can never be resolved.

B.   *"MAN'S FEAR IN THE TWENTIETH CENTURY"*

Since the beginning of man fear has always been present. Up until the Twentieth Century, man did not seem to realize the potentiality of fear to subdue the human race to a state of nonexistence. Now man can comprehend the meaning of what it is to live in a state of fear and know what must be done if he is to be happy and thankful for the life he enjoys. Although man has brought most of the fear upon himself, he can still be the master of his soul. What are the causes that have put man into a state of fear of the challenge for existence? The answer is the fear of death: ". . . the fear of death; not the normal fear of having to die which every human being experiences in the contemplation of death, but a horror of dying by which people can be possessed constantly." Man's dealing with the nuclear bombs, the powerful machines, namely the man-made automobile, plus careless cultivation and overpopulation of the land on which he lives have brought man to realize that his life is challenged and the fear of survival is the greatest hindrance to mankind.

The fear of death is possessed by all people and this fear has ruined the minds of many people. The three sub-types of fear are closely related to man's greatest fear—the fear of death.

.   .   .   .

Man realizes the cause for his fear and it is up to him to overcome the fear of death or let it haunt him for all his life. If peace could ever be assured and nuclear disarmament would occur, if man would try to take as many precautious means as he could when dealing with any type of machine, and if over-population could become decreased so the population could make the ends meet with the land from which they live, man's fear would soon dwindle down to a simple worry. But if man is not willing to accept life as he and his ancestors have made it, this fear will continue. "And what do we gain by a long life when it is full of hardships and starved of joys and so wretched that we can only welcome death as our deliverer?"

237

C.   *"KEEP GOING"*

Fortunately for Robert L. Ripley, handsomeness is not a criterion for successfulness. He is a big man with thinning hair and protruding teeth; however, he possesses a characteristic that is seldom seen in this world of pushbuttons and easy chair. This characteristic is his boundless energy.

His seemingly infinite supply of energy was apparent early in his life. Since he was very skillful in drawings and not so skillful in compositions, his high school teacher allowed him to submit an illustration in the place of each paper assigned. He drew illustrations for many of the classics which his class studied; and in doing so, he worked laboriously, studying each carefully and doing much research. This zest for accuracy and enthusiasm in his work remains with him today.

.   .   .   .

An ordinary day in the life of Robert Ripley does not leave much leisure time. In the morning he draws cartoons, often for many hours without interruption. Never does he eat a noon-time meal, and he spends the afternoon at home rearranging his estimated two million dollars worth of oddities and curios, such as shrunken heads, Buddhist shrines, and other rarities that he uses in his cartoons and on his radio programs. All day he is busy—as he has been all his life; and out of this never-idleness, he has come to believe that one who relaxes too much grows old. So it is with Robert L. Ripley. He may best be summed up by his own motto: "Keep going."

D.   *"DEGENERATION AND NATURAL SELECTION"*

Degeneration is a contributing factor toward natural selection. Degeneration is, according to the article by Henry Drummond, the regression of the human to a more primitive state of being. Drummond suggests that the individual man has the power to control his motion in life. A man's motion in life can be in one of three directions—balance, evolution, or degeneration. Drummond feels that the first of these three, balance, is hard to achieve as it calls for the person to neither progress nor regress either biologically or spiritually over a period of time. The second course open to man is evolution, which according to Charles Darwin and Henry Drummond is the process which changes man into a more adaptable, more complex, and more sophisticated being.

Drummond feels that degeneration is the natural course of nature, and it is the course demanding the least resistance and effort. Therefore the man who makes no personal effort either to evolve to a higher level of development or to maintain a consistent balance of nature must degenerate. Furthermore, it is suggested that if man permits himself to degenerate far enough he will perish. Drummond claims that dying is not an evolutionary form of nature but a degenerative form. That is, that man's existence is naturally directed toward death and not life.

. . . .

The theories of Darwin and Drummond in conjunction form an explanation for the system of evolution. The theories explain why man has advanced and changed forms from his jungle ancestors and why our world is made up of people of the same general characteristics. The fact is, that man is generally the same because those who are much different generally find life to be unadaptable to them and so by the theory of natural selection perish.

E.   *"STRUGGLES FOR EXISTENCE"*

The struggle for existence has been universal. There exists in each area of life—political, economical, social, or natural—constant opposition between oppressor and oppressed. The struggle for existence in one class is analogous with the struggle for existence in any other class. This can be proven by comparing the struggles of existence that are waged in any two areas of life, for example, the economic and natural.

In each of these two areas there is a system of subordinate gradation, in which the class at the bottom of the gradation is the oppressed, and it is the one trying to rise against the class at the top of the gradation or the oppressor. An examination of how each class of each organization achieved its position on its respective gradation scale will reveal similarities in struggles for existence in these different areas.

. . . .

From the examples given one can see that in both the economic and biological areas of life cases arise that present each with similar or identical problems. The examples also suggest that these problems are usually solved by each organization with similar defensive and offensive methods. This leads us to believe that the struggle for existence that goes on in any organization or class is also fought in all other classes, and the struggles run parallel courses.

II. Read three or four discussions of a current event, "personality in the news" or problem in three or four different sources: an AP report, editorial comment in your own newspaper and a national newspaper like *The New York Times,* a weekly news magazine like *Time* or *Newsweek,* etc. Then write a composite discussion emphasizing your own views. When writing your essay, pay special attention to your introduction and conclusion. Are they appropriate for your purpose and audience? Which standard parts do they include? Which do they omit? As an alternative to current events, you may prefer to read several reviews of the same movie, book or play, or several discussions of the same term or subject in sources like handbooks, textbooks and encyclopedias. If you take this approach, be sure to *limit* your essay and to comment on its limitations in your introduction.

Argumentation (II): Deduction

11

"**A**rgumentative" has the connotation of "contentious" or "aggressive"; but as used in rhetoric it simply means "written to prove a point." An editorial against "corruption in the city council" or "appeasement in current foreign policy" is argumentative; but so is a scientific article showing that "new evidence tends to confirm Wegener's theory of continental drift." Most argumentation falls between these two extremes.

Unless he majors in journalism or becomes a professional writer, the college graduate is more likely to be concerned with specialized and technical, rather than popular argumentation.

Argumentation by thesis and evidence has already been considered in chapters 5 and 6. The student should review these chapters to make sure that he understands clearly such terms as **proof, generalization, induction, thesis** and **evidence,** and their uses. The present chapter will concentrate on **logical** rather than **rhetorical** methods of proof, and **deduction** rather than **induction.**

11.1 INDUCTION AND DEDUCTION

Induction has already been defined as a method of proceeding from examination of particulars to general conclusions or hypotheses. This definition, although simplified, is sufficient for the needs of practical rhetoric. Deduction is the opposite of induction. **Deductive proof proceeds from general assertions to specific conclusions.** The two forms of deductive reasoning are the **syllogism** and the **enthymeme.** These forms occur constantly in conversation and writing, even when we are not conscious of using them. Because they are essential to valid argumentation, they must be considered in some detail.

11.2 SYLLOGISM

A syllogism is a logical form consisting of three parts, a major premise, a minor premise and a conclusion. Syllogisms are classified on the basis of the major premise. The most common kind is the **categorical syllogism.** In the major premise of a categorical syllogism something is unconditionally asserted or denied, as in the statements "all men are mortal" and "no cold-blooded animals are mammals." In the **conditional** (or **hypothetical**) **syllogism,** the major premise is a statement of conditions under which something is true. It can be reduced to the form

"If A, then B"; for example: "If an automobile engine burns more than a quart of oil between changes, it is inefficient." Notice that the statement can be reworded without losing its conditional form: "An automobile engine that burns more than a quart of oil between changes is inefficient"; or, "Inefficient operation results if the engine burns more than a quart of oil between regular oil changes." The major premise of a **disjunctive syllogism** is an assertion of alternatives taking the form "Either A or B"; for example: "Either the American economy must continue to grow rapidly or unemployment will increase."

There are a great many specialized forms and rules for the use of the syllogism. As in the discussion of an induction, we will limit ourselves to those matters that most directly concern the writer.

11.3 THE FORM OF THE SYLLOGISM

The **categorical syllogism** treats relations among **terms.** It consists of a **major, middle** and **minor** term. The terms are abbreviated A (Major), B (Middle) and C (Minor). They refer to successively smaller classes. The categorical syllogism may be considered a formal method of stating relations between these classes. The syllogism can be **positive** or **negative.**

1. Positive

Major premise:	B A All men are mortal.
Minor premise:	C B Socrates is a man.
Conclusion:	C A Socrates is mortal.

2. Negative

Major premise:	B A All sea water tastes salty.
Minor premise:	C Not A This water does not taste salty.
Conclusion:	C Not B This water is not sea water.

These syllogisms can be diagramed as follows:

1. **Positive**　　　　　　　　　　　2. **Negative**

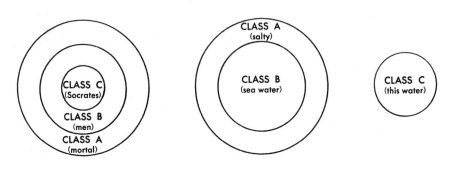

The **conditional syllogism** states relations between propositions rather than terms, and the minor premise affirms or denies one of them.

1. Positive

	A	B
Major premise:	If you are a member of the team,	you will receive a letter.

Major premise:　If you are a member of the team, you will receive a letter.

Minor premise:　You are a member of the team.

Conclusion:　You will receive a letter.

2. Negative

Major premise:　Only if you have six months' residence, can you vote.

Minor premise:　You do not have six months' residence.

Conclusion:　You cannot vote.

The **disjunctive syllogism** must have at least two but can have several propositions acting as terms.

1. Two terms:

A
Major premise: Either the Democrats control Congress
B
or the Republicans [control it].
[Or: The Congress is controlled by either the
Democrats or the Republicans.]
Not A
Minor premise: The Democrats do not control Congress.
B
Conclusion: The Republicans control Congress.

2. Several terms:

A   B
Major premise: Writing is either to entertain or [it is] to inform
C
or [it is] to persuade.
Not A   Not C
Minor premise: This passage is not intended to entertain or persuade.
B
Conclusion: This passage is to inform.

Notice that conditional and disjunctive syllogisms deal with classes that are separate: The person who is a member of the class labeled "team" is also a member of another class labeled "receive letter"; the Congress is controlled by two separate classes labeled "Democrat" and "Republican," and if one does not assert control, the other does.

11.4 LIMITATIONS AND FALLACIES

The validity of deductive argument depends on two factors, the validity of the premises and the observance of formal rules for the syllogism. Of these the first is by far the most important. **Only if the premises are true is the conclusion true.** The premises are generalizations. As we observed in chapter 6 (p. 140), they can be subjective, probable or

245

categorical. When used in an argumentative essay, they must be examined carefully. If there is likely to be any question about their meaning or truth, they must be justified. Usually, this involves giving **evidence.** The "All men are mortal" syllogism is self-evident; neither the major nor minor premise need to be explained or proved. Consider, however, the following syllogism:

Major premise: A country with widespread poverty is economically sick.
Minor premise: America has widespread poverty.
Conclusion: America is economically sick.

This syllogism is formally correct. Obviously, however, its conclusion is untrue. The fault lies not with the reasoning but with the premises. The phrase "widespread poverty" of the major premise is extremely vague. What does the writer mean by "poverty" and how wide is "widespread"? And what is meant by "economically sick"? Many underdeveloped nations with flourishing economies still have widespread poverty of the worst sort. The minor premise also needs attention. If the writer explains the major premise satisfactorily, he still has to prove that "widespread poverty" of the kind he is talking about exists in America. To do this he will need convincing evidence, probably in the form of economic statistics. However, it is likely that in the course of explaining the major premise he will encounter so many difficulties that he will recast the argument.

The formal rules for the categorical syllogism are:

1. There must be three and only three terms in the categorical syllogism. Each term must appear twice and be used in the same sense each time it appears.

2. The positive form of the categorical syllogism takes the form B-A; C-B; C-A. The form B-A; C-A; C-B results in the fallacy known as the **undistributed middle term.**

3. If both premises are affirmative, the conclusion must be affirmative. If one premise is negative, the conclusion must be negative. If one premise is limited by a word like "some" or "many," the conclusion must be so limited. Finally, if both premises are negative, no conclusion can be drawn.

Failure to observe these rules results in many common errors in logic.

1. Shifting terms:

> The mark of a true Christian is charity. There are many virtues but "the greatest of these is charity." This is one of the reasons why I consider Mr. Smith the finest man I have ever known. He has contributed more than any other member of our church to the South American Missions Fund, and without his generous support, the drive to enlarge the old rectory would never have succeeded.

Charity is used in two senses in this passage. The fallacy becomes apparent if the writer's syllogism is written formally:

Major premise: Charity is the mark of a true Christian.
Minor premise: Mr. Smith gives to charity.
Conclusion: Mr. Smith is a true Christian.

In the major premise *charity* refers to the theological virtue, which is a condition of the spirit. In the minor premise, it refers to "the act of giving money," which may or may not be a sign of the inward virtue.

2. Undistributed middle:

a. Positive

Major premise: All men are mortal. (B-A)
Minor premise: Socrates is mortal. (C-A)
Conclusion: Socrates is a man. (C-B)

b. Negative

Major premise: All men are mortal.
Minor premise: No dogs are men.
Conclusion: No dogs are mortal.

Here, the fallacy is obvious. In the positive syllogism, "Socrates" may refer to a man, but it may equally well be the name of a pet dog. The syllogism is faulty because the conclusion does not follow necessarily from the premises. The syllogism can be diagramed as follows:

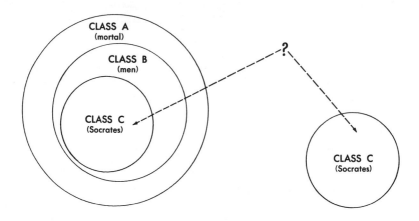

Socrates may be a member of the class "men," but this is not necessarily so. Consequently, the placing of the class indicated by the circle labeled "Socrates" remains ambiguous.

The fallacy of the undistributed middle is common and a source of real confusion to both reader and writer. Often it is difficult to detect until the syllogism is written formally.

> When Hamlet first sees Ophelia, he does not realize she is playing a role. He is mild with her. Even as he denies that he has ever loved her, he is advising her to leave the wicked world of the Danish court. Suddenly there is a noise behind the arras. Hamlet realizes that spies are watching and that Ophelia is only pretending to be sincere. His voice rises and he berates her violently as the shallow, hypocritical turncoat that she is.

Formally:

Major premise: All hypocrites are role-players.
Minor premise: Ophelia is a role-player.
Conclusion: Ophelia is a hypocrite.

The interpretation is, of course, unfair, and the syllogism reveals the source of the unfairness. Logically the fact that Ophelia is playing a role does not necessarily make her a hypocrite. It is more probable that

248

she acts out of love for Hamlet or desire to obey her father than out of a wish to deceive.

3. Both premises negative:

Everyone agrees, I suppose, that scientists are not drones in twentieth-century society. They have given us new forms of food, clothing, housing, medication, and communication. They have also given us the means of overcoming our enemies and releasing energies undreamed of in the past. Now let us turn to the humanists. What have they given us? What clothing, housing, food, medication, or communications system was devised by a humanist? The answer is plainly, none. And the conclusion is equally plain. Humanists are the drones of twentieth-century society.

Formally:

Major premise: Scientists are not drones.
Minor premise: Humanists are not scientists.
Conclusion: Humanists are drones.

The major premise and minor premise of the syllogism are both true, but since they are both negative, they lead to no conclusion. Attempting to add a conclusion results in a logical error.

11.5   ENTHYMEME

An enthymeme is a syllogism in which the major or minor premise is left unstated. In spite of its formidable label, the enthymeme is the most common form of the syllogism. It is sometimes called the **rhetorical syllogism**. Formal syllogisms are comparatively rare in discourse, but enthymemes are frequent. "It must be cold outside because there is frost on the window" is an enthymeme with the conditional major premise omitted. In expanded form:

Major premise: If there is frost on the window, it is cold outside.
Minor premise: There is frost on the window.
Conclusion: It is cold outside.

Enthymemes are useful because they are short and sound natural in everyday conversation and writing. On the other hand, because one of the premises is suppressed, the enthymeme is often ambiguous—the suppressed premise may be formulated in more than one way—and errors in logic are easy to make. It is also easy to use enthymemes to create the impression of logical proof without the substance. The statement "John Smith is wealthy because he drives an expensive car" seems reasonable at first. On analysis, it turns out to be fallacious. There are two possible ways of expressing the major premise.

First:

Major premise: Wealthy men drive expensive cars.
Minor premise: John Smith drives an expensive car.
Conclusion: John Smith is wealthy.

This version of the syllogism commits the error of the undistributed middle term.

Second:

Major premise: All drivers of expensive cars are wealthy.
Minor premise: John Smith drives an expensive car.
Conclusion: John Smith is wealthy.

The second version is logically valid, but the major premise is clearly erroneous.

▶ ## 11.6 USES OF DEDUCTION; DEDUCTION AS A METHOD OF DEVELOPMENT

Syllogisms and enthymemes are used in all kinds of writing. They are most frequent in argumentation, but they are found whenever the author needs to establish a specific point by appeal to general principles. Often several syllogisms are linked to form a **chain of inference**. It is equally common to find the premises of a syllogism supported by comments, illustrations and evidence as they are presented. Consider the following paragraph:

> (1) When two great powers confront one another, one or both must compromise or war becomes inevitable. (2) Such confrontations are moments of truth. (3) In 1939 when neither Britain nor Germany would compromise on the issue of Polish neutrality, the Second World War began. (4) In 1963 war was avoided when the Soviets agreed to withdraw their missiles from Cuba in the face of American demands. (5) A third great confrontation appears inevitable between Russia and China. (6) What its result will be is anybody's guess, but there are several ominous portents. (7) A poor nation is likely to be more intransigent than a wealthy one because it has less to lose. (8) Paradoxically, nuclear weapons tend to increase the relative advantage of poorer nations. (9) In a nation like China there are few large cities or industrial concentrations to serve as nuclear targets, and China's population is both enormous and dispersed. (10) Although a nuclear attack would cripple China, it would devastate Russia. (11) It is therefore probable that in the coming confrontation between Russia and China, either Russia will compromise or there will be a major war.

This paragraph uses a disjunctive syllogism for its overall organization:

Major premise: When two great powers confront one another, either one or both compromise or there is war.

Minor premise: In a confrontation between Russia and China, China will not compromise.

Conclusion: Therefore either Russia will compromise or there will be war.

Within the larger structure there is room for **comment, evidence** and additional deduction. The second sentence is a **comment** on the major premise. Sentences 3 and 4 are **evidence** of its validity. Sentence 5 specifies the two great powers to be cited in the minor premise. Sentence 7 is an **enthymeme.**

Formally:

Major premise: A nation that has little to lose is likely to be intransigent.

Minor premise: A poor nation has little to lose.

Conclusion: A poor nation is likely to be intransigent.

Sentence 8 restates the major premise of this syllogism, relating it to the conditions of nuclear war. Sentence 9 states that China is a "poor nation" and gives examples of the advantages this status would bring in a nuclear war. Sentence 10 contrasts China and Russia, identifying Russia with "wealthy nations." Finally, sentence 11 is the conclusion of the overall syllogism.

Deductive forms can govern major units of the essay as well as the paragraph. The whole essay can, in fact, be organized in syllogistic form. In this case the **purpose statement** or **thesis** is either the **conclusion** of the syllogism or an **enthymeme.** The following outlines illustrate three forms of syllogistic organization.

1. Organization by **categorical syllogism**; thesis based on conclusion:

	I.	Cigarette smoking can cause lung cancer.
Major premise:	II.	Irritants that cause skin cancer in animals can cause lung cancer if inhaled.
Minor premise:	III.	The irritants of cigarette smoke cause skin cancer in mice.
Conclusion:	IV.	The irritants in cigarette smoke can cause lung cancer.

Note that topics II and III are the **development** of this essay. Both need to be discussed and proved by citation of **evidence.** If, as is sometimes the case, the major premise is self-evident or can be proved in a few sentences, it can be included in the **introduction** as **background material.** The author then concentrates on proof of the minor premise, usually by giving extensive evidence. The **conclusion** need not be developed. It follows necessarily from the major and minor premises. If these are true, it must be true. If the author writes an extended conclusion, he will do so by introducing **author's comment.**

2. Organization by **disjunctive syllogism** with several alternatives; thesis based on conclusion:

    I. The best current theory of the origin of the galaxies is that of "constant creation."

    II. According to astronomers, the galaxies were formed either by a single explosion, by rhythmic contraction and expansion or by continuous creation of new matter in interstellar space.

III. The explosion theory fails to account for observed facts. (Cite evidence.)

IV. The expansion and contraction theory has internal contradictions. (Cite evidence.)

V. The constant creation theory is the most satisfactory. (Expand conclusion with author's comment: there are weaknesses in this theory, but they are not crippling.)

In this essay the major premise would probably be included in the introduction. As background material, the author might cite the three theories and briefly sketch the history of each.

3. Organization by **categorical syllogism; enthymeme** as purpose statement:

I. Machiavelli was a scientific student of politics because in *The Prince* he divorced politics from morality.

II. Political writers who divorce their subject from moral questions are scientific. (Include in introduction as background material. Give comment and illustration.)

III. Machiavelli divorced politics from morality in *The Prince*.
   a. Religion is considered a propaganda device. (Examples.)
   b. War is treated purely as a matter of expediency. (Examples.)
   c. The wise leader is advised to use cruelty as a political policy. (Examples.)
   d. He should pretend to be virtuous and be merciful, but only because these policies are useful. (Examples.)

IV. Machiavelli was a scientific student of politics.

Here the major premise is combined with the introduction. The combination may be intentional, since the major premise is dubious. Including it in the introduction allows the author to "play it down" rather than giving it the emphasis that would be necessary were it a major section of the development. On the other hand, if the arrangement is unintentional, the author should question it. If the essay is to be rigorous, the major premise needs convincing proof. In the course of attempting to prove it, the author may well decide that it is wrong or too vague, and revise the essay.

TERMS TO BE LEARNED

- ▸ Deduction
- ▸ Syllogism
- ▸ Parts of the syllogism: major premise; minor premise; conclusion (Be able to give examples.)
- ▸ Three types of syllogism: categorical; conditional; disjunctive (Be able to give examples.)
- ▸ The fallacy of the undistributed middle (with example)
- ▸ Enthymeme

Exercises & Theme Topics

I. Show the logical structure of the following passages. When the passage is not explicitly syllogistic, write out the formal syllogism(s) involved. Which passages are logically correct, and which are erroneous? Are there any passages that *cannot* be reduced to syllogistic form?

A. You can't buy a pair of shoes today because it's Sunday.

B. All oversized books are on the fourth level of the library. *Pilgrim's Progress* is on the fourth level of the library. *Pilgrim's Progress* is an oversized book.

C. . . . and what is the lesson of this educational reform movement? It is that reading is the most important subject taught in the early grades. The leaders of tomorrow will be the children who read widely today. Help your child to be one of tomorrow's leaders by filling out the enclosed order form for *A Treasury of Children's Classics*.

D. When these insects are exposed to the air, they shrivel and die within two hours. The specimens before you are quite dead, and they are obviously desiccated. They must have been exposed to the air for at least two hours.

E. Inflation is never caused by increased taxation. Mortgage rates are unrelated to increases in taxation. Therefore mortgages rates can cause inflation.

F. You've had that lump on your leg for two weeks now. You should see a doctor.

G. The plane is scheduled to arrive at 8:00 P.M. If it's late, plan to meet me in the coffee shop. If it's early, I'll wait for you in the lounge.

H. All good men are willing to come to the aid of their country. Because I know that you are a good man I am sure you will be glad to serve on the Committee to Preserve Historical Landmarks.

I. Without long-range planning, the water resources of this region will be inadequate to meet future requirements. At present no effort is being made to begin the needed surveys and projections. The Commissioners have persistently ignored requests for funds. The situation is becoming critical. It is already apparent that eventually some form of water rationing will be necessary during the summer months.

J. We must either win this game or give up the hope of a post-season invitation to one of the bowl tournaments. We will win this game. We will receive an invitation to one of the bowl tournaments.

II. Write three syllogisms and three enthymemes of your own. Expand the enthymemes to syllogistic form. Identify the type of each full syllogism.

III. Using two of your syllogisms, write two outlines that might be used for short essays.

IV. Write an essay (500-700 words) using a syllogism as the basis of your organization. The following theses will illustrate the type essay that you might write. They may be modified, and if you wish, you may use your own thesis.

A. All drivers should take a course in driver training.

B. Hamlet is mentally unbalanced during much of Shakespeare's play.

255

C. Personal (or property) rights should take precedence over property (or personal) rights.

D. College regulations should permit a student who wishes to do so to take a year's leave of absence.

E. The atomic test ban treaty should be strengthened (or repudiated).

Style (III)

12

In addition to the basic elements of style examined in chapters 3 and 9, there are a great many supplementary techniques that can clarify, emphasize and convey different shades of meaning. It would be pointless to list all of them. Several, however, are so useful that they should be familiar to all writers. They can be roughly divided into figures of speech and sound effects. Their use depends entirely on the writer's purpose.

257

A figure or sound pattern that is appropriate in one context may be inappropriate in another. In general, the writer should strive for a consistent style throughout the essay, but the principle must be used flexibly. Whatever the style, it should avoid being so artfully simple as to seem precious or so ornamented as to seem flowery.

12.1 THE THREE STYLES

Although each essay and story should have a style adapted to its purpose and expected readers, a useful distinction can be made between general types of style. Up to now, the discussion of style has concentrated on **standard style,** recognizing that variation is possible within this style from **informal** to **formal,** and from **popular** to **technical** and **specialized.** **Standard style** is, as the name indicates, the most common style for English prose. There are two other styles that can be used for special purposes: **plain style** and **ornate style.**

The characteristics of **plain style** are simple words, simple and compound sentences, little modification and minimal imagery. The writing by children has some of the characteristics of plain style, but it is usually inconsistent and relies rather heavily on imagery. To achieve a convincing plain style is extremely difficult since both the habits of the writer and the prejudice of the reader are against it. The only fully successful modern writer who frequently used the plain style was Ernest Hemingway. Hemingway began learning plain style during his work as a newspaper reporter in St. Louis, but only after a long, rigorous apprenticeship was he able to elevate simplicity to the level of art.

Standard style comes naturally. Since most of what we read—fiction, textbooks, magazine articles and specialized publications—is in standard style, we absorb its techniques from our culture. When we write we use them unconsciously as well as by choice. Standard style varies from informal to formal and technical, and to use it well demands the ability to adapt the techniques of style to the purpose at hand. Perhaps the most obvious characteristic of standard style is that it does not seem to be "style" at all. It is what we expect. Because the writer does nothing out of the ordinary, we are seldom conscious of the writing as writing, as long as there are no grammatical or rhetorical errors. The general rule for standard style is "moderation in all things." Any device can be used as long as it is appropriate to purpose and tone; but no device should be used so frequently or in such an exaggerated form that it calls attention to itself. Simple sentences are appropriate but should not predominate. Parallelism should be employed where useful, but not overused. Metaphors and other images can appear frequently, but artificial, "poetic" and extremely intricate images should appear infrequently if at all. Throughout, the writer should seek for agreeable, unforced variety.

The **ornate style** is easier to achieve and more common than the plain style. It is appropriate for ceremonial occasions, for moments of great emotional import or crisis and for subjects that demand elevated treatment. Although the ornate style is less popular today than fifty years ago, the *Congressional Record* furnishes examples of ornate speeches dealing with critical issues, commemorating national heroes and praising outstanding achievements. Some of these speeches are nothing more than hot air, but occasionally they are genuinely moving. Epic poetry uses the ornate style regularly because of its elevated subject matter—Milton's *Paradise Lost* is the best example in English—but ornate style can also be used for everyday occasions—a letter of consolation, a description of an especially moving scene or event or argument in which the author wishes to stress the significance of the subject or issue through style. The characteristics of the ornate style are long sentences with prominent structural features such as parallelism, inversion and antithesis, rich and striking imagery and emphatic sound effects. Ornate vocabulary is likely to be polysyllabic, and to use unfamiliar, somewhat exotic words.

Notice the differences in word choice, imagery and sentence structure in the following passages. Be prepared to make a few specific contrasts during class discussion.

1. **Plain style:**

> That was not a nice expression. His mother had told him not to speak with the rough boys in the college. Nice mother! The first day in the hall of the castle when she had said goodbye she had put up her veil double to her nose to kiss him: and her nose and eyes were red. But he had pretended not to see that she was going to cry. She was a nice mother but she was not so nice when she cried. And his father had given him two five-

259

shilling pieces for pocket money. And his father had told him if he wanted anything to write home to him and, whatever he did, never to peach on a fellow.

—JAMES JOYCE*

2. **Standard style** (tending to formal):

From the 1870's through the 1890's a flood of heated argument filled the press and pulpit over the controversy or warfare between science and theology. So exciting did the conflict become that Mark Twain proposed that a monument be erected to Adam before the great progenitor of the race should be entirely supplanted by Darwin's monkey. Clouds began to gather over this same conflict no longer ago than the 1920's. Between 1921 and 1929, no fewer than thirty-seven bills against the teaching of the theory of evolution were introduced in nearly half of the American state legislatures—in thirteen states in 1926 alone. In some states the battles were bitter if not bloody, as in North Carolina in 1925 and 1927 and in Minnesota in 1927, but no part of the country had a monopoly on the "Fundamentalist War." Loud rumblings of the conflict were heard in "the corridors of the American public schools." The teaching of the theory of evolution was "forbidden in approximately two-thirds of the rural districts of the Union" and a federal anti-evolution amendment "was one of the avowed goals" of two prominent fundamentalist organizations. The nation-wide campaign reported to have been proposed seems to have been thwarted, after that fateful day in October, 1929, when the great depression set in. Then both fundamentalists and modernists had to attend to more pressing matters and let up on the question whether they came from mud or monkey. In most states the fights for anti-evolution bills failed, but many teachers were dismissed from their posts for holding certain scientific views.

—EDGAR W. KNIGHT†

3. **Ornate style:**

The work of Dr. Nares has filled us with astonishment similar to that which Captain Lemuel Gulliver felt when first he landed in Brobdingnag, and saw corn as high as the oaks in the New Forest, thimbles as large as

* From *A Portrait of the Artist as a Young Man* (New York: The Viking Press, 1960), p. 9.
† From *Progress and Educational Perspective* (New York: The Macmillan Company, 1942), pp. 113-4.

buckets, and wrens of the bulk of turkeys. The whole book, and every component part of it, is on a gigantic scale. The title is as long as an ordinary preface: the prefatory matter would furnish out an ordinary book; and the book contains as much reading as an ordinary library. We cannot sum up the merits of the stupendous mass of paper which lies before us better than by saying that it consists of about two thousand closely printed quarto pages, that it occupies fifteen hundred inches cubic measure, and that it weighs sixty pounds avoirdupois. Such a book might, before the deluge, have been considered as light reading by Hilpa and Shallum. But unhappily the life of man is now three-score years and ten; and we cannot but think it somewhat unfair in Dr. Nares to demand from us so large a portion of so short an existence.

Compared with the labour of reading through these volumes, all other labour, the labour of thieves on the treadmill, of children in factories, of negroes in sugar plantations, is an agreeable recreation. There was, it is said, a criminal in Italy who was suffered to make his choice between Guicciardini and the galleys. He chose the history. But the war of Pisa was too much for him. He changed his mind, and went to the oar. Guicciardini, though certainly not the most amusing of writers, is a Herodotus or a Froissart, when compared with Dr. Nares. It is not merely in bulk, but in specific gravity also, that these memoirs exceed all other human compositions. On every subject which the Professor discusses, he produces three times as many pages as another man; and one of his pages is as tedious as another man's three. His book is swelled to its vast dimensions by endless repetitions, by episodes which have nothing to do with the main action, by quotations from books which are in every circulating library, and by reflections which, when they happen to be just, are so obvious that they must necessarily occur to the mind of every reader. He employs more words in expounding and defending a truism than any other writer would employ in supporting a paradox. Of the rules of historical perspective, he has not the faintest notion. There is neither foreground nor background in his delineation. The wars of Charles the Fifth in Germany are detailed at almost as much length as in Robertson's life of that prince. The troubles of Scotland are related as fully as in M'Crie's *Life of John Knox*. It would be most unjust to deny that Dr. Nares is a man of great industry and research; but he is so utterly incompetent to arrange the materials which he has collected that he might as well have left them in their original repositories.

—Thomas Babington Macaulay*

* From "Burleigh and his Times" (1832).

12.2 SPECIALIZED FIGURES

Figures of speech are a form of imagery. They are used to clarify, to emphasize and to intensify the author's tone. Of the many figures used in prose writing, the following are the most common: allusion, irony, paradox, personification, exaggeration, understatement, metonymy and synecdoche.

1. **Allusion** is reference to a person, place or thing, historical or literary, that adds to the understanding of the subject at hand. Macaulay alludes to *Gulliver's Travels,* the Old Testament, Guicciardini, Herodotus and Froissart in the paragraphs reprinted above. **Allusion** is also common in standard style: "Mr. Smith exhibited a Job-like patience while waiting for the testimony to end." **Quotations** and **phrases** from well-known sources are a form of **allusion.**

2. **Irony** is saying one thing and implying something else, usually the opposite of the expressed meaning. At the end of his first paragraph, Macaulay pretends to take seriously the idea that Hilpa and Shallum would have found Dr. Nares "light reading." Obviously, however, he is poking fun at the book. **Irony** is just as appropriate to everyday conversation as it is to Macaulay's ornate style. Everyone has used an expression like "It's a great day!" meaning, "It's a terrible day: it's raining, the roof is leaking and I'm down with a cold."

   When the purpose statement of an essay is ironic, the essay becomes an example of **sustained irony.** The most famous example of sustained irony in English is Swift's "Modest Proposal," defending the ironic thesis that Irish children should be fattened for the English meat trade. **Sarcasm** is a form of irony intended to hurt rather than to emphasize or amuse.

3. **Paradox** is a statement that seems contradictory or impossible but may actually be true. "The longest way round is the shortest way home" is a paradox. "An honest God's the noblest work of man" is a paradox based on the reversal of a commonplace quotation. Paradox can be used for emphasis or simply for humor. St. Paul's idea

that "the wisdom of man is the foolishness of God" is a serious paradox. **Paradoxical argument** is argument in support of a seemingly impossible thesis. Erasmus's *Praise of Folly,* defending the thesis that folly is better than wisdom, is an example with both humerous and serious elements. Freud's demonstration that the unconscious mind profoundly influences conscious behavior seemed paradoxical when first introduced.

4. **Personification** is a figure in which an inanimate object or idea is treated as a living being. The Statue of Liberty is an example of personification in sculpture. Uncle Sam is a personification of the United States. If the writer refers to a ship as *she* or capitalizes the word *nature,* he is using personification. Because personification is rather artificial it is most common in ornate writing and poetry and infrequent in standard writing.

5. **Exaggeration** and **understatement** are self-explanatory. Macaulay's comparison of the labors of reading Dr. Nares to the labors of "thieves on a treadmill" is an example of exaggeration combining emphasis and humor. Understatement for emphasis is illustrated by Knight's reference to problems of the Great Depression as "more pressing matters" than the debate over evolution. Use of the negative rather than the positive form of an expression is also understatement: "The wish to live is a not unnatural desire"; or, "I would hardly describe Mr. Jones as energetic." Macaulay's "we cannot but think it somewhat unfair . . ." is another example.

6. **Metonymy** is the substitution of a term closely associated with an object for the name of the object itself. It is closely related to **synecdoche,** which is, technically, the name of the whole for the part or the part for the whole. The two figures are closely related, and for practical purposes we can use the term **metonymy** for both. Knight uses metonymy when he remarks that "controversy filled the press" rather than "controversy filled the newspapers." We commonly refer to "hired hands" rather than "hired laborers," and "the judgment of the court" rather than "the judgment of the judge." Macaulay uses metonymy effectively when he refers to "the stupendous mass of paper which lies before us" rather than "the book which lies before us."

263

12.3 RHYTHM

In spite of the fact that most writing is intended for reading rather than oral delivery, sound effects cannot be ignored. A passage that has a jerky rhythm, a final sentence that is inconclusive or a combination of words that has an unpleasant sound creates a bad effect, even when the sentences are heard mentally rather than read aloud. In general, when he revises, the writer should check to make sure that his sentences move smoothly and sound agreeable. The writer need not concern himself with the metrics of prose. The basic metrical unit in English is the **iamb,** a light stress followed by a heavy one (as in ăbrupt; thĕ bóok), but prose is irregular and the meter usually takes care of itself.

Rhythm is another matter. Rhythm is the effect created by the timing of stressed words, phrases, clauses and sentences. All prose passages have rhythm. In some passages it is used effectively while in others it is left to chance. Three types of rhythm that are easy to use effectively are **balanced rhythm, graded rhythm** and **alternation.**

1. Two grammatical units of similar length and structure have **balanced rhythm:** "tit for tat," "the power and the glory," "not for love nor money," "you take the high road and I'll take the low road." Macaulay's "not merely in bulk but in specific gravity also" and "he produces three times as many pages . . ., and one of his pages. . . ." effectively use **balanced rhythm.**

   The impulse toward balanced rhythm is so strong that a word of caution is in order. It is easy to fall into the habit of writing **doublets** —paired words and phrases—when a single one would do. Macaulay's "Hilpa and Shallum" is a **doublet** humorously intended. On the other hand, his "industry and research" seems less functional and the doublet should probably be eliminated.

2. When several units of similar structure follow one another, they often exhibit **graded rhythm** with the last phrase or clause receiving the strongest rhythmic emphasis: "The title is as long as an ordinary preface: the prefatory matter would fill out a book; and the book contains as much as an ordinary library"; ". . . that it consists of

about two thousand closely printed quarto pages, that it occupies fifteen hundred inches cubic measure, and that it weighs sixty pounds avoirdupois."

3. Rhythm is also created by the **alternation** between long and short sentences and between sentences with emphatically different grammatical structures. Notice the effect in Macaulay's second paragraph of following two long, highly structured sentences with the brief "He chose the history."

Two points about prose rhythm are of practical interest to the writer. First, prose rhythm is a means of increasing emphasis. Words and sentences that are particularly important should receive stress. Second, prose rhythm can be used to underscore the logic of a passage and hence increase clarity. If three ideas are arranged in order of ascending logical importance, **rhythmic gradation** helps make the arrangement obvious to the reader. If two ideas are of equal importance, **balanced rhythm** is a way of making the fact plain. By the same token, a concluding sentence needs to have the quality of finality. "The solution of this problem will have significant effects on man's moral nature" is less effective than "The solution of this problem will have significant effects on the moral nature of man." The difference is that the first sentence ends weakly with a trochee (nátuře) while the second ends with an iamb, thus permitting the final word to be heavily stressed (of mán).

12.4 EUPHONY; ALLITERATION

Euphony is the stylistic effect achieved when a passage is rhythmically graceful and avoids unpleasant sound combinations.

While striving for euphony, a writer may also use sound effects in a positive way. Of the many figures of sound, only one will concern us here. **Alliteration is the repetition of like or similar sounds particularly at the beginning of stressed syllables.** Alliteration is as effective in prose as in poetry when correctly used. Too much alliteration, however, will make a passage seem artificial or slightly ridiculous, as in the sentence,

265

"The *proper proportion* of *payments* to *dependents* can be *determined* by a *definite* formula." Here the alliteration is excessive and serves no real purpose. Used with restraint and in the right place, however, alliteration can call attention to important words and link related ideas. Toward the end of his paragraph on the evolution controversy, Knight sums up the debate in the clause "whether they came from *m*ud or *m*onkey." The alliteration neatly underscores the summary and reinforces the balanced rhythm of the disjunction. Macaulay uses a similar technique in his allusion to "the choice between Guicciardini and the *g*alleys." Because it arouses interest, alliteration is frequent in titles. *Of Mice and Men* is the title of a novel; *Progress and Poverty* is the title of a book on economic theory, and *Physics and Philosophy* the title of a book explaining the implications of the theory of relativity.

12.5 A NOTE ON PROPAGANDA

Propaganda is a form of writing that seeks to persuade through appeals to emotion rather than logical proof. For this reason propaganda devices are properly devices of style rather than thought. Although the word *propaganda* has derogatory connotations, those who use it claim that it is justified if (1) the writer's purpose is a good one, and (2) rigorous logical proof would confuse rather than help the expected reader. The use of propaganda devices places a responsibility on the writer. He must evaluate his purpose and audience to be sure that propaganda is really desirable. Still more important, he must be sure that his ideas are well-founded. A good deal of propaganda is the result of the writer's own confusion. He repeats platitudes and half-truths without examining them, when a little thought would show that they are vague or simply invalid.

The devices of propaganda are most obvious in advertising and political controversy, but they can be found in all types of expository and argumentative writing. A critic who writes "Any person of taste will agree that this is a great painting" is using the device of **intimidation.** The reader does not want to think of himself as "tasteless," and so he tends to accept the assertion "this is a great painting" without proof.

"The childish notion that morality can be divorced from economics" is an example of both **intimidation** (no one likes to be considered "childish") and **begging the question** (the theory is condemned before its weakness is demonstrated).

Easily recognizable devices of propaganda include:

1. **Ad hominem.** Argument **ad hominem** appeals to the prejudices, fears and desires of the reader rather than to the merits of the issue. In a sense all propaganda devices are arguments **ad hominem,** but for present purposes **ad hominem** will be narrowly defined as appeals emphasizing the identification of the interests of writer and reader. If the reader is likely to be uneducated or poorly educated, the writer uses a colloquial style, often intentionally violating the rules of grammar and diction, rests his case on appeals to "common sense" and statements like "anybody with his head screwed on the right way can see that . . ." and may attack experts in the field as "the whiz-kids with their heads in the clouds," "muddle-headed idealists" or "the boys in the ivory tower." By the same token, an author writing for experts will use a formal style, appeal frequently to "the best author-ities" and flatter his reader with statements like "Behind these superficial panaceas and cries of anguish, the serious student can see that . . ." or "The man in the street can do many things well, but he is hardly equipped to cope with the subtleties of advanced . . .." All writing involves a certain amount of argument **ad hominem,** but if the emotional appeal is predominant or a substitute for logical proof, the result is **propaganda.**

2. **Authority.** Appeal to authority is a legitimate form of proof as long as the authority is sound and the appeal is used to reveal, not conceal. If the authority is vague or unrepresentative or not really authorita-tive, the appeal is a propaganda device. Appeals to "the Founding Fathers" or "the Christian spirit" are often propaganda for the simple reason that the "authorities" cited are so vague and subject to so many different interpretations that almost any position can be justified by reference to them. Before the Second World War certain German scientists were paraded before the German people to assure them that the "Aryan race" was "biologically superior" to all other

267

races, while the Jewish race was "biologically inferior." These scientists were "authorities" in the sense that they had university training and advanced degrees, but they were entirely unrepresentative of the best scientific opinion in Germany itself, not to mention the rest of the world. The "nonauthoritative authority" is a familiar figure in advertisements. An advertisement for a deodorant features an actor dressed in a white coat surround by chemical apparatus, the implication being that the advertisement comes straight from the company laboratory and the actor has a Ph.D. in organic chemistry. The **testimonial** is a special case of appeal to authority. The fact that a well-known baseball player signs a statement that he eats Happy Daze Corn Flakes has no bearing whatever on whether they are nourishing and taste good.

3. **Bandwagon.** The bandwagon device plays on the desire of the reader to do the popular thing. "Everybody's doing it" is capable of infinite variation: "The 1966 Condor is the most popular car in the Condor Company's history"; "Why don't you do it: your friends do"; "Lively folks prefer Pep lemonade"; "20 million satisfied customers can't be wrong." **Consensus** is a variation of the bandwagon device: "As everybody knows, this idea is ridiculous"; "From the days of Jefferson to the twentieth century, Americans have agreed that . . .." (Complete the sentence with anything you want to prove.)

4. **Begging the question.** Begging the question is a way of stating a conclusion before the conclusion has been proved: "This socialistic notion that we can have our cake and eat it too will ruin the nation." **Circular reasoning** is a special case of begging the question: "The practice of passing sentence without jury trial in contempt-of-court cases is bad because it is fascistic. The chief difference between fascist countries and democracies is that fascist countries ignore due legal process."

5. **Glittering generality.** When a writer rests his case on half-truths, unprovable generalizations and popular commonplaces, he is using the devices of the glittering generality. Appeals to "the sanctity of the individual," "manifest destiny," "the class conflict," and slogans

like "all's fair in love and war" or "John Smith is a man of the people" can obscure issues rather than clarify them. Historically, glittering generalities have often had unfortunate social consequences. During the late Middle Ages the idea "usury is evil" seriously retarded the development of legitimate and desirable free-enterprise capitalism; and the vague appeal to *Lebensraum* ("living space") was used to convince the German people of the need for territorial expansion by aggression.

6. **Intimidation.** Intimidation is any device that makes the reader afraid or ashamed not to accept the writer's assertions. An advertisement directed to teen-agers implies that not to use the advertised product is "kid stuff." A political speech implies that anyone in favor of a particular program is in favor of dictatorship. A maker of hair spray implies that women who do not use his product will be unpopular with men. A civic reformer writes, "All patriotic citizens know how important it is to clean up our slums," implying that anyone who disagrees with his proposals is "unpatriotic." **Name-calling** is a type of intimidation. Words with favorable connotations are associated with what the writer favors, and words with unfavorable connotations are associated with what he dislikes. A general is called "resourceful and bold" by his friends, but "eccentric and foolhardy" by his enemies. A program is called "liberal" by its supporters but "subversive" by those opposed.

TERMS TO BE LEARNED

- Three styles (with characteristics): plain; standard; ornate
- Figures of speech (Cite three with illustrations.)
- Rhythm
- Euphony
- Alliteration
- Propaganda
- Propaganda devices (Cite three with illustrations.)

Exercises & Theme Topics

I. Identify the style of each of the following passages and discuss the effects of figures of speech, rhythm and sound effects.

A.

Swept as we are into the vortex of this war-time, our information one-sided, ourselves too near to focus the mighty transformations which have already taken place or are beginning to take place, and without a glimmering of the inchoate future, we are incapable of apprehending the significance of the thronging impressions, and know not what value to attach to the judgments we form. We are constrained to believe that never has any event been destructive of so much that is valuable in the common wealth of humanity, nor so misleading to many of the clearest intelligences, nor so debasing to the highest that we know. Science herself has lost her passionless impartiality; in their deep embitterment her servants seek for weapons from her with which to contribute towards the defeat of the enemy. The anthropologist is driven to declare the opponent inferior and degenerate; the psychiatrist to publish his diagnosis of the enemy's disease of mind or spirit. But probably our sense of these immediate evils is disproportionately strong, and we are not entitled to compare them with the evils of other times of which we have not undergone the experience.

The individual who is not himself a combatant—and so a wheel in the gigantic machinery of war—feels conscious of disorientation, and of an inhibition in his powers and activities. I believe that he will welcome any indication, however slight, which may enable him to find out what is wrong with himself at least. I propose to distinguish two among the most potent factors in the mental distress felt by non-combatants, against which it is such a heavy task to struggle, and to treat of them here: the disillusionment which this war has evoked; and the altered attitude towards death which this—like every other war—imposes on us.

—SIGMUND FREUD*

* From "Thoughts for the Times on War and Death," tr. by E. Colburn Mayne, in *On Creativity and the Unconscious* (New York: Harper Torchbooks, 1958), pp. 206-7.

B.

History, I think, ladies and gentlemen, history will say that this great trust was not abused. American testimony about the early period of the Monroe Doctrine is upon record. There was the suppression of the slave trade and piracy. During our prolonged naval supremacy, undeterred by the rise of foreign tariffs, we kept our ports freely open to the commerce of the world. Our colonial and oriental empire, even our coastal trade, was free to the shipping of all the nations on equal terms. We in no way sought to obstruct the rise of other states or navies. For nearly the whole of the nineteenth century the monopoly of sea power in British hands was a trust discharged faithfully in the general interest. But in the first decade of the twentieth century, with new patterns of warships, naval rivalries became acute and fierce. Civilized governments began to think in dreadnoughts. It was in such a setting very difficult to prevent the First World War, far more difficult than it would have been to have prevented the Second.

There was, of course, one way to prevent it—one way then *as now*—the creation of an international instrument, strong enough to adjust the disputes of nations and enforce its decisions against an aggressor. Much wisdom, eloquence, and earnest effort was devoted to this theme in which the United States took the lead, but we only got as far as the World Court at the Hague and improvements in the Geneva Convention. The impulses toward a trial of strength in Europe were far stronger at this time. Germany, demanding her "place in the sun," was faced by a resolute France with her military honor to regain. England, in accordance with her foreign policy of three hundred years, sustained the weaker side. France found an ally in the Russia of the Czars, and Germany in the crumbling Empire of the Hapsburgs. The United States, for reasons which were natural and traditional, but no longer so valid as in the past, stood aloof and expected to be able to watch as a spectator the thrilling, fearful drama unfold from across what was then called "the broad Atlantic." These expectations, as perhaps you may remember, were not wholly borne out by what happened.

After four years of hideous mechanical slaughter, illuminated by infinite sacrifice, but not remarkably relieved by strategy or generalship, the victorious allies assembled at Versailles. High hopes and spacious opportunities awaited them. War, stripped of every pretension of glamour or romance, had been brought home to the masses of the peoples and brought home in forms never before experienced except by the defeated. To stop another war was the supreme object and duty of the statesmen who met

271

as friends and allies around the peace table. They made great errors. The doctrine of self-determination was not the remedy for Europe, which needed then above all things, unity and larger groupings. The idea that the vanquished could pay the expenses of the victors was a destructive and crazy delusion. The failure to strangle Bolshevism at its birth and to bring Russia, then prostrate, by one means or another into the general democratic system lies heavy upon us today. Nevertheless, the statesmen at Versailles, largely at the inspiration of President Wilson, an inspiration implemented effectively by British thought, created the League of Nations. This is their defense before history, and had the League been resolutely sustained and used, it would have saved us all.

—WINSTON S. CHURCHILL*

C.

Fourscore and seven years ago our fathers brought forth on this continent a new nation conceived in liberty and dedicated to the proposition that all men are created equal. Now we are engaged in a great civil war testing whether that nation, or any nation so conceived and so dedicated, can long endure. We are met on a great battlefield of that war. We have come to dedicate a portion of that field as a final resting-place for those who here gave their lives that that nation might live. It is altogether fitting and proper that we should do this. But, in a larger sense, we cannot dedicate, we cannot consecrate, we cannot hallow this ground. The brave men, living and dead, who struggled here have consecrated it far above our poor power to add or detract. The world will little note nor long remember what we say here, but it can never forget what they did here. It is for us the living rather to be dedicated here to the unfinished work which they who fought here have thus far so nobly advanced. It is rather for us to be here dedicated to the great task remaining before us—that from these honoured dead we take increased devotion to that cause for which they gave the last full measure of devotion—that we here highly resolve that these dead shall not have died in vain, that this nation under God shall have a new birth of

* From "The Twentieth Century—Its Promise and Its Realization," an address delivered 31 March, 1949, at the Boston Garden on the occasion of the Massachusetts Institute of Technology Mid-Century Convocation on the Social Implications of Scientific Progress. Published in *Mid-Century, The Social Implications of Scientific Progress*, ed. John Ely Burchard (Cambridge, Mass.: M.I.T. Press, 1950), pp. 970-6.

freedom, and that goverment of the people, by the people, for the people, shall not perish from the earth.

—ABRAHAM LINCOLN*

D.

. . . One day when I went out to my wood-pile, or rather my pile of stumps, I observed two large ants, the one red, the other much larger, nearly half an inch long, and black, fiercely contending with one another. Having once got hold they never let go, but struggled and wrestled and rolled on the chips incessantly. Looking farther, I was surprised to find that the chips were covered with such combatants, that it was not a *duellum*, but a *bellum* a war between two races of ants, the red always pitted against the black, and frequently two red ones to one black. The legions of these Myrmidons covered all the hills and vales in my wood-yard, and the ground was already strewn with the dead and dying, both red and black. It was the only battle which I have ever witnessed, the only battle-field I ever trod while the battle was raging; internecine war; the red republicans on the one hand, and the black imperialists on the other. On every side they were engaged in deadly combat, yet without any noise that I could hear, and human soldiers never fought so resolutely. I watched a couple that were fast locked in each other's embraces, in a little sunny valley amid the chips, now at noon-day prepared to fight till the sun went down, or life went out. The smaller red champion had fastened himself like a vice to his adversary's front, and through all the tumblings on that field never for an instant ceased to gnaw at one of his feelers near the root, having already caused the other to go by the board; while the stronger black one dashed him from side to side, and, as I saw on looking nearer, had already divested him of several of his members. They fought with more pertinacity than bulldogs. Neither manifested the least disposition to retreat. It was evident that their battle-cry was Conquer or die. In the meanwhile there came along a single red ant on the hill-side of this valley, evidently full of excitement, who either had despatched his foe, or had not yet taken part in the battle; probably the latter, for he had lost none of his limbs; whose mother had charged him to return with his shield or upon it. Or perchance he was some Achilles, who had nourished his wrath apart, and had now come to avenge or rescue his Patroclus. He saw this unequal

* Gettysburg Address (1863).

combat from afar,—for the blacks were nearly twice the size of the red,—
he drew near with rapid pace till he stood on his guard within half an
inch of the cambatants; then, watching his opportunity, he sprang upon
the black warrior, and commenced his operations near the root of his right
fore-leg, leaving the foe to select among his own members; and so there
were three united for life, as if a new kind of attraction had been invented
which put all other locks and cements to shame. I should not have wondered
by this time to find that they had their respective musical bands stationed
on some eminent chip, and playing their national airs the while, to excite
the slow and cheer the dying combatants. I was myself excited somewhat
even as if they had been men. The more you think of it, the less the
difference. And certainly there is not the fight recorded in Concord history,
at least, if in the history of America, that will bear a moment's comparison
with this, whether for the numbers engaged in it, or for the patriotism and
heroism displayed. For numbers and for carnage it was an Austerlitz or
Dresden. Concord Fight! Two killed on the patriots' side, and Luther
Blanchard wounded! Why here every ant was a Buttrick,—"Fire! for God's
sake fire!"—and thousands shared the fate of Davis and Hosmer. There was
not one hireling there. I have no doubt that it was a principle they fought
for, as much as our ancestors, and not to avoid a three-penny tax on their
tea; and the results of this battle will be as important and memorable to
those whom it concerns as those of the battle of Bunker Hill, at least.

—Henry David Thoreau*

E.

Once (it was in Mississippi, in May, in the flood year 1927) there were
two convicts. One of them was about twenty-five, tall, lean, flat-stomached,
with a sunburned face and Indian-black hair and pale, china-colored out-
raged eyes—an outrage directed not at the men who had foiled his crime,
not even at the lawyers and judges who had sent him here, but at the
writers, the uncorporeal names attached to the stories, the paper novels—
the Diamond Dicks and Jesse Jameses and such—whom he believed had
led him into his present predicament through their own ignorance and
gullibility regarding the medium in which they dealt and took money for,
in accepting information on which they placed the stamp of verisimilitude
and authenticity (this so much the more criminal since there was no sworn
notarised statement attached and hence so much the quicker would the
information be accepted by one who expected the same unspoken good

* From *Walden* (1854).

faith, demanding, asking, expecting no certification, which he extended along with the dime or fifteen cents to pay for it) and retailed for money and which on actual application proved to be impractical and (to the convict) criminally false; there would be times when he would halt his mule and plow in midfurrow (there is no walled penitentiary in Mississippi; it is a cotton plantation which the convicts work under the rifles and shotguns of guards and trusties) and muse with a kind of enraged impotence, fumbling among the rubbish left him by his own and only experience with courts and law, fumbling until the meaningless and verbose shibboleth took form at last (himself seeking justice at the same blind fount where he had met justice and been hurled back and down): Using the mails to defraud: who felt that he had been defrauded by the third-class mail system not of crass and stupid money which he did not particularly want anyway, but of liberty and honor and pride.

—WILLIAM FAULKNER*

F.

You could dictate that, but you could not dictate the Place Contrescarpe where the flower sellers dyed their flowers in the street and the dye ran over the paving where the autobus started and the old men and the women, always drunk on wine and bad marc; and the children with their noses running in the cold; the smell of dirty sweat and poverty and drunkenness at the Café des Amateurs and the whores at the Bal Musette they lived above. The Concierge who entertained the trooper of the Garde Republicaine in her loge, his horse-hair plumed helmet on a chair. The locataire across the hall whose husband was a bicycle racer and her joy that morning at the Crémerie when she had opened L'Auto and seen where he placed third in Paris-Tours, his first big race. She had blushed and laughed and then gone upstairs crying with the yellow sporting paper in her hand. The husband of the woman who ran the Bal Musette drove a taxi and when he, Harry, had to take an early plane the husband knocked upon the door to wake him and they each drank a glass of white wine at the zinc of the bar before they started. He knew his neighbors in that quarter then because they all were poor.

—ERNEST HEMINGWAY†

* From "The Old Man" in *The Portable Faulkner* (New York: The Viking Press, 1948), pp. 541-2.

† From "The Snows of Kilimanjaro" in *The Short Stories of Ernest Hemingway* (New York: Charles Scribner's Sons, 1938), p. 69.

G.

I deny not but that it is of greatest concernment in the Church and Commonwealth to have a vigilant eye how books demean themselves as well as men; and thereafter to confine, imprison, and do sharpest justice on them as malefactors. For books are not absolutely dead things, but do contain a potency of life in them to be as active as that soul was whose progeny they are; nay, they do preserve as in a vial the purest efficacy and extraction of that living intellect that bred them. I know they are as lively, and as vigorously productive, as those fabulous dragon's teeth; and being sown up and down, may chance to spring up armed men. And yet, on the other hand, unless wariness be used, as good almost kill a man as kill a good book: who kills a man kills a reasonable creature, God's image; but he who destroys a good book, kills reason itself, kills the image of God, as it were in the eye. Many a man lives a burden to the earth; but a good book is the precious life-blood of a master spirit, embalmed and treasured up on purpose to a life beyond life. 'Tis true, no age can restore a life, whereof perhaps there is no great loss; and revolutions of ages do not oft recover the loss of a rejected truth, for the want of which whole nations fare the worse. We should be wary, therefore, what persecution we raise against the living labors of public men, how we spill that seasoned life of man, preserved and stored up in books; since we see a kind of homicide may be thus committed, sometimes a martyrdom; and if it extend to the whole impression, a kind of massacre, whereof the execution ends not in the slaying of an elemental life, but strikes at that ethereal and fifth essence, the breath of reason itself, slays an immortality rather than a life. But lest I should be condemned of introducing licence, while I oppose licensing, I refuse not the paints to be so much historical as will serve to show what hath been done by ancient and famous commonwealths against this disorder, till the very time that this project of licensing crept out of the Inquisition, was caught up by our prelates, and hath caught some of our presbyters.

—JOHN MILTON*

II. Identify propaganda devices in selections B, D and G in exercise I.

* From *Areopagitica* (1644).

III. Bring several magazine advertisements to class. Be prepared to identify the propaganda devices used in each.

IV. Select one of the first four essays submitted to your English class this semester. Rewrite it, concentrating on improvement of style. Consider the principles covered in chapters 3 and 9, as well as those in the present chapter.

The Research
Paper

The purpose of the research paper is to present truth as far as the author is able to discover it. This simple principle explains both the value of research and the specialized techniques of research writing. It takes precedence over all other principles and techniques and provides a guide in cases where standard practices are inadequate. It is, unfortunately, often forgotten in the struggle to master source material, take notes

279

and provide documentation. It will therefore bear repeating: A research paper is valuable only to the extent that it presents the best, most rigorous version of the truth of its subject that the writer can offer.

Occasionally there is confusion over the matter of "subjectivity" and "objectivity" in the research paper. An "objective" paper is not a paper that is "unrelated to the author's personal beliefs." If the paper is truly the best, most rigorous version of the truth that the author can offer, it must, by definition, represent his personal beliefs. It is "objective" rather than "subjective" because it presents *proof* of its conclusion in the form of *deductions* and verifiable *evidence*. Confusion also sometimes arises over the matter of "originality." A good research paper always has an element of originality, otherwise there could be no point in writing it. The originality is evident in the use of sources, the development of thesis, the choice of evidence, and the use of such techniques as definition and deduction and in the style.

13.1 TYPES OF RESEARCH PAPERS

Research papers fall into two categories, **recovery of information** and **presentation of a thesis.**

Recovery of information is the assembling of already available information on a given topic. To be worthwhile, an essay recovering information must be based on comprehensive knowledge of available information and should offer more information than standard reference works and readily accessible book-length treatments of the topic. It should also be selective, eliminating the obvious, the eccentric and the trivial, and concentrating on the essential. Recovery of information is necessary for two reasons. First many specialized topics are so limited or obscure that before advanced study of them can begin, a search must be made of previous literature to recover what is known. This task usually requires dogged perseverance and a knowledge of bibliography and several languages. Second, many topics, both specialized and general, have been treated so often and in so many different ways that consolidation

280

is necessary. A treatment is needed that sifts the good from the bad, defines possible lines of approach and points out the limitations of current knowledge.

Recovery of information is extremely demanding. It is normally a job for experts only. Yet, paradoxically, students are often encouraged to write essays of recovery of information as their introduction to the research paper. This is nonsense. A student without formal training in historical scholarship simply cannot write a worthwhile "research paper" on "The Life and Times of Alexander Hamilton." If forced to do so, he will produce what is known as a "cut-and-paste" essay composed of bits of information haphazardly assembled from commonplace sources—two encyclopedias, a few popular articles listed in *The Reader's Guide to Periodical Literature,* and one or two biographies selected because they happen to be available rather than because of their quality. The result will be especially unfortunate for the writer. The writer knows that what he is doing is pointless except as a mechanical exercise. He may come to think of it as "shifting bones from one grave to another," which is exactly what it is. If he assumes this is true of *all* research writing, some of the most rewarding opportunities in college course-work will be closed to him.

Research writing that **presents a thesis** is both less and more demanding than **recovery of information.** It is less demanding because it does not assume the sort of mastery of a subject that can come only with years of study. It is more demanding because it requires the writer to discover his own thesis. Naturally, a thesis can be a platitude or something quite original. The more original it is, the greater scope it allows for expression of the writer's own insights, interests and creative abilities. This is another way of saying that the more original it is (assuming it is proved convincingly), the more exciting it will be to develop, and the more stimulating it will be for the reader.

Presentation of a thesis does not always require a background in depth. The more one knows about a subject the better. That is obvious. But by properly limiting his approach, a writer can substitute intensive analysis of a limited body of material for extensive knowledge of a whole field. For example, the writer assigned a research paper on Alexander Hamilton could limit himself to one good biography and write a demonstration of a thesis like "In spite of his reputation, Alexander Hamilton

281

was a man of the people"; or "Alexander Hamilton misunderstood Thomas Jefferson on several important occasions." Another possible approach would be to read three biographies noting points of difference. The research paper could then support the thesis, "There are four major points on which Hamilton scholars differ"; or, if the writer decides that one account is best, "On three of the four major points at issue between Hamilton scholars, Professor Smith's biography is superior." Another alternative would be to write about Hamilton's correspondence or the *Federalist Papers*. In this case the thesis would be something like "The three major themes of the *Federalist Papers* are . . ." or "Hamilton's style is skillfully adapted to his purpose in the *Federalist Papers*." The possible variations are so numerous that the difficulty is not in finding a thesis but in selecting the most stimulating one. In general, the thesis of a research paper should be sufficiently limited to be proved within the space available, emphatic and unambiguous and of genuine interest to the writer. The methods of developing the thesis of a research paper are the same as those for argumentation (see chapters 6, 11).

13.2 EVIDENCE IN THE RESEARCH PAPER

In a research paper, the presentation of **evidence** must be rather formal. The writer of the paper is interested in truth, not merely persuasion. Therefore, he uses his evidence as fairly as possible and presents it in such a way as to permit the interested reader to verify it by referring to the writer's own sources. **Documentation** is the device used to insure the possibility of verification. If the reader feels that an item of evidence is unrepresentative, inaccurate or cited out of context, documentation allows him to check the original for himself. Note that if he checks the evidence and decides that it is, indeed, in error, he has performed a service for the writer as well as himself. If the writer is genuinely interested in truth, he will welcome correction. In this sense, writing a research paper is saying "Here is the best version of the truth that I can offer; if anyone can improve on it, all the better."

13.3   KINDS OF EVIDENCE

The uses of evidence and the methods of criticizing it have been considered in chapter 6, which the reader should now review. Since the chief difference between the use of evidence in general argumentation and in research is that of formality, it is necessary now to differentiate between the kinds of evidence normally used in research.

The simplest kind of evidence in research is **personal observation.** In many situations **personal observation** cannot be verified. Therefore it is of limited value. The reader has to take the word of the writer; if he feels that the writer has made an unintentional or intentional distortion, he can only criticize the evidence indirectly, by suggesting that it is improbable or impossible. On the other hand, when the writer makes personal observations of a situation that can be duplicated by the reader, this type of evidence is entirely satisfactory. A laboratory report, for example, is based on **personal observation.** The conditions of the experiment are exactly specified in the report so that the reader can duplicate them if he wishes and test the accuracy of the observations for himself. "Laboratory conditions" are, however, difficult to attain outside of the physical sciences. A sociologist would never base general conclusions about behavior on a single case history, no matter how suggestive.

When conditions of observation cannot be duplicated, or when the subject must be considered in terms of general patterns, **personal observation** can be formalized by means of a **survey.** When making a **survey** the writer accumulates a large number of specific cases by means of a poll, a questionaire or interviews. He then examines the cases for significant trends and patterns, usually presenting his conclusions in the form of statistics. The Gallup Poll, the reports of the Census Bureau, the Kinsey Reports and the reports on smoking and lung cancer are all based on **surveys.** This is not the place to discuss the limitations of surveys. Proper use of them is extremely difficult, and demands, in addition to mathematical sophistication, an elaborate methodology. Even the most careful surveys—the Kinsey Reports are an example— can be criticized. "Figures don't lie but liars do figure" expresses a well-founded suspicion of the survey technique in its cruder forms. Unless the writer is trained in the mathematics and methodology of the survey, he should not attempt his own survey and should be extremely cautious when using the results of other people's surveys.

Consensus, authority and **testimony** are all based on something other than personal observation. Each has its limitations and dangers. **Consensus is appeal to the opinion of mankind at large or of a specialized group of experts** such as "all (or most) biologists," "all (or most) specialists in constitutional law," or "all (or most) *Hamlet* scholars." "Common sense tells us that without sound public education a democracy cannot function" is an example of **consensus.** The statement that a truth is "self-evident" is another form of **consensus:** "We hold these truths to be self-evident, that all men are created equal, that they are endowed . . ." In its general form, **consensus** is of limited value and easily converted into a propaganda device. The fact is that there are few (if any) positions on which a majority of men can agree, and few truths that are really "self-evident." Appeal to the **consensus** of a specialized group is also liable to become propaganda. It is, however, somewhat more reliable provided that the author is in a position to have accurate knowledge of current opinion on his subject. If there really is a **consensus** it is quite legitimate to indicate the fact. If the point is important to the author's proof, documentation should be provided citing the experts—or a representative group of them—who accept it. "Recent scholarship has shown that Donne makes frequent use of the Jesuit meditation in his poetry" is a legitimate appeal to the **consensus** of experts. If it is an important point for the author, it should be followed by a footnote number, and the footnote should cite (and perhaps quote) several representative examples of "recent scholarship." Without the footnote, the reader has no way of checking the accuracy of the statement.

Authority is appeal to an individual or work that has special validity in the area treated. A Moslem appeals to the **authority** of the Koran, a Catholic to the **authority** of St. Thomas Aquinas, a lawyer to the **authority** of the Constitution or Blackstone, a literary scholar to the **authority** of Aristotle's *Poetics*. In most fields, there are writers whose statements and opinions carry special weight. They are the current **authorities,** and their opinions are often used as evidence. In English literature, for example, E. K. Chambers and Douglas Bush have the status of authorities. While citing their opinions does not constitute absolute proof, it considerably reinforces the author's case.

284

Research papers use **authority** for two reasons. First, it is impossible for an author to know everything. If it is important for him to use material from an area of which he has only limited knowledge, he must accept the opinions of the specialists in that area. Obviously he needs the best opinions available. Second, **authority** can be used to reinforce the author's case in those areas that he knows well. A historian writing a book to show that the French Revolution was caused by the growing prosperity of the middle classes takes the burden of proof on himself, but it certainly strengthens his argument to point out that Georges Lefevre holds the same opinion.

Like **consensus,** citation of **authority** demands care. In a research paper, when an authority is cited, the citation is normally documented. To avoid weakening an argument by improper use of authority, the writer should make sure of two things. (1) The authority must be a genuine authority. One of the most common errors of beginning research papers is the assumption that publication is a guarantee of authority. The author consults the library card catalogue and *The Reader's Guide to Periodical Literature,* arbitrarily selects two books and three articles, and then cites the opinions expressed as "authoritative." In any important field a high proportion of published material is superficial popularization, out-of-date, erroneous or sheer trash. If the writer is not thoroughly familiar with the literature of the field he should consult someone who is. In any college course, the instructor will be able to identify the authoritative books and articles; if consultation is impossible, selective bibliographies such as are usually included in textbooks are useful. (2) The view attributed to the authority should be the view he holds. Knowledge advances and writers change their minds; an opinion considered authoritative in 1948 may be quite different from the best current opinion. Intentional distortion is still more pernicious. If a prominent critic writes "This play is an outstanding example of dullness; for sheer stupidity it surpasses any other play of the season," he should not be quoted as saying "This play is . . . outstanding . . . it surpasses any other play of the season." Although the example is extreme, misrepresentation and quotation out of context are, unfortunately, common. They convert the research paper from a search for truth to the cheapest form of propaganda.

Testimony is the use of quotation to reinforce **observation, consensus** or **authority.** "Toynbee has long held that most cultures follow a cyclical

285

pattern of birth, growth and decline" is strengthened by the addition of, "In the first volume of *A Study of History*, he writes . . .."

13.4   SOURCES

Almost all research papers rely on **sources** for much of their evidence. A historian writing about Mary Queen of Scots, may cite her letters and the writings of authors contemporary with her, as well as works written in the twentieth century. A writer discussing voter registration in Oregon may use statistics from state publications, published articles by Oregon political leaders and formal studies by political scientists.

Sources are either **primary** or **secondary.** A **primary source** is a document exhibiting the subject as directly as possible and with a minimum of distortion arising from prejudice, misinformation or lack of information. To a biographer, for example, the life records and writings of the man he is studying are primary, whereas comments on and appraisals of the man—even those by the man's contemporaries—are secondary. Both Mary, Queen of Scots' letters and published statistics on Oregon voter registration could serve as **primary sources.** For a critic writing about Hemingway's *Farewell to Arms,* the novel, itself, is the **primary source;** for an economist writing on "Free Enterprise in Economic Thought, 1800-1825," any discussion of economics published between 1800 and 1825 is a **primary source.**

A **secondary source** is a document commenting on the subject being considered. A comment on Mary Queen of Scots by one of her contemporaries, an article by a political scientist on Oregon voting patterns, a critical article on *A Farewell to Arms,* and a book entitled *A History of Economics in the Nineteenth Century* would all be **secondary sources** in the examples given. Notice that what is **primary** in one essay may become **secondary** in another. For an article on "Jeremy Bentham's Attitude toward Free Enterprise" only Bentham's writings and speeches would be primary; other comments on free enterprise contemporary with Bentham would be secondary.

As a general rule, **in research writing the author should base his proof on primary rather than secondary sources.** When using primary

286

sources, the author has an opportunity to form his own judgments. The results will be more authoritative, and the opportunities for original insights much greater, than if he relies on the interpretations of others. When using secondary sources the author must rely on the honesty and perceptiveness of another person. A historian of the year 2500 could make a fair evaluation of Stalin as a political theorist by studying Stalin's own writings; he would produce a hopelessly inaccurate picture if he relied primarily on comments *about* Stalin's political ideas appearing during Stalin's lifetime in the Soviet press. By the same token, a student writing a term paper about *Paradise Lost* must recognize that in the course of a single semester, he cannot master the many important books and articles dealing with the poem. He will be well advised to read a few recommended books and articles, but he should invest most of his time in reading and rereading the poem itself. If he bases his paper mostly on his **primary source** (i.e., *Paradise Lost*), the validity of his argument will depend on evidence presented rather than on the secondary sources that he has or has not read. His thesis will be original as far as he is concerned, since he developed it himself; and if his evidence is sound it will meet the requirement that the research paper be the best version of truth that the author can offer. Later, if the student does further work on Milton in graduate school, he may qualify or change his earlier view, but this is natural. It happens to professionals as well as students. The alternative is mental stagnation.

13.5   "SOURCE BOOKS"

It is common for courses in composition and research writing to use **source books**—collections of primary and secondary material on a specific subject. Source books enable the student to gain facility in research techniques without requiring that he master all available material on the subject. Source books are useful because they focus on the real problems of research—analysis of sources, development of an original thesis and proof of the thesis in a clear, rigorous essay. A novel or play can serve as an informal source book, with or without an appended collection of secondary sources commenting on the work selected.

Although not all courses use source books, they are increasingly popular. The student using a source book should realize that such a book does not in any way interfere with the opportunity for original, creative insight. In fact, it increases this opportunity. The responsibility for developing a stimulating original thesis from the materials in the source book is squarely on the shoulders of the student. He can use the materials in an obvious, trite way to produce mediocre essays that are a chore to write and boring to read; or he can accept the challenge to discover an interesting thesis and produce essays that are stimulating to write and enjoyable to read.

13.6   TAKING NOTES

Notes containing quotations should be clear and double-checked for accuracy. The original spelling and punctuation should be followed. If a note omits any part of the original, the omission should be indicated by three points (points of ellipsis—see below). In addition to the quotation, the note should identify the source and page number. If the author does not keep a separate bibliography file, the identification should be in bibliographic form (see below). Notes may contain a summary or précis as well as a quotation. If note cards are used, not more than one quotation or summary should appear per card. This will allow the note cards to be rearranged as the essay is developed.

Subheadings on note cards are sometimes convenient as long as they do not force the essay into an inflexible mold before the author has thoroughly considered his materials. Since note taking can become an end in itself, the writer is cautioned against accumulating too many notes before he has decided on purpose and method.

13.7   DOCUMENTATION

Documentation (see sample research paper for examples) is the writer's way of making sure that the reader can verify his evidence. Perhaps the most frequently asked question concerning documentation is

"What needs to be documented?" A simple rule for this is that **documentation should be used whenever an authority, opinion or item of evidence is essential to the proof of the author's thesis.** "Common knowledge" need not be documented if it is really common and if it is uncontroversial. In a paragraph that is mostly composed of references to one source, a single footnote at the end of the paragraph can be used in place of footnotes after every sentence.

Informal documentation consists of brief citations usually in parentheses, following the reference. Informal documentation is based for (1) works like the Bible, (2) works cited continuously throughout a paper, after the first footnote. In a research paper on *Huckleberry Finn,* for example, the first documented reference to the novel would be a footnote; the later references would probably be in the form "Huck later (p. 37) decides to leave home."

Formal documentation in a paper is provided by **footnotes** and **bibliography.** There are a number of possible forms to follow in composing a footnote citation or a bibliographical entry. The rules given here are based on one widely accepted style and will fit most cases. For ambiguous cases, consult your instructor or a full-scale discussion of documentation like the University of Chicago *Manual of Style* or Skillin and Gay's *Words into Type.**

1. Footnotes are indicated by numbers in the text. The footnote number is elevated above the line and *follows* the reference or quotation.
2. The footnote itself can be placed at the bottom of the page where the reference occurs. It is sometimes more convenient, however, to type the notes consecutively on separate sheets and place them at the end of the paper.
3. In writing footnotes, the general rule is "be clear and consistent."
4. Use the forms given below for first citation:

Book

[1] Richard Chase, *The Quest for Myth* (Baton Rouge: Louisiana State University Press, 1949), pp. 20-3.

---

* University of Chicago Press, *A Manual of Style*, 11th ed. (Chicago: University of Chicago Press, 1949), 522 pp.; Marjorie E. Skillin and Robert M. Gay, *Words into Type*, new rev. ed. (New York: Appleton-Century-Crofts, 1964), 596 pp.

Article

[2] Martin Scheerer, "Problem Solving," *Scientific American*, CCVIII (April, 1963), 118.

Chapter or section of a book

[3] Harry Levin, "Some Meanings of Myth," in *Myth and Mythmaking*, ed. Henry A. Murray (New York: George Braziller, 1960), pp. 118-21.

Newspaper story

[4] "Laboratory Launched in Space," *Greensboro Daily News*, April 3, 1964, A.3.

Multi-volume work

[5] Hippolyte Taine, "Introduction," *A History of English Literature*, tr. H. Van Laun (New York: Henry Altemus Co., 1908), I, 12.

5. The following **abbreviations** may be used for second and later citations:
   a. *Ibid.* (abbreviation of *ibidem*, "the same") means that the work is the same as the one cited in the previous footnote.
   b. When a work has been cited, but not in the preceding footnote, *op. cit.* (*opere citato*, "in the work cited") may be used. It is less confusing, however, to abbreviate the author's name and the work's title.
   Continuing the sequence of footnotes begun in section 4 we thus have:

[6] Chase, *Quest,* p. 35. [Or: [6] Chase, *op. cit.*, p. 35.]
[7] Levin, "Some Meanings," p. 120. [Or: Levin, *op. cit.*, p. 120.]
[8] *Ibid.*, pp. 123-4.
[9] Scheerer, "Problem Solving," p. 119. [Or: [9] Scheerer, *op. cit.*, p. 119.]

6. Most short research papers do not need a bibliography. If one is necessary, arrange the items alphabetically according to the author's last name in the forms given below:

Chase, Richard. *The Quest for Myth*. Baton Rouge: Louisiana State University Press, 1949.
"Laboratory Launched in Space." *Greensboro Daily News*. April 3, 1963, A.3.

Levin, Harry. "Some Meanings of Myth." In *Myth and Mythmaking*. Ed. Henry A. Murray. New York: George Braziller, 1960, pp. 103-24.

Murray, Henry A., ed. *Myth and Mythmaking*. New York: George Braziller, 1960.

Scheerer, Martin. "Problem Solving." *Scientific American*. CCVIII, April, 1963, 118-28.

Taine, Hippolyte. *A History of English Literature*. Tr. H. Van Laun. New York: Henry Altemus Co., 1908, 3 vols.

7. Footnotes often contain references to several authors and books. They can also include **quotation** and **author's clarification.** In the latter case the author comments on a point raised in the text to show its implications, qualify it or otherwise supplement the text.

13.8 QUOTATION

Quotation is one of the most effective forms of **evidence.** It should be used freely. Occasionally novice writers feel that quotation should be used infrequently because it is "not their own work." This is wrong. The "work" involved in using quotation is in finding the right quotation. Quotations vary in length from a word or phrase to several paragraphs. A quotation should be 'the minimum length necessary to illustrate or prove the author's point, and "minimum length" obviously depends on the circumstances. An essay that is a mosaic of quotations strung together on transitional sentences is unsatisfactory. However, an essay that fails to make effective use of quotation is almost as bad.

Quotations, whether in the text or in footnotes, should be accurate and representative of the context from which they are taken. The language, spelling and punctuation of the source should be preserved. If there is an obvious error in the source, this can be indicated with the word *sic* (Latin "thus"—no period) in square brackets following the error. If the author omits words in the original, the omission is indicated by three points (**points of ellipsis**) at the beginning and in the middle of a sentence, and four points at the end if the sentence is declarative.

Short quotations—from a phrase to one or two sentences—are usually combined with the text. They can be **continuous** with the author's comment, or they can be introduced with an **"identifying label."** In either case they are set off with quotation marks. Longer quotations are usually indented and single-spaced. Since this form clearly indicates that the material is quoted, no quotation marks are used. **Documentation** always *follows* the quoted material. Note the following examples:

1. Quotation **continuous** with author's comment:

    When Cordelia tells her father that she lacks "that glib and oily art,/To speak and purpose not" (I, i, 227-8), she is beginning to sound hostile.

2. Quotation in text, but introduced with an **"identifying label"**:

    King Lear is incapable of recognizing that nature is indifferent to human suffering. Just as the storm begins he says, "And thou, all shaking thunder,/Smite flat the thick rotundity o' the world!" (III, ii, 6-7). Later, he becomes still more violent. . . .

3. **Inset quotation** (note the use of **points of ellipsis**):

    Considering the problem of Shakespeare's religious attitudes in *King Lear*, A. C. Bradley concluded that Shakespeare was not concerned with theology, as were Dante and Shelley:

    > Nor do I mean that *King Lear* contains a revelation of righteous omnipotence . . . or even a promise of the reconciliation of mystery and justice. . . . Any theological interpretation of the world on the author's part is excluded. . . .[1]

▶ 13.9 ANNOTATED EXAMPLE

The following research paper illustrates several typical characteristics and techniques. It has been selected for three reasons. First, although it is on an author and book that have received a great deal

---

[1] A. C. Bradley, *Shakespearean Tragedy* (London: Macmillan and Co., Ltd., 1904), pp. 278-9.

of critical attention—the bibliography of *Tom Jones* is very large—it develops an original thesis almost entirely on the basis of a close reading of the single **primary source,** the novel itself. Second, its organization is essentially that of "argumentation by thesis and evidence," the type of argumentation explained in chapter 6. Third, its organization is exceptionally clear, and techniques such as definition, devices of coherence and transitions are emphasized. It shows that original and perceptive research is possible with a very limited subject and careful analysis of a single primary source. While it should not be considered a model for all types of research, it sets a high standard that is, at the same time, within the reach of any writer willing to examine a limited subject thoroughly.

TITLE PAGE

VERBAL IRONY IN TOM JONES

by Eleanor N. Hutchens*

Without its verbal irony, <u>Tom Jones</u> would be quite a different book: massive and well made

BACKGROUND

but lacking the high polish and the effect of urbane control which do much to preserve it as a major classic. Its realism, its satire, and even its much-praised plot keep their unified brilliance through being governed by an ironic style that forms as important a contribution to

PURPOSE

the English novel as any Fielding made.

A variety of sources beginning with Lucan

BACKGROUND
(HISTORY)

can be cited for Fielding's uses of irony. The

* Reprinted by permission of the Modern Language Association from Eleanor N. Hutchens', "Verbal Irony in *Tom Jones*," *PMLA*, LXXVII (March, 1962), 46-50.

Scriblerus group were his acknowledged masters in his own time, and French prose romance was not without its influence.[1] But Fielding, in _Tom Jones_, was the first English novelist who employed verbal irony to hold a huge body of realistic material, including a straightforward narrative and a set of believable characters commanding the sympathetic interest of the reader, under the dual scrutiny of comedy and morality. As an ironist he is generally held

BACKGROUND (CONTRAST TO SWIFT)

inferior to Swift in subtlety, intellectuality, and force. But Swift creates an abstract world—the nonexistent lands visited by Gulliver, the weird mind of the Modest Proposer, etc.—into which he draws selected materials from the real world for ironic treatment. Fielding treats people, events, and ideas in their native settings, amid the mitigations and qualifying circumstances that blunt the edge of any but the most skillfully applied irony.

FOOTNOTE (CITATION OF AUTHORITY)

[1]On the French influence, see Wayne C. Booth, "The Self-Conscious Narrator in Comic Fiction before _Tristram Shandy_," _PMLA_, LXVII (1952), 163-185.

That his verbal irony is best exemplified in Tom Jones may be questioned by readers who think of Jonathan Wild first in connection with it. But the irony in Jonathan Wild has no basic

straightforward text to operate upon; the whole text is ironic, like that of A Modest Proposal; morover, the irony is not so urbane and mature. The long and greatly-admired passage on honor (I, 13), besides owing much to Falstaff, has not the subtle ease of a casually-dropped remark to the same end in Tom Jones: "his lordship, who was strictly a man of honour, and would by no means have been guilty of an action which the world in general would have condemned, began to be much concerned for the advice which he had taken" (XVIII, 11). There is verbal irony in Joseph Andrews; but it does not prevail there, and the style therefore has a more yielding surface; Amelia too has it, but it is mired in the emotionalism which renders the text boggy. Only in Tom Jones does it achieve the triumphant mastery that taught Fielding's successors.

PRACTICAL RHETORIC

BACKGROUND
(DEFINITION)

Verbal irony takes several forms. As irony, it is one of two main varieties—verbal and substantial—of the sport of bringing about a conclusion by indicating the opposite one. It is effected by a choice or arrangement of words which conveys the ironist's meaning by suggesting its reverse. The suggestion clashes with the context or with some view presumably shared by author and reader (or at least known by the reader to be held by the author), and the clash comically invalidates the suggestion and thereby strengthens the view with which it conflicts. The forms of verbal irony are the

STATEMENT OF
METHOD

ways in which the suggestion may be made: by the denotation, connotation, tone, or implied reference of the words or of their arrangement. In <u>Tom Jones</u> Fielding persistently employs all these forms. Narration, description, characterization, and exposition receive

END OF INTRODUC-
TION (NOTE EXTRA
SPACE BETWEEN
PARAGRAPHS)

constant polish from them, and to them the book may well be said to owe its enduring brilliance.

INTRODUCTION TO "DENOTATIVE IRONY" (NOTE DEFINITION)

Of the four, denotative irony is the simplest and least subtle, consisting merely in the use of a word to mean its literal opposite, as "noble" is used in these passages:

EVIDENCE (INSET QUOTATIONS; NOTE INFORMAL CITATIONS AND USE OF POINTS OF ELLIPSIS)

> [Mrs. Partridge] was . . . a professed follower of that noble sect founded by Xantippe of old. . . . (II, 7)

> The great are deceived if they imagine they have appropriated ambition and vanity to themselves. These noble qualities flourish as notably in a country church . . . as in the drawing room. . . . (IV, 7)

> The noble bumtrap, blind and deaf to every circumstance of distress, greatly rises above all the motives to humanity, and into the hands of the gaoler resolves to deliver his miserable prey. (VII, 3)

or as "good" is used in these:

> 'Every man must die some time or other,' answered the good woman; 'it is no business of mine. I hope, doctor, you would not have me hold him while you bleed him.' (VII, 3)

> Among other good principles upon which this society was founded, there was one very remarkable; . . . that every member should, within twenty-four hours, tell at least one merry fib, which was to be propagated by all the brethren and sisterhood. (XV, 3)

297

Denotative irony sounds a brief, sharp crack
of sarcastic humor, without those reverberative
qualities that carry the effect of other kinds
of verbal irony beyond the boundaries of the
ironic words themselves. When Squire Western's

OTHER EXAMPLES
AS EVIDENCE

demeanor as a magistrate is called wise, when
Partridge's remarks are called sage, when
a hideous chambermaid is called fair, the
flat contradiction of truth makes its brief
impact and dies, with no probing into relative
validities (as connotative irony is likely to
probe) and no transfiguring effect on the
context.

Yet this is not to say that it has no part
in the larger effects of <u>Tom Jones</u>. These
recurring snaps of the whip have their function
in helping to keep the novel within its appointed
bounds—that is, within the pale of comedy
and morality at once. Take away "noble," take
away "good" from the passages cited, and in
most cases Fielding's moral comment is lost
or dulled. Substitute "base" or "bad," the

298

straightforward truthful words, and moral
criticism is retained but the comedy is lost.
Where there is no moral criticism, as in the
case of the "fair" chambermaid, there is only
comedy to be lost; but the loss of one passage
in the novel from the comic view is a loss
to the whole effect. Denotative irony, then,
although in itself less interesting and
stimulating than connotative irony, is a
useful auxiliary in the work of producing the
total impression of the novel as well as in
enhancing the liveliness of individual
passages. That Fielding himself felt it to
be an inferior device is suggested by the fact
that in <u>Tom Jones</u> he uses it sparingly, only
about one third as often as connotative irony.

TRANSITION TO
"CONNOTATIVE
IRONY"
DEFINITION

This form, the one by which Fielding does
most to achieve the verbal brilliance of <u>Tom
Jones</u>, differs from the denotative in that the
ironic word retains its literal meaning but
clashes with truth in its connotaions. I have
attempted to show, in another place, how

299

connotative irony is used to carry out one of the major themes of the book;[2] for present purposes, a demonstration of its mechanics will perhaps suffice.

EXAMPLE FOR
DEFINITION

Fielding shows an analytical awareness of connotative irony in the first chapter of <u>Jonathan Wild</u>, where he takes pains to remove the connotation of goodness from the word "greatness." (Despite this explicit separation the comic impact of "great" as applied to Wild rests in its connotative irony as we continue to associate goodness, or worthiness, with greatness and are therefore struck by a comical incongruity in the application.) In <u>Tom Jones</u>, besides bearing specific themes (the nature of prudence, honor, etc.), connotative irony in its nature reflects Fielding's governing comic-moral view that a thing may be good or true in one sense but bad or false in others. His use of "proper"

[2]"'Prudence' in <u>Tom Jones</u>," <u>PQ</u>, XXXIX (October, 1960), 496-507.

EXAMPLE (QUOTA-
TION IN TEXT)
illustrates this point: "The captain was

indeed as great a master of the art of love as

Ovid was formerly. He had besides received

proper hints from his brother, which he failed

INFORMAL
CITATION
not to improve to the best advantage" (I, 10).

The conspiracy of the Blifil brothers is thus

dignified with a word which, while legitimately

used to mean appropriate (to the attainment

of the end in view), carries connotations

of laudable conduct which are comically

inapplicable to the Blifil game. Squire

Western's indecorous behavior, Partridge's

gluttony and self-interest, and the rapacity

of the Man of the Hill's fellow gamblers

receive similar treatment:

EVIDENCE (INSET
QUOTATIONS)
> The squire, however, sent after his
> sister the same holloa which attends the
> departure of a hare, when she is first
> started before the hounds. He was indeed
> a great master of this kind of vociferation,
> and had a holloa proper for most occasions
> in life. (VII, 3)
>
> Partridge thought he had now a proper
> opportunity to remind his friend of a
> matter which he seemed entirely to have
> forgotten; what this was the reader will
> guess, when we inform him that Jones had
> eaten nothing more than one poached egg
> since he had left the alehouse. . . .
> (XII, 13)

> [Partridge] no sooner discovered the
> principles of his fellow-traveller than
> he thought proper to conceal and outwardly
> give up his own to the man on whom he
> depended for the making his fortune. . . .
> (VIII, 9)

> 'I mean . . . those gross cheats which
> are proper to impose upon the raw and
> unexperienced. . . .' (VII, 13)

COMMENT ON
EVIDENCE

In each case, an element of the literal meaning of "proper" can be applied faithfully to the context. The idea of fitness, in some form, is always present; but the straightforward expression would differ in each instance. "Cunningly aimed" for Dr. Blifil's hints; "adapted" for the squire's holloa (though even here there might be some irony in the ideal of rational choice usually associated with the word); all of the examples which range in subject matter from harmless eccentricity through opportunism to actual criminality, could have been rendered unironically in terms not carrying the favorable connotations of "proper."

Usually the moral criticism is adverse, as in the buying of Molly Seagrim's favors: "some well-chosen presents from the philosopher

EXAMPLES AS
EVIDENCE (QUOTA-
TIONS IN TEXT)

so softened and unguarded the girl's heart,
that . . . Square triumphed . . ." (V, 5).
"Softened" and "unguarded" apply in some slight
literal sense to Molly's coming to terms, but
the connotations direct the reader to contrast
her case with that of the innocent victim of
seduction. Sometimes, on the other hand, the
connotations are worse, rather than better,
than the subject warrants, when Fielding wishes
to excuse rather than to blame: "This hare he
had basely and barbarously knocked on the head,
against the laws of the land, and no less
against the laws of sportsmen" (III, 10).
Here Fielding shifts downward into the view
of the game-preserving squires, who while
they save the game from the hungry poor "will
most unmercifully slaughter whole horse-loads
themselves" (III, 2). "Basely" and "barbarously"
do not lose all their literal meaning, since
the act is illegal and a violation of the
rights of property which, Fielding would have
been the last to deny, constitute a foundation
stone of civilized society; but the connotations

of self-righteousness they carry, in their unwarrantable severity, clash comically with the real moral position of the squires. Thus Black George comes off the better for them.

TRANSITION TO "IRONY OF TONE" (NOTE SHORT PARAGRAPH)

The technique of connotative irony is Fielding's chief means of accomplishing the stylistic effect of <u>Tom Jones</u>. Denotative, tonal, and referential irony mesh with it, but they are not so frequently used, are not so closely adapted to his realistic materials, and all in all are not so well calculated to give the whole its high polish.

IRONY OF TONE
DEFINITION

Irony of tone stands somewhere between connotative and denotative irony in subtlety and staying power. One of the great life-giving excellences of Fielding's prose is that in it we hear continually the cadences, the modulations, the pauses and accelerations of the human voice.[3] Here, as elsewhere, his presence as author allows him full play, permitting him a

FOOTNOTE USED
FOR COMMENT

[3] Some readers seem not to have the inward ear with which others hear whatever they silently read. To them, what is here called tonal irony may appear to be purely a matter of syntax or sentence structure.

wide range of tones not only in his own voice but in the voices to which he shifts for ironic effect. (To deplore Fielding's "intrusiveness" is to wish away his verbal irony, which would

be impossible without it.) Tonal irony has little to do with the words used; it does not depend on the raising or lowering of diction, though one of these sometimes accompanies it. It is achieved by the sequence in which words are arranged, by the ordering of clauses and phrases, and sometimes by punctuation. When it does partially depend on the words used, this dependence is owing to the fact that those words demand a certain tone of voice when they occur at a given point in the sentence. "In deed," "at least," "never," "only," and many other words and phrases in English take on standard tones when they are placed in certain relations

with other parts of a given utterance.

> . . . that surprising sect, who are
> honourably mentioned by the late Dr. Swift
> as having, by the mere force of genius
> alone, without the least assistance of
> any kind of learning, or even reading,
> discovered that profound and invaluable
> secret that there is no God. . . . (VI, 1)

305

"Mere," "alone," "least," and other words in this passage require, in the positions they occupy, tones of wonder and admiration. These tones clash, of course, with Fielding's real contempt, ironically driving it home. In contrast to their emphasis, here is a dependent clause which makes its effect by virtue of its subordination:

> It was Mr. Western's custom every afternoon, as soon as he was drunk, to hear his daughter play on the harpsichord. . . . (IV, 5)

The perfunctory, matter-of-fact tone demanded by the "as soon as" clause is in comic conflict with its meaning as statement and thus comments ironically upon Squire Western's way of life.

At its noisiest, as in Squire Western's sudden irruptions into scenes of courtesy or sentiment, the tonal irony of <u>Tom Jones</u> reaches the burlesque. It is worth noting that in the "Homerical" churchyard battle the tone, alternately soaring and lurching like a schoolboy's translation, participates in the effect as fully as do the diction and the

referential irony of classical allusion:

> Recount, O Muse, the names of those who fell on this fatal day. First, Jemmy Tweedle felt on his hinder head the direful bone. Him the pleasant banks of sweetly-winded Stour had nourished, where he first learnt the vocal art, with which, wandering up and down at wakes and fairs, he cheered the rural nymphs and swains when upon the green they interweaved the sprightly dance; while he himself stood fiddling and jumping to his own music. How little now avails his fiddle! He thumps the verdant floor with his carcass. (IV, 8)

COMMENT

In its total range, irony of tone approaches

that of connotation as a contributor to the

persistent effect of authorial mastery that

controls the reader's impression of the novel.

In exposition it enables Fielding not only

to create variety by going beyond his own

appointed range of tones as straightforward

lecturer but to introduce points of view other

than his own in such ways that their possessors

seem to be present and exposing themselves to

ridicule rather than being exposed by him. Thus

avoiding the appearance of ill humor and

narrow-mindedness, he seems to be letting them

307

have their say with perfect good grace and leaving it to the reader to judge them. In characterization it operates similarly as a device for making speakers condemn themselves: "No, no, friend, I shall never be bubbled out of my religion in hopes only of keeping my place under another government; for I should certainly be no better, and very probably might be worse" (XII, 7). Readers more sensitive to tone than to substance are capable of taking this speech as one of stout religious loyalty, so well does the tone envelop the statement. The tone of resolution created by the linking of "never" with "religion" and the tone of deprecation in the linking of "only" and "place" overwhelm the sense of the final reflection, which thus subordinated sounds as righteous as the rest while actually marking the exciseman's motive as altogether self-interested. Narrative and descriptive passages likewise demand alertness to clashes between tone and statement if the reader is to keep up with the irony or even, in some cases, with the action; for Fielding shows a perfect willingness to couch important information in casual tones that make it sound not only insignificant but probably untrue: "In plain language, the only way he could possibly find to account for the possession of this note was by robbery; and to confess the truth, the reader, unless he should suspect it was owing to the generosity of Lady Bellaston, can hardly imagine any other" (XIII, 8). We learn in the next paragraph that Lady Bellaston is indeed the source of Tom's new affluence, the slyness of the foregoing hint yielding to a contrasting and equally ironic openness and enthusiasm in regard to the giver's charitable impulses.

TRANSITION TO
"IRONY OF REF-
ERENCE"

Whereas tone, it must be acknowledged, is sometimes elusive and often subject to question because of differences in receptivity and ear among readers, the irony of reference lends itself rather more readily to objective

309

discussion. In its verbal form, it consists in the use of words which by implication compare or refer a subject to something else which in its comic dissimilarity points up the real nature of the subject. Fielding's customary use of this device calls in the terminology of a body of learning—law, medicine, classical literature, politics, science, or military craft—to give the subject an air of dignity, method, reason, or importance which does not belong to it and thereby to emphasize its lack of the quality suggested.

EXAMPLES (INSET QUOTATIONS)

> Tom was now mounted on the back of a footman, and everything prepared for execution, when Mr. Allworthy, entering the room, gave the criminal a reprieve. . . . (III, 8)

> [Square] soon found the means of mitigating her anger . . . partly by a small nostrum from his purse, of wonderful and approved efficacy in purging off the ill humours of the mind, and in restoring it to a good temper. (V, 5)

> An ancient heathen would perhaps have imputed this disability to the god of drink, no less than to the god of war; for, in reality, both the combatants had sacrificed as well to the former deity as to the latter. . . . (IX, 6)

> Now there was a certain office in the gift of Mr. Fitzpatrick at that time

vacant, namely, that of a wife: for the
lady who had lately filled that office
had resigned, or at least deserted her
duty. Mr. Fitzpatrick therefore, having
thoroughly examined Mrs. Waters on the
road, found her extremely fit for the place,
which, on their arrival at Bath, he
presently conferred upon her, and she
without any scruple accepted. (XVII, 9)

In not every case, however, is the subject

dignified: the shift may be downward, as in

Squire Western's application of hunting terms

**BRIEF EXAMPLES
IN TEXT**

to the lovely Sophia—"We have got the dog fox,

I warrant the bitch is not far off" (X, 7),

". . . I'll unkennel her . . ." (XV, 5)—and

as in Fielding's use, in his chapter headings,

of the jargon of advertisers and publishers of

sentimental literature. Here the irony operates

in favor of the subject by seeming to classify

it in a clearly inferior category.

**SPECIAL TYPES;
COMMENT**

Fielding's use of referential irony extends

the conceptions within which his material is

considered, relating his incidents and his

characters to greater matters or general ideas

or established institutions or bodies of

thought; it is more than metaphor in that

311

its comparisons swell or diminish their subjects in significant ways, assisting in the continuous work of keeping them under comic and moral surveillance. Thus it makes a special contribution of its own in addition to joining the other three forms of verbal irony in the management of total effect.

CONCLUSION (NOTE
SPACING BETWEEN
PARAGRAPHS)
AUTHOR'S
COMMENT

Substantial irony is outside the scope of this discussion, which seeks to show only how verbal irony in <u>Tom Jones</u> operates in the creation of the whole impression made by the novel. Let it nevertheless be noted that substantial irony functions as a huge complement to the verbal kind in unifying and holding together as living tissue the materials of <u>Tom Jones</u>. The tripartite structure of the book, so often credited with giving it superior form and purposefulness, is as naught beside the constant play of large and small ironies of action and thought that keep reaching backward and forward to draw its multitudinous events and persons into relation

RESTATEMENT (I.E., "VERBAL IRONY IS IMPORTANT IN TOM JONES") —

with one another under the comic-moral view. Again, however, <u>Tom Jones</u> would be a vastly different novel if its irony were substantial only. Much of it would be grim, much sentimental. (Take away the descriptions of Blifil as a prudent youth, and the like, and the blackness of his character would seriously darken the book; take away the mock-reverential tones in which Sophia is sometimes treated, and at points she would dissolve into the sentimental heroine.) However expert the writing, the whole

CONCLUDING SENTENCE

thing could not be carried off with the air of urbane triumph that does in fact distinguish it.

TERMS TO BE LEARNED

▸ Two types of research paper
▸ Three kinds of evidence
▸ Two kinds of sources
▸ Standard footnote forms for citation of a book and an article

Exercises & Theme Topics

I. Assume that the following items are to be footnotes in a research paper. Give them in proper footnote form. Then write the bibliography for the paper.

A. Reference to page five of a book called The Christian Scholar in the Age of the Reformation published in 1956 by Charles Scribner's Sons of New York. The author is E. Harris Harbison.

B. Reference to a book translated by James P. Pettegrove and printed in London by Thomas Nelson and Sons in 1953. The book is by Ernst Cassirer and is called The Platonic Renaissance in England. The citation is of pages 129 to 135.

C. Reference to pages fifty-six and fifty-seven of Professor Harbison's book.

D. Reference to page sixty of Professor Harbison's book.

E. Reference to an article by George B. Parks entitled The First Italianate Englishmen published in the journal Studies in the Renaissance. The article appeared in the 1961 issue, which was volume eight, on pages 197 to 216. The citation of this footnote is pages 198 to 200.

F. Reference to page 98 of Professor Cassirer's book.

G. Reference to page 210 of Professor Parks's article.

H. Reference to lines 469 to 490 of Book Five of Paradise Lost by John Milton. These lines appear on page 313 of the edition by Merritt Y. Hughes entitled John Milton: Complete Poems and Major Prose published in 1957 by The Odyssey Press, Inc., of New York.

I. Reference to pages one through seven of Professor Cassirer's book.

J. Reference to the entry Platonism in A Handbook to Literature by William Flint Thrall, Addison Hibbard and C. Hugh Holman. The book was published in 1960 by The Odyssey Press, Inc., of New York, and the entry appears on pages 354 to 356.

K. Reference to pages 272 to 273 of the first volume of the two-volume edition of John Calvin's Institutes of the Christian Religion, translated by Henry Beveridge and published in London in 1953 by James Clarke & Co., Limited.

L. Reference to page 272 of Calvin's Institutes.

M. Reference to page 272 of Calvin's Institutes.

N. Reference to an article by Paul Oskar Kristeller entitled The Place of Classical Humanism in Renaissance Thought and reprinted in a collection of articles edited by Karl H. Dannenfeldt entitled The Renaissance: Medieval or Modern? The article appears on pages 75 to 78 of this volume, and the citation is of page 76. The volume was published by D. C. Heath and Company of Boston in 1959.

O. Reference to page 210 of Professor Parks's article.

II. The following suggestions for essays are intended to provide preliminary experience in selecting and evaluating source materials, taking notes, formulating a thesis, presenting results and documenting. You should include notes, outline and bibliography with your essay.

A. Choose a play or novel that interests you. Using this as your primary source, decide on a limited aspect that you wish to treat (e.g., a theme, a character or technique, a stylistic feature) and take notes on it. Formulate a thesis based on your analysis and write an essay (500-750 words) demonstrating your thesis. Feel free to use quotation, and document all important citations.

B. Select an important political or social event of the past year. Read several independent accounts such as the AP and UP stories, the analysis of the event in editorials and "The News of the Week in Review" section of *The New York Times,* and comment in news magazines such as *Time, Newsweek, The Reporter* and *U.S. News and World Report.* After analyzing and evaluating the sources, write a documented paper (500-750 words) on press reaction to the event selected. Note: do not attempt to deal with too many sources. Your paper will be judged more on the quality and depth of the analysis than on its breadth.

C. Develop a bibliography of ten to fifteen significant items on a currently controversial subject. Include key primary sources as well as secondary ones. In compiling your bibliography consult such standard reference guides as the *Readers' Guide to Periodical Literature*, the *International Index to Periodicals*, *The New York Times Index*, *Facts on File* and the library card catalogue. Typical subjects include: The Drain on the Gold Reserve, Federal Aid to Education, Disarmament, China versus Russia, Birth Control, Civil Rights, a recent, controversial book or movie. After completing a preliminary bibliography, read the items listed and take notes. Then write an essay (1000-1500 words) analyzing and evaluating the various points of view encountered or supporting the point of view you consider best. Include a formal bibliography with two sections, one for primary and one for secondary sources.

D. Using sources contemporary with the subject as well as recent comment, write a research paper (1000-2000 words) on a significant historical event or person. Concentrate on primary rather than secondary sources and limit your approach so that you can make a clear, emphatic case in the space given. The following list will suggest a few possibilities:

1. Northern (or Southern) Reaction to the Firing on Fort Sumter
2. Steam Engines Before 1800
3. The Federal Government in *The Federalist Papers*
4. A Critical Analysis of *The Communist Manifesto*
5. The Fulbright Act: A Short History
6. Roosevelt's First Presidential Campaign
7. Contemporary Reactions to *Huckleberry Finn,* 1884-1900
8. Knowledge of Anatomy During the Sixteenth Century
9. English Poetry of World War I
10. Henry Ford's Pacifism

Rhetoric and
Criticism

14

The present text is intended primarily for writers, but inevitably, in the process of developing skill in writing, one also develops skill in reading in the same way that an amateur artist, by undertaking his own experiments with oils and canvas, learns to appreciate professional painting more deeply. In addition to increasing enjoyment, critical appreciation of skilled accomplishment—whether in painting or writing—

317

can improve the performance of the person doing the appreciating. We learn not only by precept and practice; we also learn by example and imitation.

The principles of rhetoric have thus far been treated in terms of their practical application to common writing problems. Since they apply to all writing, they can be used equally well as aids to the appreciation of literature. When we appreciate a movie, play or book silently, we become informal critics speaking to an audience of one. When we talk or write about literature, we become formal critics and what we say becomes **criticism.** Criticism is simply speech or writing about literature. It does not imply a negative approach—one that emphasizes the inadequacies of a literary work—although it includes negative criticism as one of its forms. Criticism may, in fact, be entirely descriptive. In this case the critic simply explains what the author is doing without passing judgment or offering a formal evaluation. Since a critic usually will not waste time on a work that, after being given a fair trial, seems worthless, essays of **descriptive criticism** usually imply that the literature discussed is successful and enjoyable, but the critic's objective is not **proof** that it is successful. The essay on *Tom Jones* reprinted in chapter 13 is **descriptive criticism.** Professor Hutchens assumes that the novel is enjoyable; her purpose is to describe its use of a specific rhetorical device. Often, of course, the critic's purpose is to demonstrate either excellence or failure. When this is so, he is practicing **judicial criticism.** There are many other types of criticism, but they need not be discussed here.

Rhetoric is a particularly valuable tool of descriptive and judicial criticism. Again the essay on *Tom Jones* is a case in point. Using a single stylistic device, *irony,* and an extended definition of the device, the author writes a descriptive analysis of its use in a well-known novel. Because irony is an important part of the novel, the essay contributes to our understanding and hence to our appreciation. Notice that any other rhetorical device from such general ones as organization and imagery to highly specific ones like personification, allusion or use of periodic sentences could also be made the basis of an essay of descriptive or judicial criticism.

This leads to another point about criticism. From the reader's point of view, criticism is valuable because it reveals new aspects of the literature in which he is interested. It corrects misconceptions, and it enriches his appreciation of the range of the work's ideas, themes, characters and background. From the writer's point of view, this kind of criticism contributes to his awareness of the resources of language. When he has noticed, for example, the variety of effects that Henry Fielding can achieve by irony, he can increase the effectiveness of his own uses of irony. This does not mean that he will slavishly imitate Fielding, although he may wish to try some out-and-out imitations for his own private benefit. It means rather that when he encounters writing problems similar to those encountered by Fielding, he will be aware that irony is one effective solution. This is another way of saying that reading improves writing, and the more analytical the reading, the greater the likelihood of improvement.

The present chapter is an introduction to a few of the standard methods of literary criticism. It is offered in the hope that it will encourage the student to make use of what he already knows and eventually seek to extend his knowledge to the many areas of criticism that are beyond the limits of practical rhetoric.

14.1   THE LIMITS OF RHETORICAL CRITICISM

The writer has the opportunity to control his own writing. Usually, the finished product is a combination of conscious **intention** plus elements that come—for better or for worse—without planning. At any rate, for the writer of expository or argumentative prose, what he has done in a given essay is usually fairly unambiguous. He consciously formulates his **intention** and expresses it in his purpose statement. For the literary critic, **intention** is less simple. Some literary artists are highly self-conscious, but others feel that what happens in their writing is best left to instinct or inspiration. Even self-conscious writers are apt to be reluctant to discuss their work or are (as in the case of William Faulkner) positively misleading. When we move from the contemporary period to the literature of the past, the question of intentions is further complicated, because most authors have not left convenient explanations (false or true) for the guidance of later readers. The problem created by this situation can be illustrated by supposing that Shakespeare had written a letter toward the end of his life saying that *Hamlet* was intended to be a

319

comedy. What would we do with such a document? It would force us to reexamine the play, but we would not use the document to judge the play. The reverse is true. Whether or not *Hamlet* is a comedy depends on what *Hamlet* contains, not on what Shakespeare or anyone else says about it. As a rule then, **the intentions and methods used in a literary work should be discovered in the work itself, and not in statements by the writer, his contemporaries or later critics about the work.** Statements can be useful guides, but they must always be tested against the work.

This rule provides a basis for objectivity in criticism. It also sets limits to what criticism can do. When we are planning our own essay, we can be reasonably certain of what we are doing. When we judge the writing of another person, we are capable of misinterpretation, and differences of opinion are inevitable. If criticism is objective, why are there so many different interpretations of *Hamlet* or the Bible or the Constitution? The answer is that different interpretations are inevitable as long as human beings are not omniscient. The existence of different interpretations does not, however, mean that all interpretations are of equal value. Some are probable, some are highly improbable; some are profound, some superficial. **Criticism is objective because it offers verifiable proof of its conclusions, not because everyone agrees on every point.**

14.2 INTENTION AND FUNCTION

The intention of a literary work is the most general theme or impression that the work conveys. As we have noted, it is judged by the work itself, not by what the author or a critic may state the intention to be. The intention of the work is sometimes called its "main point" or "meaning." Rhetorically speaking, the **intention** of a literary work is equivalent to the **purpose statement** of an expository or argumentative essay.

The function of a character, descriptive passage, image or other element of a literary work is the way in which it contributes to the expression of the work's intention. Discussion of **function** is an important aspect of criticism. It assumes that the literary work is shaped

320

to meet a specific end or create a specific effect. Even when the writer draws on a source, as Shakespeare did when writing *Hamlet,* he has freedom to suppress or enlarge elements in the original, change motivation and add new material. For most criticism the question is not "Where did this material come from?" but "How is it used, and how does this particular usage contribute to the total effect?" Why, for example, is Ophelia necessary to the play *Hamlet?* Why is it appropriate for her to be obedient to her father rather than—like Juliet—defy him? Why is her mad scene appropriate? That is, her madness could have been reported rather than acted out at considerable length in a scene where Hamlet does not even appear. In the abstract, one might think the mad scene digressive since it shifts the focus of attention from the main character to a minor one. By the same token, instead of showing the scene where Hamlet is saved by the pirates from Rosencrantz and Guildenstern, Shakespeare has it reported secondhand. Again, in the abstract, the treatment might seem inappropriate. Each of these examples represents a challenge to the critic. If he can show that the treatment is **functional**—that it is appropriate and even necessary to the work's **intention**—he will increase his own appreciation as well as that of other readers.

Notice that any aspect of a work, from a single word or image to the entire plot, can be treated in terms of function. Speaking of one of his early teachers, Samuel Taylor Coleridge wrote in the first chapter of his *Biographia Literaria:*

> I learned from him that Poetry, even that of the loftiest and, seemingly, that of the wildest odes, had a logic of its own, as severe as that of science; and more difficult, because more subtle, more complex, and dependent on more, and more fugitive causes. In the truly great poets, he would say, there is a reason assignable, not only for every word, but for the position of every word. . . .

The only reservation necessary about this passage is that, although some problems of criticism are extremely subtle, others demand only care and thoughtful reading. As in any other discipline, the critic can begin with relatively easy methods and problems and learn to deepen his approach as he gains skill.

Notice also that analysis in terms of function can be used in both descriptive and judicial criticism. If the critic assumes that the work is unified—that its components all contribute to the expression of its intention—he may be content to describe the function of one or more of its parts without heavily emphasizing its excellence. This approach is particularly useful in criticism of works generally regarded as literary masterpieces. If reader and writer both know that the work in question is outstanding, there is no need to labor the point. The interest will be in *why* and *how* it is outstanding. On the other hand, if the writer finds that the work in question is deficient, functional analysis gives him a means for showing its inadequacies. To demonstrate that a given element is digressive, tangential or inadequate to its function, is to show that the work is flawed.

A last word of caution is needed here. The quality of negative criticism depends entirely on the quality of the critic's analysis. If his understanding of the work's intention is superficial or erroneous, his discussion of function will obviously reflect deficiencies in his own analysis rather than deficiencies in the work being criticized. Literary works become "masterpieces" because they have satisfied a great many readers—critics as well as laymen—over long periods of time. While revaluation goes on continually, the beginning critic usually does best to assume that if a work has the status of a masterpiece, its parts are functionally related to its intention. A writer who dismisses Ophelia's mad scene as irrelevant to the main point of *Hamlet,* for example, is simply demonstrating that he has not fully understood the play's intention. Not only will his criticism be weak, but he will also deny himself and his reader the chance for increased understanding of Shakespeare's art. This does not mean that masterpieces are sacrosanct—that they should *never* be subjected to negative criticism. It *does* mean that the critic should proceed with caution. Whether he is discussing a masterpiece or the latest best-seller, he has a responsibility to understand the work as thoroughly and as sympathetically as possible before he writes about it.

14.3   ANALYSIS OF PLOT

In narrative literature, whether poetry or prose, **plot** is the equivalent of **structure** in the expository or argumentative essay. **Plot is an arrangement of episodes according to a definite pattern and having**

the quality of unity. In some plots the episodes are arranged chronologically, following the sequence A-B-C-D-E and so forth. Often, however, the author will suppress some episodes of a chronological sequence and stress others, so that the plot has the form A-B-(C)-D-(E)-F-G, where the letters in parentheses stand for episodes that are logically necessary but omitted or mentioned only briefly. In Thomas Hardy's *Mayor of Casterbridge,* for example, the first episode shows the protagonist as a poor, semi-alcoholic willing to sell his wife. The next episode shows him the respected, energetic mayor of an English town. The intervening episodes—the story of how he came to be Mayor—are suppressed. The plot has the form A-(B-C-D)-E-F.

Another typical arrangement of episodes involves chronological distortion. Two episodes that occur **simultaneously** must be presented separately in a literary work. One must follow the other. For example, in Shakespeare's *Henry IV, Part I,* Shakespeare follows the activities of two distinct sets of characters, those associated with Prince Hal and those associated with Hotspur. To do this requires scenes at the Boarshead tavern featuring Hal, Falstaff and company, and other scenes in which Hotspur and his companions plot treason. The tavern scenes and the rebel scenes occur at roughly the same time. If we call the Boarshead scenes X and the rebel scenes Y, it is clear that Shakespeare can present them as $X_1, Y_1; X_2, Y_2$ and so forth; as $Y_1, X_1; Y_2, X_2$, or as $X_1, X_2; Y_1, Y_2$. The critic must then be able to answer the question, "Why is the arrangement that is used better than other possible arrangements?" Still another form of chronological distortion is **interrupted time.** The flashback is a good example of interrupted time. The episodes depicted have a chronological order of A-B-C-D-E, but the author's plot has the form C-D-A-B-E. In epic poetry interrupted time is a convention (called technically "beginning *in medias res,*" "in the middle of things"). Thus Milton's *Paradise Lost* begins chronologically with the revolt of Satan in Heaven (A), proceeds to his expulsion (B), then to his experience in Hell (C), then to his visit to Paradise (D), then to the angel Raphael's visit to Paradise (E), and then to the later episodes (F, etc.). As everyone knows, Milton begins with Satan in Hell; it is not until much later that the revolt and expulsion from Heaven are related. The poem has the plot structure C-D-E-A-B-F, etc. Again the critic must ask, "Why this arrangement? What does it accomplish that chronological arrangement could not do better?"

Chronology is only one element involved in the arrangement of episodes. In addition to **sequence,** the critic must consider **movement.** The most common form of plot movement is **movement toward climax.** If the episodes have an ascending movement and the climax is a reversal (catastrophe) leading to failure or death, the plot is **tragic,** although not all tragedies have precisely this form. If the episodes have a descending movement and the climax is a reversal (crisis) leading from apparently inevitable failure to resolution of problems, the plot is **comic,** although, again, not all comedies have this form. If the episodes have an ascending order and the climax is a "culminating success," or triumph, the plot has **epic** form; if the episodes show a series of failures leading to an ultimate one, the plot may be called **descending** although the term is a makeshift used only for lack of a better one. The plot of *Macbeth* is tragic; of *Twelfth Night* comic. The *Odyssey* has an epic structure, and *The Mayor of Casterbridge* is "descending."

In addition to having sequence and movement, the episodes of a plot must have **unity.** They must all be related directly or indirectly to the **intention.** In a play like Sophocles' *Oedipus Rex,* which focuses almost exclusively on one figure, **unity** is self-evident. In *Hamlet* or *Henry IV, Part I,* however, the playwright divides his attention among several characters. In these cases the episodes have unity because they are all means of expressing a larger **theme,** which is the play's intention, rather than because they are all related to a single character. Because literary narratives that focus on a single character are usually chronological, they are sometimes said to have "chronological form"; whereas works using several different characters or groups of characters to express a single theme are said to have "spatial form." The terms, while suggestive, need not be considered essential.

▶ ## 14.4 CHARACTER

Character is one of the most perplexing notions in criticism. Everything a literary figure does and says is a means of revealing character. In this sense, plot and style, as well as motivation and personality traits are parts of **character**. To avoid questions that cannot be answered without going beyond the limits of rhetorical criticism, we will define character as **those motives and attitudes of a fictional person that convey or emphasize intention, or increase verisimilitude** (i.e., "likeness to truth"). Notice that even when working from a source, an author has great latitude in treatment of character. Shakespeare's source, for example, included the fact that Hamlet desires to kill the King and that the act is deferred for an extended period. Shakespeare followed his source in these matters. Following the source did not, however, predetermine the **character** of Hamlet. There are a great many ways in which one can regard blood revenge; and there are a great many reasons, personal and circumstantial, that might be used to explain delay. Hamlet could have been presented as a sadist, dallying with his victim before slaughtering him; he could have been a coward, horrified by blood, who kills Claudius more by accident than by design; or he could have been a passionless agent of justice, killing to redress a crime rather than for direct personal satisfaction. Given the plot, each of these different **characterizations** would convey a different **intention**. The choice of motives and attitudes to be ascribed to Hamlet can therefore be understood functionally only in terms of the intention that they do, in fact, emphasize or reinforce. As the reader of *Hamlet* will realize, Shakespeare uses none of the characterizations just mentioned. The motives and attitudes of Hamlet the character are more complex, but this fact merely makes the need for a working definition of character all the more urgent.

Practically speaking, we cannot treat a literary character as though he existed apart from the work in which he appears. He is not separate, but a unit in the total design. To discuss the character, we must consider his relation to that design. This means asking how his motives and attitudes are related to the work's intention. Is Hamlet strongly tempted to commit suicide? Why is this so? What end is served by having him dally with a bare bodkin during the "To be or not to be" soliloquy? Notice that we are not asking whether he is neurotic or suffers from an Oedipus complex—these questions are beyond our present scope. We are asking only one kind of question. To what degree is a given motive or attribute **functional**, and if it is **functional**, what does it contribute?

From the most strictly functional point of view, only those motives and attitudes that convey intention are part of character. Fortunately,

325

we need not be quite so strict as this. A literary character needs to be believable as well as functional, and for this reason, most characters have what will be called **secondary attributes** that are included to give them **verisimilitude**. It is necessary, for example, to the intention of *Henry IV, Part I,* that Falstaff be motivated by the desire to corrupt Prince Hal. If he were *only* shown in the role of tempter, however, he would become unbelievable—an allegorical stereotype. To be believable, even as tempter, he needs a variety of attributes unrelated to temptation, in the same way that a living human being is made up of a great many traits and attitudes rather than only one or two. Thus in addition to having the functional attribute of "desire to corrupt," Falstaff has a ready wit, a love of horseplay, a great fondness for eating and drinking and a shrewd, if somewhat cynical philosophy of life. These secondary attributes are so vivid that for some unwary readers they have totally obscured the functional attribute. Without falling into this error, we can admit that Falstaff's secondary attributes do much to elevate the tavern scenes of *Henry IV, Part I,* to the plane of great comic drama.

On the basis of functional and secondary attributes we can distinguish between different modes of characterization. The first mode is **allegory**. In pure allegory, characters are personified abstractions. They have *only* functional attributes, and usually only one of these. A lady representing temptation is simply "Lust" or "Luxuria"; a figure representing salvation is "Good Spirit" or "Repentance." As secondary attributes begin to enter, they soften the allegory, making it seem less like a disguised lesson in philosophy and more like "an imitation of life." Still close to allegory is **caricature**, in which characters are dominated by obvious, sometimes grotesque "ruling passions." Ben Johnson's comedies abound in such figures, called "humours characters." As their names indicate, Thwackum and Square, the preacher and schoolmaster in *Tom Jones,* are **caricatures**. A great many stock characters in such forms as the Western movie and the television soap opera are also in this category. The fact that they are stock characters means that they come with ready-made motivations—the gunslinger, the conniving bank president, the rancher's daughter, the prostitute-with-the-heart-of-gold. Allegorical figures, caricatures and stock characters are not in themselves either bad or good art. *Everyman, The Faerie Queene* and William Golding's *Lord of*

326

the Flies are medieval, Renaissance and modern works respectively. They are all successful, and all use **allegory.** By the same token Lady Politic Would-Be (in Ben Jonson's *Volpone*), Mr. Micawber (in Dickens' *David Copperfield*), and Tom Buchanan (in F. Scott Fitzgerald's *The Great Gatsby*) are characters dominated by ruling passions, but possessing some secondary attributes. The techniques of allegory and caricature become bad literature when (a) the work is intended to seem realistic, (b) the characters are so flat or stereotyped as to have no interest, or (c) the intention itself is insignificant.

The more prominent "**secondary attributes**" become in a character, the closer he will come to having the complexity of a living person. Hamlet and Falstaff are good examples. Even when a literary character has a great many secondary attributes, however, he must by definition have an underlying **functional attribute** if he is really a part of the work in which he appears. It is impossible to treat Falstaff as a jolly, harmless old fellow unless his relation to the play as a whole is ignored. At the same time, not all characters in a literary work can be as complex as Hamlet or Falstaff. If they were, the intention of the work would be lost. The sense of the whole would give way to bewilderment at the sheer variety of the parts.

A final qualification: to say that secondary attributes contribute to **verisimilitude** is accurate as long as we recognize that what passes for "likeness to truth" in one context may be entirely out of harmony in another. In this sense "**verisimilitude**" is better understood as "what enhances the reader's acceptance of the work" rather than "what is true to life." In a realistic novel—for example, Henry James's *The American* or John Galsworthy's *Forsyte Saga*—we expect the use of secondary attributes to suggest the complexities and attitudes of real people living in the period and social classes described. In a musical comedy, on the other hand, realistic secondary attributes would be out of place. Few of us break into song when saying "I love you"; but it is natural for a character in a musical comedy to do so, and we will be disappointed if he doesn't. To say "I love you" in prose in a musical comedy would be a breach of verisimilitude. Coleridge defined the appreciation of a literary work as "willing suspension of disbelief"; and perhaps the best definition of verisimilitude is "that which encourages our suspension of disbelief."

327

▶ 14.5 NONNARRATIVE FORMS

Devotional, impressionistic and lyric modes of expression, whether prose or poetry, rely heavily on methods other than narrative. Many approaches to these forms lie within the scope of rhetorical criticism. In fact, in the previous chapters, several passages for analysis have been poetry or prose selections of a high degree of artistic merit. Although analysis of these passages has had development of practical writing skill as its objective, the process of analyzing them in order to understand their use of rhetorical devices is essentially the same as the process of rhetorical criticism. Any nonnarrative passage can be analyzed in terms of purpose; methods of organization; presentation of subtopics; use of details, examples and evidence; and use of logical forms. As in the case of narrative forms, the criticism can be descriptive or judicial.

▶ 14.6 STYLE

We have observed several times that there is no such thing as a sentence without **style**. Whether good or bad, simple or complex, undisciplined or controlled, anything written has style. This being the case, it is foolish and misleading to think of literature as having more style than other forms of writing. We may be more conscious of style in literature than in other forms of writing either because we have been taught to be (a bad reason) or because literary authors generally use style with particular skill, so that we notice it (a good reason).

Style in literature is judged in exactly the same way as style in other forms of writing. A literary work has a **tone**. If it is long it may have several different **tones** depending on who is speaking, where and when. The tone or tones are functional if they are appropriate to the intention, and discordant if they are not.

In literary prose, word choice, sentence structure, imagery and sound effects are used to control tone just as they are used in descriptive and expository writing. Since literary prose often treats a variety of subjects with marked differences of emotional coloring, the range of

328

effects—and consequently the range in the devices of style used—is usually somewhat greater than in expository prose. Since literary writers are often men of great talent, the devices are also often used with greater effectiveness and sensitivity than is common in everyday exposition. Because of this, the critic will find style a particularly fruitful subject for analysis. The essay reprinted in chapter 13 on "Irony in *Tom Jones*" is a case in point.

Poetic style is an extension of prose style. It is similar in kind, but differs in having resources not available to the prose writer. In addition to all the devices of style that can be found in prose, poetry uses special devices to control structure, rhythm and sound effects. Verse and stanza forms are essentially devices to control overall structure. The simplest pattern is blank verse, in which the line is controlled by the pattern, but in which there is no control of larger units, so that a poem in blank verse can be anywhere from a few to one thousand or more lines long. After blank verse come the couplet and the quatrain, and after them still more elaborate forms—the sonnet, the sestina, ottava rima and the Spenserian stanza to name only a few. We cannot examine these forms here, but it should be recognized that they act as structural elements. When used effectively they emphasize the progress and division of thought within the poem, and if they are conventional forms like the sonnet, they help to emphasize the feeling of "achieved unity" at the end.

Just as verse and stanza forms supplement rather than replace other methods of organization, so meter and controlled line length supplement the devices of prose rhythm. Most traditional English poetry is composed in regular meters in which effects are varied by *substitution,* the device of inserting unexpected metrical units at points of emphasis. *Free verse* abandons the meter but not the control of rhythm. Whereas in traditional poetry line length is determined by verse form and stanza, in free verse it is determined by sentence rhythm, as in Walt Whitman's *Leaves of Grass.* Again, discussion of specifically poetic devices of controlling rhythm is impossible here. Because so many devices of rhythm are the same in poetry as in prose, however, a good deal of poetic analysis is possible without consideration of meter and free verse techniques. By and large, poetic rhythms are more striking and more pronounced than prose rhythms, but they are analyzed on the basis of the same starting assumption: whatever the effect, it is to be understood in terms of its contribution to intention.

329

PRACTICAL RHETORIC

Poetry has an especially large repertory of sound effects. Most of these can be used in prose, although they are infrequent. The one sound effect common in poetry but almost never found in prose is rhyme. Being a part of verse and stanza form, rhyme is essentially a structural device. In the couplet, rhyme joins two lines together as a unit. In the quatrain, alternate rhymes perform the same service for four-line units. In addition to emphasizing structure, rhyme—because it calls attention to the rhymed words—can emphasize ideas and logic.

TERMS TO BE LEARNED

- ▶ Descriptive criticism
- ▶ Judicial criticism
- ▶ Limitation in criticism
- ▶ Intention
- ▶ Function
- ▶ Plot
- ▶ Sequence
- ▶ Movement
- ▶ Unity
- ▶ Character
- ▶ Functional attribute
- ▶ Secondary attribute
- ▶ Verisimilitude

Exercises & Theme Topics

I. Using one or more rhetorical principles considered in previous chapters, write a critical essay on one of the following selections. *Do not* refer to secondary sources, and *do* document your references informally by citing line number(s) in parentheses.

A.

Since there's no help, come let us kiss and part,
Nay, I have done, you get no more of me;
And I am glad, yea glad with all my heart,
That thus so cleanly I myself can free;
Shake hands for ever, cancel all our vows,   5
And when we meet at any time again,
Be it not seen in either of our brows
That we one jot of former love retain.
Now at the last gasp of Love's latest breath,
When his pulse failing, Passion speechless   10
   lies,
When Faith is kneeling by his bed of death,
And Innocence is closing up his eyes:
Now if thou would'st, when all have given
   him over,   15
From death to life thou might'st him yet
   recover.

—MICHAEL DRAYTON*

B.   **"ODE ON A GRECIAN URN"**

Thou still unravish'd bride of quietness,
   Thou foster-child of silence and slow time,
Sylvan historian, who canst thus express
   A flowery tale more sweetly than our rhyme:
What leaf-fring'd legend haunts about thy shape   5
   Of deities or mortals, or of both,
     In Tempe or the dales of Arcady?
   What men or gods are these? What maidens loth?
What mad pursuit? What struggle to escape?
     What pipes and timbrels? What wild ecstasy?   10

Heard melodies are sweet, but those unheard
   Are sweeter; therefore, ye soft pipes, play on;
Not to the sensual ear, but, more endear'd,
   Pipe to the spirit ditties of no tone:

* From *Idea*, Sonnet 61 (1619).

15 Fair youth, beneath the trees, thou canst not leave
        Thy song, nor ever can those trees be bare;
            Bold Lover, never, never canst thou kiss,
        Though winning near the goal—yet, do not grieve;
            She cannot fade, though thou hast not thy bliss,
20   For ever wilt thou love, and she be fair!

        Ah, happy, happy boughs! that cannot shed
            Your leaves, nor ever bid the Spring adieu;
        And, happy melodist, unwearied,
            For ever piping songs for ever new;
25   More happy love! more happy, happy love!
            For ever warm and still to be enjoy'd,
                For ever panting, and for ever young;
        All breathing human passion far above,
            That leaves a heart high-sorrowful and cloy'd,
30   A burning forehead, and a parching tongue.

        Who are these coming to the sacrifice?
            To what green altar, O mysterious priest,
        Lead'st thou that heifer lowing at the skies,
            And all her silken flanks with garlands drest?
35   What little town by river or sea shore,
            Or mountain-built with peaceful citadel,
                Is emptied of this folk, this pious morn?
        And, little town, thy streets for evermore
        Will silent be; and not a soul to tell
40   Why thou art desolate, can e'er return.

        O Attic shape! Fair attitude! with brede
            Of marble men and maidens overwrought
        With forest branches and the trodden weed;
            Thou, silent form, dost tease us out of thought
45   As doth eternity: Cold Pastoral!
            When old age shall this generation waste,
                Thou shalt remain, in midst of other woe
        Than ours, a friend to man, to whom thou say'st,
        "Beauty is truth, truth beauty,"—that is all
50   Ye know on earth, and all ye need to know.

                                    —JOHN KEATS

C. *"WHEN LILACS LAST IN THE DOOR-YARD BLOOM'D"*

1.

When lilacs last in the door-yard bloom'd,
And the great star early droop'd in the western sky in the night,
I mourn'd—and yet shall mourn with ever-returning spring.

O ever-returning spring! trinity sure to me you bring;
Lilac blooming perennial, and drooping star in the west,   5
And thought of him I love.

2.

O powerful, western, fallen star!
O shades of night! O moody, tearful night!
O great star disappear'd! O the black murk that hides the star!
O cruel hands that hold me powerless! O helpless soul of me!   10
O harsh surrounding cloud, that will not free my soul!

3.

In the door-yard fronting an old farm-house, near the white-wash'd
    palings,
Stands the lilac bush, tall-growing, with heart-shaped leaves of rich
    green,   15
With many a pointed blossom, rising, delicate, with the perfume
    strong I love,
With every leaf a miracle . . . and from this bush in the door-yard,
With delicate-color'd blossoms, and heart-shaped leaves of rich green,
A sprig, with its flower, I break.   20

4.

In the swamp, in secluded recesses,
A shy and hidden bird is warbling a song.
Solitary, the thrush,
The hermit withdrawn to himself, avoiding the settlements,
Sings by himself a song.   25
Song of the bleeding throat!
Death's outlet song of life—(for well, dear brother, I know
If thou wast not gifted to sing, thou would'st surely die.)

333

5.

Over the breast of the spring, the land, amid cities,

30 Amid lanes, and through old woods, (where lately the violets peep'd
    from the ground, spotting the gray debris;)
Amid the grass in the fields each side of the lanes—passing the endless
    grass;
Passing the yellow-spear'd wheat, every grain from its shroud in the

35   dark-brown fields uprising;
Passing the apple-tree blows of white and pink in the orchards;
Carrying a corpse to where it shall rest in the grave,
Night and day journeys a coffin.

6.

Coffin that passes through lanes and streets,

40 Through day and night, with the great cloud darkening the land,
With the pomp of the inloop'd flags, with the cities draped in black,
With the show of the States themselves, as of crape-veil'd women,
    standing,
With processions long and winding, and the flambeaus of the night,

45 With the countless torches lit—with the silent sea of faces, and the
    unbared heads,
With the waiting depot, the arriving coffin, and the somber faces,
With dirges through the night, with the thousand voices rising strong
    and solemn;

50 With all the mournful voices of the dirges, pour'd around the coffin,
The dim-lit churches and the shuddering organs—where amid these
    you journey,
With the tolling, tolling bells' perpetual clang;
Here! coffin that slowly passes,

55 I give you my sprig of lilac.

7.

(Nor for you, for one, alone:
Blossoms and branches green to coffins all I bring:
For fresh as the morning—thus would I carol a song for you, O sane
    and sacred death.

All over bouquets of roses,   60
O death! I cover you over with roses and early lilies;
But mostly and now the lilac that blooms the first,
Copious, I break, I break the sprigs from the bushes;
With loaded arms I come, pouring for you,
For you, and the coffins all of you, O death.)   65

8.

O western orb, sailing the heaven!
Now I know what you must have meant, as a month since we walk'd,
As we walk'd up and down in the dark blue so mystic,
As we walk'd in silence the transparent shadowy night,
As I saw you had something to tell, as you bent to me night after   70
    night,
As you droop'd from the sky low down, as if to my side, (while the
    other stars all look'd on;)
As we wander'd together the solemn night, (for something, I know
    not what, kept me from sleep;)   75
As the night advanced, and I saw on the rim of the west, ere you
    went, how full you were of woe;
As I stood on the rising ground in the breeze, in the cold transparent
    night,
As I watch'd where you pass'd and was lost in the netherward black   80
    of the night,
As my soul, in its trouble, dissatisfied, sank, as where you, sad orb,
Concluded, dropt in the night, and was gone.

9.

Sing on, there in the swamp!
O singer bashful and tender! I hear your notes—I hear your call;   85
I hear—I come presently—I understand you;
But a moment I linger—for the lustrous star has detain'd me;
The star, my departing comrade, holds and detains me.

10.

O how shall I warble myself for the dead one there I loved?
And how shall I deck my song for the large sweet soul that has gone?   90
And what shall my perfume be, for the grave of him I love?

Sea-winds, blown from east and west,
Blown from the eastern sea, and blown from the western sea, till
there on the prairies meeting:
95 These, and with these, and the breath of my chant,
I perfume the grave of him I love.

11.

O what shall I hang on the chamber walls?
And what shall the pictures be that I hang on the walls,
To adorn the burial-house of him I love?

100 Pictures of growing spring, and farms, and homes,
With the Fourth-month eve at sundown, and the gray smoke lucid
and bright,
With floods of the yellow gold of the gorgeous, indolent, sinking sun,
burning, expanding the air;
105 With the fresh sweet herbage under foot, and the pale green leaves of
the trees prolific;
In the distance the flowing glaze, the breast of the river, with a wind-
dapple here and there;
With ranging hills on the banks, with many a line against the sky,
110 and shadows;
And the city at hand, with dwellings so dense, and stacks of chimneys,
And all the scenes of life, and the workshops, and the workmen
homeward returning.

12.

Lo! body and soul! this land!
115 Mighty Manhattan, with spires, and the sparkling and hurrying tides,
and the ships;
The varied and ample land—the South and the North in the light—
Ohio's shores, and flashing Missouri,
And ever the far-spreading prairies, cover'd with grass and corn.
120 Lo! the most excellent sun, so calm and haughty;
The violet and purple morn, with just-felt breezes;
The gentle, soft-born, measureless light;
The miracle, spreading, bathing all—the fulfill'd noon;
The coming eve, delicious—the welcome night, and the stars,
125 Over my cities shining all, enveloping man and land.

13.

Sing on! sing on, you gray-brown bird!
Sing from the swamps, the recesses—pour your chant from the bushes;
Limitless out of the dusk, out of the cedars and pines.

Sing on, dearest brother—warble your reedy song;
Loud human song, with voice of uttermost woe.   130

O liquid, and free, and tender!
O wild and loose to my soul! O wondrous singer!
You only I hear . . . yet the star holds me, (but will soon depart;)
Yet the lilac, with mastering odor, holds me.

14.

Now while I sat in the day, and look'd forth,   135
In the close of the day, with its light, and the fields of spring, and the
    farmer preparing his crops,
In the large unconscious scenery of my land, with its lakes and forests,
In the heavenly aerial beauty, (after the perturb'd winds, and the
    storms;)   140
Under the arching heavens of the afternoon swift passing, and the
    voices of children and women,
The many-moving sea-tides,—and I saw the ships how they sail'd,
And the summer approaching with richness, and the fields all busy
    with labor,   145
And the infinite separate houses, how they all went on, each with its
    meals and minutia of daily usages;
And the streets, how their throbbings throbb'd, and the cities pent—
    lo! then and there,
Falling upon them all, and among them all, enveloping me with the   150
    rest,
Appear'd the cloud, appear'd the long black trail;
And I knew Death, its thought, and the sacred knowledge of death.

15.

Then with the knowledge of death as walking one side of me,
And the thought of death close-walking the other side of me,   155
And I in the middle, as with companions, and as holding the hands
    of companions,

I fled forth to the hiding receiving night, that talks not,
Down to the shores of the water, the path by the swamp in the
160   dimness,
To the solemn shadowy cedars, and ghostly pines so still.

And the singer so shy to the rest receiv'd me;
The gray-brown bird I know, receiv'd us comrades three;
And he sang what seem'd the carol of death, and a verse for him
165   I love.

From deep secluded recesses,
From the fragrant cedars, and the ghostly pines so still,
Came the carol of the bird.

And the charm of the carol rapt me,
170 As I held, as if by their hands, my comrades in the night;
And the voice of my spirit tallied the song of the bird.

—WALT WHITMAN*

D.   *OF MARRIAGE AND SINGLE LIFE*

He that hath wife and children hath given hostages to fortune; for they are impediments to great enterprises, either of virtue or mischief. Certainly the best works, and of greatest merit for the public, have proceeded from the unmarried or childless men, which both in affection and means have married and endowed the public. Yet it were great reason that those that have children should have greatest care of future times, unto which they know they must transmit their dearest pledges. Some there are who, though they lead a single life, yet their thoughts do end with themselves and account future times impertinences. Nay, there are some other that account wife and children but as bills of charges. Nay more, there are some foolish rich covetous men that take a pride in having no children, because they may be thought so much the richer. For perhaps they have heard some talk, "Such an one is a great rich man," and another except to it, "Yea, but he hath a great charge of children," as if it were an abatement to his riches. But the most ordinary cause of a single life is liberty, especially in certain self-pleasing and humorous minds, which are so sensible of every restraint as they will go near to think their girdles and garters to be bonds and shackles.

Unmarried men are best friends, best masters, best servants; but not always

* From *Leaves of Grass* (1865-66).

best subjects: for they are light to run away, and almost all fugitives are of that condition. A single life doth well with churchmen for charity will hardly water the ground where it must first fill a pool. It is indifferent for judges and magistrates; for if they be facile and corrupt, you shall have a servant five times worse than a wife. For soldiers, I find the generals commonly in their hortatives put men in mind of their wives and children; and I think the despising of marriage amongst the Turks maketh the vulgar soldier more base. Certainly wife and children are a kind of discipline of humanity; and single men, though they be many times more charitable, because their means are less exhaust, yet on the other side they are more cruel and hardhearted (good to make severe inquisitors because their tenderness is not so oft called upon).

Grave natures, led by custom, and therefore constant, are commonly loving husbands, as was said of Ulysses: *Vetulam suam praetulit immortali-tati.* Chaste women are often proud and forward as presuming upon the merit of their chastity. It is one of the best bonds, both of chastity and obedience, in the wife if she think her husband wise, which she will never do if she find him jealous. Wives are young men's mistresses, companions for middle age, and old men's nurses. So as a man may have a quarrel to marry when he will. But yet he was reputed one of the wise men, that made answer to the question when a man should marry, "A young man not yet, an elder man not at all."

It is often seen that bad husbands have very good wives, whether it be that it raiseth the price of their husbands' kindness when it comes or that the wives take a pride in their patience; but this never fails, if the bad husbands were of their own choosing, against their friends' consent, for then they will be sure to make good their own folly.

—Sir Francis Bacon*

II. Write a critical essay based on plot analysis of one of the following short stories or a short story approved by your instructor:

A. James Joyce, "The Dead"
B. William Faulkner, "Turnabout"
C. Ernest Hemingway, "The Snows of Kilimanjaro"
D. Ring Lardner, "Haircut"
E. Nathaniel Hawthorne, "Young Goodman Brown"

* From *Essays, or Counsels Civil and Moral* (1625).

III. Write a critical essay based on character analysis of a character in one of the following novels or a novel approved by your instructor:

A. Charles Dickens, *Great Expectations*
B. Ernest Hemingway, *The Sun Also Rises*
C. J. D. Salinger, *The Catcher in the Rye*
D. Mark Twain, *The Adventures of Huckleberry Finn*
E. Nathaniel Hawthorne, *The Scarlet Letter*

Glossary

Numbers in parentheses indicate sections of the text containing relevant discussion and illustration. Cross-references are indicated by italics.

Adaptation.   Presenting material in a way that will be clear and interesting to the anticipated readers. (1.3)

Ad hominem.   Argument based on appeals to the prejudices, desires and fears of the reader rather than to the merits of the issue. (12.5).

Alliteration.   The repetition of like or similar sounds at the beginning of stressed syllables. (12.4)

Allusion.   Reference to a person, place or thing, historical or literary, that adds to the force or clarity of the subject at hand. (12.2)

Alternation.   Variation for the sake of rhythmic effect between long and short syntactical units and between units with emphatically different grammatical structures. (12.3)

Alternative outlines.   Outlines on the same subject using different (or alternative) methods of development. (1.3)

Analogy.   An image based on *comparison* and used to clarify or explain. (3.5)

Analysis.   The division of a large subject into smaller, logically distinct components. (1.5) Analysis related to definition. (8.4)

Antithesis.   The juxtaposition of two syntactical units similar in structure but opposed in content. (9.4)

Approach step.   A device appearing at the beginning of the essay and intended to secure the reader's attention. Usually an anecdote, striking quotation or an interesting fact or generalization. (1.4, 10.1) See *introduction*.

Argumentation. One of the standard *forms of discourse*. An argumentative essay is one that seeks to persuade or convince the reader of the truth of a *thesis*. (5.5, 6.6, 6.7, 11.6)

Arrangement. The order of the topics in the developing section of the essay (1.5) or the paragraph (2.4). The standard types of arrangement are *inherent* (space, time, process) and *imposed*, or *logical* (cause-effect, climax).

Attribute. In *definition*, a quality other than a *differentia* associated with the term being defined. (8.3) In criticism, a quality associated with a literary character. (14.4)

Authority. In research writing, a source having particular relevance, prestige or validity. (13.3) If abused, appeal to authority can become a *propaganda* device. (12.5)

Author's comment. Discussion of the implications of a point already presented or demonstrated. A common part of the *conclusion*. (1.4, 10.3)

Background material. Explanatory material necessary to the understanding of a point or of the essay as a whole. A common part of the *introduction*. (1.4, 10.1)

Balance. An effect created by two sentence elements of approximately similar length and structure. (9.4)

Bandwagon device. A *propaganda* device based on the reader's desire to identify himself with what is popular. (12.5)

Basis. In *comparison*, the common factor between the *terms* of the comparison. (7.1)

Begging the question. A *propaganda* device for evading the issue. (12.5)

Body. In rhetoric, a synonym for *development*.

Buried imagery. Many words have been used in their figurative senses for such a long time that their literal meanings have been forgotten and can only be discovered by reference to their etymologies. The imagery concealed in such words is called *buried imagery*. (3.5)

Categorical generalization. A generalization that holds true in all cases meeting a stipulated set of conditions. (6.4)

Chain of inference. A unit of writing formed by *enthymemes* or by *syllogisms* arranged so that the first leads to the second, the second to the third and so forth. (11.6)

Character. In criticism, the motives and *attributes* of a fictional character that convey or emphasize *intention* or increase *verisimilitude*. (14.4)

Chronological arrangement. Arrangement in which events are given in the order of occurrence. The usual order of *narrative*. An *inherent arrangement*. (1.5, 2.4)

Circular reasoning. A *propaganda* device similar to *begging the question*.

Clarification. Comment intended to aid comprehension. (5.4)

342

Class. In definition, the genus or category within which the *term* is placed. (8.3)

Classification. The assigning of a detail, fact or component to a larger category or "class." (1.5) In definition. (8.4)

Coherence. The effect achieved when material in the paragraph is arranged clearly and the method of arrangement is emphasized by *transitions* and *verbal links*. (2.4)

Colloquial imagery. Imagery that is clearly figurative but so commonplace that it is often used unconsciously. (3.5)

Comic plot line. The comic plot line moves through a descending action to a turning point or climax and ends with emphasis on the successful resolution of all complications. (14.3)

Comparison. A technique for emphasizing points in common between two *subjects* or between a *subject* and *object*. (7.1) A standard *method of development*. (7.3) See also *contrast*.

Complex sentence. A sentence consisting of one main clause and one or more subordinate clauses. (9.1)

Composite paragraph. A paragraph using two or more methods of development. (2.3)

Compound sentence. A sentence consisting of two or more main clauses. (9.1)

Compound-complex sentence. A sentence with two or more main clauses and one or more subordinate clauses. (9.1)

Concluding sentence. The last sentence of the essay. The concluding sentence should be emphatic and have the quality of finality. (10.3)

Conclusion. The last section of the standard essay. A conclusion can include *restatement*, *summary* and *author's comment*. In many essays the closing sentences take the place of a formal conclusion. (1.4, 10.3)

Concreteness. The use of specific rather than general details. (4.4)

Connotation. The implied overtones of a word—the coloration or shade of meaning the word suggests. (3.2)

Consensus. The opinion of mankind at large or of a specialized group. (12.5) A form of evidence in the research paper. (13.3)

Continuous comparison. Comparison in which the *points of comparison* are grouped together in the form A_1B_1; A_2B_2; A_3B_3; etc. Contrasted to *discontinuous comparison*. (7.1)

Contrast. A technique for emphasizing points of difference between two *subjects*. (7.1)

Coordination. Linking ideas of syntactical units of equal importance, usually with a coordinate conjunction. (9.1)

Criticism. Speech or writing about literature. Criticism may be favorable or unfavorable, or may be entirely descriptive. See ch. 14, p. 318.

Deduction. A method of *proof* proceeding from general assertions to specific conclusions. The normal forms of deductive reasoning are *syllogism* and *enthymeme*. (11.1) Deduction is also a *method of development*. (11.6)

Definition. An explanation of the meaning of a term. Formal definition requires giving *term, class* and *differentia*. (8.1) *Extended definition* is a standard *method of development*. (8.5, 8.6) Definitions should have precision and relevancy. (8.2) Among the techniques of definition are definition by contrast, historical definition, definition by enumeration, definition by example and definition by synonym. (8.1, 8.2, 8.3).

Deliberate imagery. Imagery used consciously for a desired effect. (3.5)

Denotation. The literal or dictionary meaning of a word. (3.2)

Description. One of the standard *forms of discourse*. *Pure description* seeks to convey an accurate impression of the object or scene described. *Literary description* seeks primarily to move and/or entertain. (2.3, 4.3, 4.4)

Detail. A single fact, impression or observation related to the subject being treated. (2.3, 4.3)

Development. The section of the essay in which the author develops and/or proves his major points. The development is usually the longest part of the essay. The standard *methods of development* are development by *detail*, development by *example*, development by *comparison* and *contrast* and development by *definition*. The developing section is often called the *body* of the essay. (1.4, 1.5)

Differentia. In *definition*, the basis for distinguishing the *term* from other terms in the same *class*. (8.1)

Digression. Straying from the point. Normally a rhetorical error involving violation of *unity*. (1.1, 1.2)

Discontinuous comparison. Comparison in which the *points of comparison* are grouped in separate units or paragraphs in the form $A_1A_2A_3$; $B_1B_2B_3$. Contrasted to *continuous comparison*. (7.1)

Discourse. See *forms of discourse*.

Division. See *statement of method*.

Documentation. In research writing, the author's reference to his source materials. Documentation can be either *formal* or *informal*. (13.7)

Doublet. Two coordinate words used when one would suffice. (12.3)

Economy. Using the smallest number of details or examples consistent with the desired effect. (4.4)

Effect. In *comparison*, the main point of the comparison. (7.1)

Ellipsis. See *points of ellipsis*.

Enthymeme. A *syllogism* in which the major or minor premise is left unstated. Often called a *rhetorical syllogism*. (11.5)

Epic plot line. A plot line moving in ascending order through complications to a final, climactic success. (14.3)

Etymology. See *historical definition.*

Euphony. The effect achieved when a passage is rhythmically graceful and avoids unpleasant sound combinations. (12.4)

Evidence. Details or examples used to prove a generalization. (5.5) Argument by thesis and *evidence.* (6.6) Use of evidence in the research paper. (13.2, 13.3) Among the types of evidence are personal observation, *consensus, authority,* survey and testimony. (13.3)

Exaggeration. Overstatement for effect. Hyperbole is a form of exaggeration. (12.2)

Example. A detail or instance illustrating a *generalization.* (2.3) Development by example. (2.3, 5.1) Example as a method of *definition.* (8.6) Example in *conclusions.* (10.4) Examples are usually devices of *illustration, clarification* or *proof.* (5.2)

Explicit unity. Paragraph unity emphasized by means of a *topic sentence.* Contrasted to *implicit unity.* (2.1)

Exposition. One of the standard *forms of discourse.* Exposition explains, clarifies and informs. (4.4)

Extended definition. A *method of development.* See *definition.*

Fallacy. A logical error. A fallacious *syllogism.* (11.4)

Filler. Material added to the essay for the sole purpose of increasing word length. (4.2)

Formal definition. See *definition.*

Formal documentation. Documentation by means of footnotes and bibliography. (13.7)

Forms of discourse. The standard forms of discourse are *description, narration, exposition* and *argumentation.*

Function. In criticism, the reason for the inclusion of a passage, scene, character, etc., in a literary work; the way in which it contributes to the work's *intention.* (14.2, 14.4)

Functional arrangement. Synonym for arrangement by *process.* See *inherent arrangement.*

Generalization. An assertion about a group or *class.* (5.1) Generalizations may be *subjective, probable* or *categorical.* (6.4)

Genus. See *class.*

Glittering generality. A propaganda device based on the substitution of an attractive generalization for logical *proof.* (12.5)

Gradation. Arrangement of sentence elements in order of ascending importance. (9.4)

Graded rhythm. When elements are arranged in order of *gradation,* they often exhibit graded rhythm, with the last element receiving the strongest rhythmic emphasis. (12.3)

Historical definition. Definition based on the history of the term. Etymology is a form of historical definition. (8.3)

Hyperbole. A form of *exaggeration.*

Iamb. The most common metrical unit in English, consisting of a light stress followed by a heavy, as in the word prŏmóte. (12.3)

Illustration. A standard technique of literary description, narration and exposition. (5.2, 5.3)

Imagery. Any figurative use of language (not necessarily visual) for emphasis, ornament or sense appeal. (3.4, 12.2) See *buried imagery, colloquial imagery, deliberate imagery.*

Immediacy. Using details or examples that are meaningful to the reader. (4.4)

Implicit unity. Paragraph unity implied rather than stated. A paragraph having implicit unity lacks a *topic sentence* but is unified because its material clearly relates to a single idea, theme or mood. (2.1) Contrasted to *explicit unity.*

Imposed arrangement. A method of *arrangement* imposed by the writer on his material. The imposed orders include cause-effect, least to most familiar, climax, question and answer. Often called *logical arrangement.* Contrasted to *inherent arrangement.* (1.5, 2.4)

Inadequate development. The inadequate "filling out" of the topics of the outline. (4.2)

Induction. A method of proof proceeding from examination of particulars to general conclusions. Contrasted to *deduction.* (6.2, 11.1)

Inference. See *chain of inference.*

Informal documentation. Brief citation of source, usually in parentheses following the reference. (13.7)

Inherent arrangement. *Arrangement* inherent in the subject matter, including arrangement by space, time and process. Contrasted to *imposed arrangement.* (1.5, 2.4)

Instance. A specific member of a group or *class* used to represent that group or class. (5.1)

Intention. In *criticism,* the most general impression, mood or idea the literary work conveys. The *intention* of a literary work is similar to the *purpose statement* of an expository essay, but it is usually implied rather than stated. (14.2)

Interruption. A deviation from standard sentence order. (9.2)

Intimidation. A *propaganda* device. (12.5)

Introduction. The first section of the standard essay, the other two being the *development* and the *conclusion.* There are four elements that occur frequently in introductions: *statement of purpose, statement of method, background* and *approach step.* (1.4, 10.1)

346

Inversion. A deviation from standard sentence order. (9.2)

Irony. Saying one thing and implying something else. (12.2) See also *sustained irony.*

Levels of usage. There are four common levels of usage: technical and formal, standard, colloquial and slang. (3.3, 9.1)

Limitation. Selecting an aspect of a subject small enough to be manageable. (1.3, 10.1)

Listing. An arbitrary *arrangement* of points or items using neither *inherent* nor *imposed order.* (1.5, 2.4, 10.3)

Literary description. See *description.*

Litotes. A form of *understatement.*

Logical arrangement. Arrangement using *imposed order.* See *arrangement.*

Logical proof. Proof that seeks to convince by logical reasoning and evidence. (6.1)

Loose sentence. A sentence ending with one or more elements not essential to the completion of the meaning of the main clause. Contrasted to *periodic sentence.* (9.2)

Metaphor. An implied *comparison* without "like" or "as." Contrasted to *simile.* (3.5)

Method of arrangement. See *arrangement.*

Method of development. See *development.*

Metonymy. The substitution of a word closely associated with an object for the name of the object itself. Related to *synecdoche.* (12.2)

Movement. The progression of episodes in a *plot.* Plot movement is usually ascending or descending, especially toward or away from a climax, catastrophe or turning point. (14.3)

Multiple example. Two or more *examples* used to illustrate or prove the same generalization. Contrasted to *representative example.* (5.6)

Narration. One of the standard *forms of discourse.* Narration "tells a story," and normally uses *chronological arrangement.* (4.4)

Necessity. The quality achieved when each detail or example adds something essential and when no detail or example can be deleted without loss of meaning. (4.4)

Notes. Advice on taking notes. (13.6)

Object. In comparison, that to which the *subject* is compared. (7.1)

Order. See *arrangement* and *sentence order.*

Ornate style. The most elaborate of the three styles of English prose. Ornate style uses artificial devices such as highly figured sentence structure, emphatic rhythm, formal and exotic words and elaborate imagery. See *style.* (12.1)

Paragraph. A paragraph is a unit of thought. (2.1) See also *composite paragraph.*

Parallelism. The use of like grammatical structures in two or more sentences. (2.4, 9.4) Parallelism is also useful in larger units of the essay. (9.4, 9.5)

Partition. A synonym for *statement of method.*

Periodic sentence. A sentence in which the meaning of the main clause is not completed until the end. (9.2)

Personification. A figure in which an inanimate object or abstract idea is treated as a living being. (12.2)

Plain style. The simplest of the three styles of English prose. Its characteristics are simple words, simple and compound sentences, little modification and minimal imagery. See *style.* (12.1)

Plot. In cricticism, an arrangement of episodes in a definite pattern having the quality of *unity.* (14.3)

Points of comparison. When two *subjects* are being compared, the various similarities that they reveal are called the *points of comparison.* (7.1)

Points of ellipsis. Periods used to indicate omitted material. (13.8)

Precision. Exactness of detail, example or definition. (4.4)

Process. See *inherent arrangement.*

Probable generalization. A *generalization* that is true in most cases but not in all. (6.4)

Proof. Logical demonstration based on *induction* or *deduction.* (5.5)

Propaganda. Writing that seeks to persuade through appeals to emotion rather than logical *proof.* (12.5)

Purpose. The most general point the essay is intended to convey. (1.2)

Purpose statement. See *statement of purpose.*

Quotation. Quotation may be used for ornament, *illustration* and *proof.* Quotations may be coordinated with the author's own text or set off from it and given in block form. (13.8)

Representative example. A single example used to illustrate, clarify or prove a generalization. Contrasted to *multiple example.* (5.6)

Restatement. A repetition or rephrasing of a point already made. A common part of the *conclusion.* (1.4, 10.3)

Rhetorical proof. Proof using *propaganda* devices rather than *evidence* and rigorous logic. (6.1) See *propaganda* and *proof.*

Rhetorical syllogism. See *enthymeme.*

Rhythm. The effect created by the timing and stress of words, phrases, clauses and sentences. (12.3)

Rigor. Logical validity. (6.3)

Sentence order. The standard sentence order in English is subject-verb-object.

Variation from this order is achieved through *interruption* and *inversion*. (9.2)

Sentence types. The standard English sentence types are *simple, compound, complex* and *compound-complex.* (9.1)

Sequence. The order of episodes in a *plot.* Sequence can be chronological, interrupted or discontinuous. (14.3)

Simile. A *comparison* made explicit by the use of "like" or "as." Contrasted to *metaphor.* (3.5)

Simple sentence. A simple sentence consists of one main clause. (9.1)

Source. A source is a document cited by an author containing information relevant to the subject being treated. A primary source is a document directly related to the subject and contemporary with it. A secondary source is only indirectly related to the subject or a comment about it. (13.4)

Source book. A collection of primary and secondary source material on a specific subject. (13.5)

Spatial arrangement. Arrangement of details in terms of space relations inherent in the subject. An *inherent arrangement.* (1.5, 2.4)

Standard style. The usual *style* of English prose. Standard style varies from informal to formal. Contrasted to *plain* and *ornate* style. (12.1)

Statement of method. A statement telling how the author plans to treat his material. Often it consists of a brief outline (*partition*) giving the order in which the main points will be taken up. It is usually part of the *introduction.* (1.4, 10.1)

Statement of purpose. A statement telling the main point of the essay. A statement of purpose has two parts: it indicates the *subject* of the essay, and it makes an assertion about the subject. It is usually part of the *introduction.* (1.2, 10.1)

Stipulative definition. The author states (or "stipulates") the definition appropriate to his essay. The definition can be his own or one derived from an authoritative source such as a dictionary. (8.2)

Style. The way in which an author adapts his expression to his purpose. Style is affected by word choice, *imagery* and sentence structure. (ch. 3, pp. 61 ff.) . The three "styles" of English are *plain, standard* and *ornate.* (12.1) Criticism of style in literary works. (14.6)

Subject. The topic or subject matter of the essay. (1.1, 2.2, 2.3) In comparison-contrast, the *subject* is what the author is immediately concerned with and is compared or contrasted to the *object.* (7.1)

Subjective generalization. A *generalization* that depends so heavily on personal attitudes that it cannot be logically proved or disproved. (6.4)

Subordination. The use of subordinate clauses to emphasize the fact that one idea is of less importance than, or contingent on another. (9.1)

PRACTICAL RHETORIC

Summary. A concise statement of important points already covered. A common part of the *conclusion*. (1.4, 10.3)

Sustained irony. *Irony* continued through a section of an essay or an entire essay. (12.2)

Syllogism. A logical form consisting of a major premise, a minor premise and a conclusion. (11.2) A syllogism can be hypothetical, disjunctive or categorical. (11.2, 11.3) For *rhetorical syllogism* see *enthymeme*.

Synecdoche. Using the name of the whole for the part, or the part for the whole. Related to *metonymy*. (12.2)

Synonym. A method of *definition*. (8.3)

Term. In *definition*, the word to be defined. (8.3) Also used in relation to *syllogism*. (11.4)

Thesis. The *purpose statement* of an argumentative essay. (5.5) Argument by *thesis* and *evidence*. (6.6)

Tone. In relation to *style*, the quality that controls the response of the reader to the subject matter. (3.1)

Topic sentence. A sentence stating the dominant theme or idea of a *paragraph*. (2.1)

Tragic plot line. The tragic plot line conventionally includes an ascending action, a climax or catastrophe and an ending emphasizing the failure of the protagonist, although the failure may be qualified. (14.3)

Transition. A link between two units of thought. Paragraphs can be used as transitions between sections of an essay. (1.10, 2.5)

Understatement. The opposite of *exaggeration*. (12.2)

Unity. The effect achieved when all parts of the essay contribute to the author's purpose and when nothing has been left out that should be included. (1.1, 9.5)

Unity of purpose. The effect achieved when the *subject* is treated in a manner consistent with the *purpose statement*. (1.2)

Unity of subject. The effect achieved when all parts of the essay are clearly related to the main *subject*. (1.1)

Usage. See *levels of usage*.

Verbal link. A device of *coherence* used to clarify and emphasize relationships within the paragraph. (2.4)

Verisimilitude. "Likeness to truth." A literary device. (14.4)

ERROR	CORRECTION SYMBOL		EXPLANATION
	Standard	Alternative	
1. CASE	*ca.*		Improper case of noun, pronoun
2. VERB	*v.f.*		Improper verb form
	t.		shift of tense; improper tense sequence
	p.v.		unnecessary shift of tense, mood, person, number
	agr.		lack of agreement between subject and ve
3. PRONOUN	*ref.*		Vague antecedent; lack of antecedent
	agr.		Lack of agreement between pronoun and antecedent
4. MODIFIERS	*dang.*		Dangling modifiers
	ad.		Adjective used as adverb; adverb used as adjective
5. SPELLING	*sp.*		Word misspelled
	cap.		Lack of capitalization; improper capitalization
6. MECHANICS	*apos.*		Apostrophe omitted
	⊙		Comma error:
	⊙	*a*	(a) in compound sentence
	⊙	*b*	(b) after long introductory clause or phrase
	⊙	*c*	(c) in series
	⊙	*d*	(d) to set off nonrestrictive elements
	⊙	*e*	(e) for clarity